George MacDonald

The Gold Coast, Past and Present

A short description of the country and its people

George MacDonald

The Gold Coast, Past and Present
A short description of the country and its people

ISBN/EAN: 9783337231545

Printed in Europe, USA, Canada, Australia, Japan

Cover: Foto ©ninafisch / pixelio.de

More available books at **www.hansebooks.com**

THE GOLD COAST

PAST AND PRESENT

A SHORT DESCRIPTION OF THE COUNTRY AND ITS PEOPLE

BY

GEORGE MACDONALD

LATE H.M. DIRECTOR OF EDUCATION FOR THE GOLD COAST COLONY AND PROTECTORATE
INSPECTOR OF SCHOOLS; MEMBER OF THE BOARD OF EDUCATION; ORGANISER
AND MANAGER OF THE GOVERNMENT SCHOOLS, ETC., ETC.

WITH ILLUSTRATIONS

LONGMANS, GREEN, AND CO.
39 PATERNOSTER ROW, LONDON
NEW YORK AND BOMBAY
1898

All rights reserved

PREFACE.

IN the compilation of the historical portion of the present volume the following authorities have been consulted:—

Bosman.	*Coast of Guinea*	1705.
Snelgrave.	*New Account of Guinea*	1734.
Benezet.	*Some Account of Guinea*	1787.
Bowdich.	*Mission to Ashanti*	1817.
Cruickshank.	*The Gold Coast*	1853.
Burton.	*Wanderings in West Africa*	1863.
Gordon.	*Life on the Gold Coast*	1874.
Burton and Cameron.	*To the Gold Coast for Gold*	1883.
Ellis.	*Tshi-speaking People on the Gold Coast*	1887.

I am indebted to Messrs. Chatto & Windus and to the proprietors of *Black and White* for descriptions of the Lake Village in Apollonia, and also to Messrs. Skuse & Hughes, Photographers, of Cape Coast Castle, for many of the illustrations, which are from photographs taken by those gentlemen, during my tours of service in the Gold Coast Colony (1893-97).

Should the present volume help to draw attention to one of our most important West African Colonies, its object will have been attained by

THE AUTHOR.

LONDON, *July*, 1898.

CONTENTS.

CHAPTER I.

PAGES

The Gulf of Guinea—Divisions—Early Expeditions to the Coast—French and Portuguese Claims—Early English Trading Companies—The Gold Coast in Bosman's Time—The Gold Coast of To-day—General View of the Colony . . . 1-29

CHAPTER II.

The Early Inhabitants of the Gold Coast—Their Traditional Origin—The Dominant Powers—Manners—Customs—Superstitions—Occupations—Religion—Manual Arts—The Aggrey Bead 30-61

CHAPTER III.

The Seasons—Climate—The Harmattan—Productions—Vegetation—Animal Life—Exports—Imports—Habitations—The Slave Trade—Its Rise and Fall—The Labour Question 62-89

CHAPTER IV.

Gold in West Africa—Antiquity of the same—Gold-producing Areas—Present Gold Mines—How Obtained—Gold Work—Gold Weights—The Future of West Africa as a Gold-producing Country 90-121

CHAPTER V.

Half Assini to Axim—Apollonia—The Lake Village—Axim and its Neighbourhood—The Ante Country—Cape Three Points—Chama and the Prah—The Kingdoms of Wassaw, Denkira and Sefwi 122-150

CONTENTS.

CHAPTER VI.

Chama to Elmina—Commendah, British and Dutch—Cape Coast Castle—Landing—The Town in General—The Lighthouse—The Resting-place of "L. E. L."—A Memoir—The Road to Kumasi—Mouri and Fort Nassau—Anamaboe and Saltpond—The Tufel and Assin Countries 151-177

CHAPTER VII.

Appam—The Devil's Mount—Winnebah—Bereku—Accra or Akra—The Akra People—Manners and Customs—The Adangme Tribe—Names—The Present Town—Christiansborg—Meridian Rock 178-207

CHAPTER VIII.

The Akim and Kwahu Countries—Begoro, Kyebi and Abetifi—The Akim Forests—The Tshi People—Manners and Customs—The Future of Akim—Native Traditions—Akwamu or Aquamboe 208-234

CHAPTER IX.

The Aquapim, Adangme, Awoonah, Krobo and Akwamu Countries—Their Peoples—Pram Pram—Ada and Kwitta—Krepi and Peki Countries—The Volta River—Anglo-French Convention, 1898 235-261

CHAPTER X.

The Kingdom of Ashanti—Its People—Origin—History—Dwaben—The Capital, Kumasi—Wars down to 1817—The Town—Constitution and Laws—Roads from Kumasi . . 262-291

CHAPTER XI.

Monthly Notes—Wars with England, 1807-1817—Mission to Ashanti—Second Ashanti War, 1824—Third Ashanti War, 1863—Fourth Ashanti War, 1873—The Last Ashanti War—Downfall of Prempeh, 1896 292-315

CONTENTS.

CHAPTER XII.

Progress of the Colony—Education—The Basle Mission—The Wesleyans—The Roman Catholic Mission—The Schools of the Colony—The Future of the Colony—Want of Railways and Central Harbour 316-338

APPENDICES.

A. Ashanti Kings, Battles and Wars 339-340
B. Distances between Coast Towns, Windward and Leeward 341-342
C. Fares for Hammockmen, Carriers and Canoemen . 342-343
D. Distances between Interior Towns 344-345
E. Governors on the Gold Coast 346-349
F. Outfit for the West Coast 350-352

LIST OF ILLUSTRATIONS.

1. Native Majesty on the Gold Coast		*Frontispiece*
		PAGE
2. Map of the Gold Coast of the Present Day	*opposite*	1
3. The Gold Coast of the Seventeenth Century		13
4. A Fetish Priest		48
5. Native Pottery and Silverwork of the Ashantis		52
6. Native Loom for Weaving Cloth		54
7. Gold Coast Beetles: The Goliath		77
8. Typical Native Huts	*opposite*	81
9. A Group of Labourers		87
10. Ashanti Gold Weights		101
11. Ashanti Gold Weights		113
12. Fort St. Anthony, Axim		136
13. Squaring Mahogany on the Beach, Axim		141
14. Interior of Wesleyan School, Chama		146
15. A Street Scene in Elmina	*opposite*	153
16. Cape Coast Castle	*opposite*	157
17. The Lighthouse, Cape Coast		160
18. Interior Courtyard of Cape Coast Castle		169
19. View of the Town of Cape Coast	*opposite*	177
20. View of the Beach at Cape Coast	*opposite*	185
21. Christiansborg Castle, Accra		190
22. Town Travelling in Accra		201
23. A Group of Officials and Merchants		203
24. Basle Mission Station, Begoro		214
25. Base of a Big Tree, Aburi		241
26. The Road to Kumasi	*opposite*	265
27. The Town of Kumasi (1817)		285
28. Roads from Kumasi		291
29. Group of Native Women	*opposite*	304
30. British Resident at Kumasi and Officers		313
31. A Native Beauty		320
32. A Wedding Group		329

h

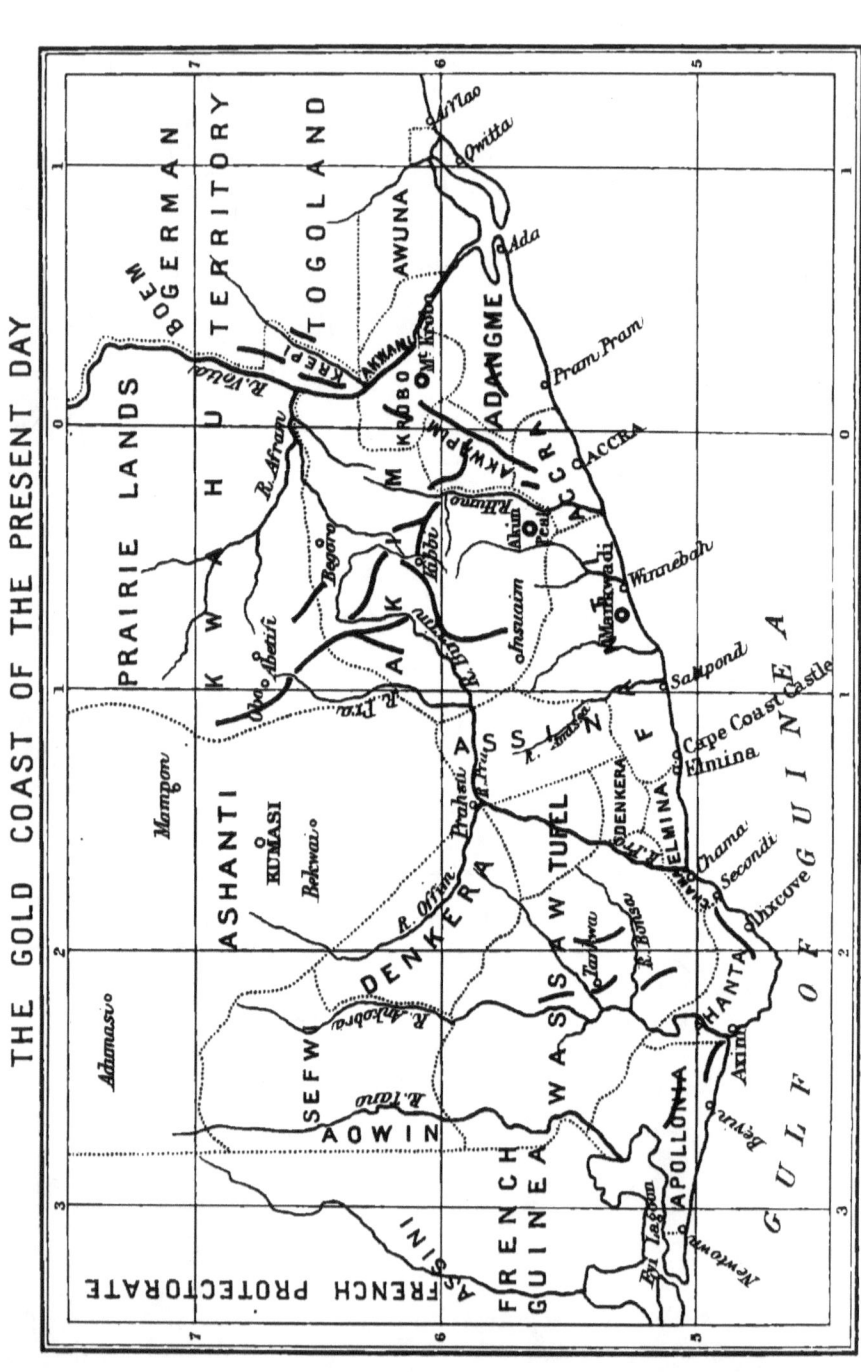

THE GOLD COAST PAST AND PRESENT.

CHAPTER I.

The Gulf of Guinea—Divisions—Early Expeditions to the Coast—French and Portuguese Claims—Early English Trading Companies—The Gold Coast in Bosman's Time—The Gold Coast of To-day—General View of the Colony.

IN all the old maps of Africa, and indeed in many of those of more recent times, that part of the African continent known as the *Guinea Coast* was marked as occupying the strip of shore running almost due east from *Sierra Leone* to the *Bight of Biafra*. It had a seaboard of some 1400 miles, stretching roughly for 10° of longitude on either side of the meridian of Greenwich, and at no part being more than 9° north of the Equator.

According to Monsieur Dubois in *Timbuctoo the Mysterious* (1897), the name Guinea owes its origin to the ancient town of Jenne, the capital of Jenneris, a country upon the banks of the River Niger, some distance south-west of Timbuctoo. In olden times this town sent her merchandise to the coast, and when the first Europeans trading between Benin and Cape Palmas asked where the gold and produce offered them for sale came from, the natives answered "From Jenne". Her name was thus given to our present Gulf of Guinea, and also indirectly to an English coin, the guinea, so called from the first pieces being struck from the gold that came from there.

This strip of coast was generally sub-divided into four minor territories, which received their designations from the commercial commodities they then furnished to the European adventurers of the sixteenth, seventeenth and eighteenth centuries, who risked their lives among the perils and dangers of this part of the then almost unknown continent, for the traffic in grains, ivory, slaves and gold.

These four divisions, extending eastward from the *Isles de Los*, were severally known as *The Malaguetta or Grain Coast, The Tooth or Ivory Coast, The Gold Coast,* and *The Slave Coast;* of which, at the present day, one only retains and deserves the name that was bestowed upon it by these ancient navigators, *viz.*, *The Gold Coast.*

The Grain or Malaguetta Coast of these early times is now known under the more modern title of the *Free State of Liberia*, and extends from Sierra Leone to Cape Formosa. Why the ambiguous name of the Grain Coast was given to this territory it is difficult to say, for the grain for which this part of Guinea was once famous was a condiment and not a cereal. The late Sir R. F. Burton thus describes it in his *Wanderings in West Africa* (1863). "It is a real cardamon, of which many varieties grow along the whole length of the western coast of intertropical Africa. The flower is of great beauty, the shrub is cane-like, and the fruit, which appears close to the ground with a pyriform pod with crimson skin, enclosing black-brown seeds, is surrounded by a juicy placenta. On a long and thirsty march, nothing is more pleasant than a handful of these cardamons, the acidity of the pulp contrasting most pleasantly with the pungency of the spice." By the Dutch they were called *Guinea Grains;* and by the trade, Malaguetta pepper; and the demand in Europe in the sixteenth century led to the discovery of many ports on "the coast". The grains were then principally used for giving the fire and flavour to spirituous liquors and in the adulteration of beer. At last the importation into England was forbidden; cases of poisoning being attributed to it. The natives of the West Coast still use this cardamon extensively as a condiment and a medicine; it is a stomachic, a carminative, and also an external irritant. The people of the Gold Coast, when suffering from headache, rub over the forehead a paste made from Malaguetta pepper, and the powder is applied during the hot stage of fever. In earliest times these grains were supposed to have been derived from cochineal, which was then thought to be a parasitical plant instead of an insect. In Martin's *History of the British Colonies* (1834) we find the following explanation for the name given to the Grain Coast. "The species of pepper to which it owes its name is produced from a small parasitical plant, with beautiful green leaves, and the fruit of which, resembling a fig, presents, when opened, aromatic grains, forming the valuable part. At its first introduction into Europe, where such articles were little known, it received the flattering appellation of 'Grains of Paradise'. After the diffusion, however, of the finer species from India, it fell into total disrepute; and this coast, producing no other articles of export, has been the least frequented of any part of Guinea."

"The first of these grains is Malaguetta, otherwise called Paradise Grains, or Guinea Pepper, a fruit which is not generally known. It grows on shrubs in red shells or husks, which at a distance afford a very pleasant prospect. Within these husks is contained the Malaguetta, separated into four or five divisions and covered by a white film. This Guinea pepper grows also in a different manner, not unlike large grass reeds.

" Here also grows a fruit on shrubs, which in taste and figure resembles cardamon, which I doubt not but it is."

The Ivory Coast extended from Cape Formosa eastward to Assinie, but the name is now entirely a misnomer; the animals that once supplied Europe with tusks having been either exterminated or driven away by the ravages of the hunter; the ivory of the present day coming from ports much farther to the south. On the old *Ivory Coast* there were but few settlements; Fresco, Cape Lahou, Jack-a-Jack, Grand Bassam and Assinie were among the chief, the last two being French. The teeth obtained in olden times were of good quality and often very large, some weighing as much as 200 pounds.

This part of West Africa is now known as French Guinea; it is under the administration of Senegal, and includes the country east and west of Cape Palmas for some 150 miles; of which the chief part is at present distinguished as the *Kru Coast*. This name is variously written Kru, Kroo, Croo and Krou. It would hardly be fair to leave this part of the Guinea Coast without saying something about the peculiar tribes which inhabit the Kru country, and the part they have played and still play in this rapidly civilising part of Africa.

Bishop Payne describes "the Krus as a small tribe,

occupying that part of the coast lying half-way between Cape Mesurado and Cape Palmas, with a seaboard extending some twenty or thirty miles, and stretching perhaps as far into the interior. Originally they possessed but five settlements—Little Kru, Settra Kru, Krubah, Nanna Kru and King Will's town. Of the inhabitants of this part of the coast they were the first to leave their country and go to sea; but soon other tribes followed their example, until, at the present day, some twenty or more tribes, numbering perhaps some 20,000 souls, are largely engaged in the various spheres of labour throughout the whole of Upper and Lower Guinea under the common name of Kru men, but more commonly known as Kru boys, whether their age be twelve or forty. One most noticeable feature about them is that they never enslave one another; yet in past days they were the life and soul of the Spanish and Portuguese slave traders, and might well have been considered the greatest kidnappers on the coast. On the decline of the slave trade they offered as seamen to the ships of war and merchantmen then on the coast, and have at the present day practically become the 'coolies' and 'lascars' of West Africa."

The tribes now supplying the boys for this work come from Sinou, Sette Kru, Niffu, Grand Cess, Cavally and Cape Palmas, and from the surrounding country for some forty miles inland. Their language and physique prove them to be cognate tribes, and from their intercourse, general morals and behaviour they may all be included under the one name of Kru boys.

The features of these people are distinctly African, the skin is very dark, the hair short and kinky, and often cut and shaved into peculiar patterns, which gives the cranium a very grotesque appearance to European eyes.

The skull is often remarkably flat at the back, and sometimes narrows much towards the crown, thus appearing almost pyramidical in shape. The face is always cut and tattooed, the variation in the marks proclaiming the tribe from which the individual comes. The teeth, which are very fine, are cut, sharpened and sometimes extracted. This cutting is most often seen in the shape of an inverted letter V, which is done between the middle incisors of the upper jaw. All this disfigurement is done in the roughest possible manner, the implement being simply a knife or rough piece of iron, and the process, instead of helping to destroy the teeth, seems to act rather as a preservative, and appears opposed to the views once held by dentists and physiologists, that destruction of the tooth enamel involved the loss of the tooth. After food, the mouth is always rinsed and the teeth cleansed, and it is rare that a day passes without the whole body being bathed, thus greatly reducing the unpleasant odour which always exists. The tooth stick, too, is largely used.

Of all the African tribes belonging to the West Coast, the Kru boy lends himself most readily to imitation of the European. In his native state he is a fine-looking savage, with the muscles of the shoulders, chest and arms finely developed, a single cloth round the middle being his only covering, a rude chain of coloured string or even a strip of hairy skin or beads round the neck, whilst ankles and wrists are variously adorned with ivory, brass or iron rings. One of his greatest weaknesses is a hat, and this covering embraces every kind and colour that can be included from an old "top hat" to a cotton nightcap.

A few years away from home, however, changes all this, and when he returns again to his country, which he must always do, he is transformed in the most grotesque manner. His wages have been spent upon his outfit, and he returns to "we country," as he calls it, in the most glaring colours of Manchester cotton clothes, or in cast-off European garments either too large or too small; and with personal impedimenta in the shape of a wooden box the size of a tool chest—in which are secreted all the odds and ends he has managed to appropriate during his term of service—two or three kegs of gunpowder, a case or two of Hamburg gin, brass and iron pans, brush, comb and looking-glass, all of which are duly appreciated and quickly divided by the members of his expectant family, who have been awaiting his return.

By many of the other races on the West Coast the Kru boys are despised, and yet they are doing all the rough work along this western part of Africa, from Sierra Leone to the mouth of the Niger. They work the cargoes of the vessels plying between these points, and are to be found in every factory down the coast, preparing the palm oil, the palm kernels, and the rubber for the export trade. When trained, they make fairly good personal servants, but would be of little or no use as soldiers, too large a proportion of cowardice being found in their nature. They make excellent canoe and surf-boat men, being apparently neither afraid of the water nor of the sharks that abound in it.

When away from their own country they adopt, or more often are given by their new masters a new name, which to European ears sounds in many cases most ludicrous, but by which in future they are always known. Thus in every coast town will be found Kru boys answering to such names as Seabreeze, Jack Savage, Half-Dollar, No. 1, Bottle o' Beer, Prince of Wales, Best Man, and so on, *ad libitum.*

The one object of the Kru boy in leaving home is to make money, in order to return again to his own country as a " fine gentleman ". For the first few years of his voluntary exile, he is fleeced of his earnings and belongings by the various members of his family and the headmen of his village, every time he returns to " we country," but after five or six voyages he learns enough English to become a headman, and then he is able to fleece others in place of being fleeced himself.

The Kru women seldom or never leave their country. I have seen but two offer themselves for service on the Gold Coast. This was to the Roman Catholic Mission at Cape Coast Castle; but without the aid of the Kru boy, much of the present trade of West Africa would entirely cease.

The Gold Coast is the third division of Guinea, and, as before stated, is the only part that now retains the name that was first bestowed upon it, as early as the fourteenth century. Since that time it has seen many changes, until at the present day it has become one of the chief centres of interest, both in the diplomatic and the commercial world. The Gold Coast has well deserved its name, for from the beginning of the sixteenth century, and on through the two succeeding centuries, it poured a steady flow of the yellow metal into Europe, and attracted to its shores the adventurers of all nations, until down to the present time, it is estimated that between sixty and seventy million pounds of gold sterling have been scraped from this auriferous tract of the Guinea Coast.

As this little work is to treat specifically of the Gold Coast and the history of its inhabitants, so far as I have been able to gather it, I will not introduce in this slight description any further particulars concerning it, but proceed at once to the fourth and last division of the old Guinea Coast, which was one of the three great depôts, as it were, of African slavery, and appropriately named *The Slave Coast.*

That part of the Guinea territory known as the Slave Coast extended in early times from the Volta River in the Gold Coast eastward to Biafra, and included in its area the now well-known countries of Togo, Dahomey, Lagos, Yoruba and Benin, and formed, together with Ashanti, one of the three great slave-producing parts of the African continent. In these early times Ashanti, Dahomey, Yoruba and Benin were among the most powerful states to be found in this part of Africa. Ruled by savage despots, and maintaining what might be termed large standing armies, well armed and disciplined in their own native fashion, and used for raids and forays upon their weaker neighbours, they supplied the European adventurers who visited the coast for this purpose, with their cargoes of " black ivory," in exchange for those commodities most tempting to these wily savages. Without exception, each of these once most powerful nations has fallen in its turn before the march of European progress, which has slowly but steadily pushed its way throughout the whole West Coast. The last to go were Ashanti and Benin, the latter of which will be long remembered for the brutal murder of Acting-Consul Philips and his party, when on a mission of peace to Benin city early in 1897.

The two other great centres of the African slave trade lay in the countries immediately surrounding the Gambia and Senegal Rivers on the one part, and the territories along the whole mouth of the Congo upon the other, but with these it is not my intention to deal.

Early Expeditions.—So far as is known, and according to their own writers, the French were the first Europeans to visit the Gulf of Guinea. This is stated to have been sometime between 1364 and 1413, in the reign of Charles the Fifth, when they explored as far as the present Elmina of the Gold Coast. This claim to be the first navigators of what was then an unknown region is upheld by many French writers, who state that a company of Dieppe merchants visited Guinea and founded the trading stations at Goree, Verde and Grand Cess. The date of this visit is said to have been 1364, and the expedition to have consisted of only two vessels of one hundred tons each. Some eighteen years later, in 1382, a combined fleet from Rouen and Dieppe, consisting of three ships, again visited the coast, one of which, the *Virgin*, is stated to have reached Commendah and Mina, and to have obtained large supplies of gold from these places. More than this, it is alleged that the French were the builders of the first fort at Elmina in 1383, which was afterwards rebuilt by the Portuguese in 1481, and named St. George del Mina or Ora del Mina—the mouth of the mines. This occupation by the Rouen and Dieppe merchants is reported to have been the means of importing large quantities of gold, ivory and Malaguetta pepper into France, and of establishing a flourishing trade between the two countries, which lasted for about half a century, when European continental disturbances caused the French to abandon their West Coast settlements. This would be somewhere about 1413, when the attention and resources of France were drawn away from her colonial enterprise, and concentrated upon her European wars, which continued to occupy her till nearly the end of the fifteenth century (1490).

This claim of early discovery and the establishment of trade by the French is strongly disputed by the Portuguese, who claim (and, according to early English authorities, are supported in their claim) the honour of being the first to visit and to trade with this part of the world.

Their claim is based upon the fact that Prince Henry of Portugal, the navigator, was the first European power that directed attention to the West Coast of Africa, and caused it to be explored as far as Sierra Leone, and that in 1442 Gonzales Baldeza, after an absence of two years, returned to Portugal, bringing with him ten slaves and a large amount of gold dust. The slaves are reported to have been presented to Pope Martin the Fifth, who thereupon conferred upon Portugal the sovereignty and right over all the lands that might be discovered in this part of the world.

Prince Henry died in 1463, and up to this date no point of discovery further than Sierra Leone is claimed in this account by the Portuguese. In 1481, however, a second expedition under the patronage of King John the Second of Portugal, is reported to have been sent, with a force of some 700 men. This expedition reached the present Gold Coast, landed at the Elmina of our time, and built the Fort of St. George of that name. That the Portuguese built this fort there is no doubt, but because no mention is made of the existence, or traces found, of the ruins of the fort previously alleged to have been built by the French, it does not follow that the French had not been there before them, as they claim to have been in 1383.

Another Portuguese account says that in 1471 Fernâs Gomez, a well-known Lisbon merchant, obtained the permission of his Government to trade upon the West Coast for five years under the following conditions: an annual payment to the Portuguese Government of £44 9s., and an annual voyage along the coast for not less than 300 miles. They then claim that in the five years some 1500 miles of coast were discovered and Elmina established.

These various accounts prove the establishment of the Portuguese at Elmina, but the actual year seems somewhat in doubt, for Bosman, writing in 1705, says: "I cannot pretend to inform you exactly when they (the Portuguese) began to build the castle, but can only tell you that we took it from them in 1638; and it is indeed justly become famous, for to speak the fair truth of it, for beauty and strength, it hath not its equal upon the whole coast".

I will not attempt to decide upon the rival claims of France and Portugal to the right of first discovery, but leave the reader to form his own opinion. However it may have been, neither one nor the other enjoyed the sole rights thus obtained for very long, for the commencement of the traffic in slaves and gold attracted other nations to the Guinea Coast, notably among whom were the Dutch, the Danes and the English.

The advent of these three nations, the gold produce, and the excitement of the slave trade soon caused that

GOLD COAST OF SEVENTEENTH CENTURY.

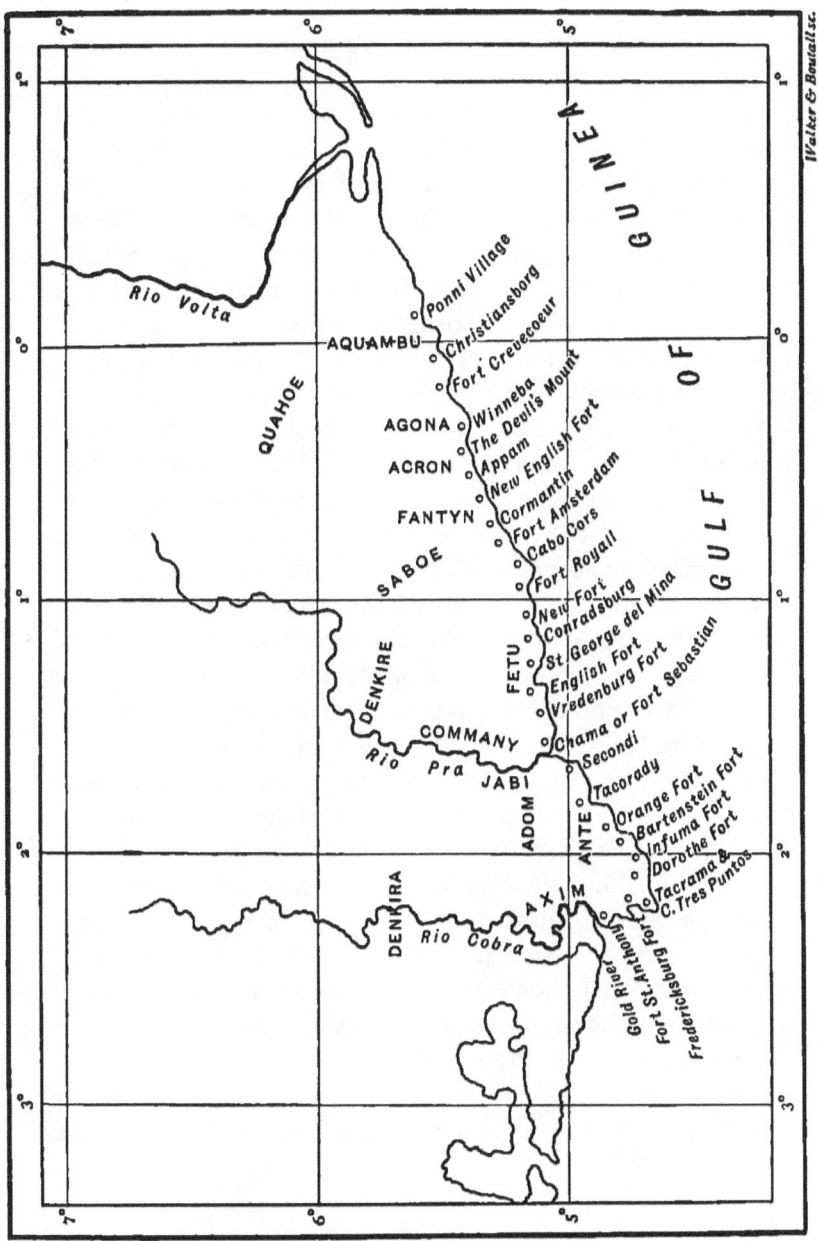

THE GOLD COAST OF THE SEVENTEENTH CENTURY.

part of Guinea known as the Gold Coast to be studded with forts and factories from end to end. A glance at the map on page 13 will show a total of twenty-five, three of which were Danish, two Brandenburgers and seventeen Dutch and English. There were probably more. The Rev. Mr. Reindorf gives the total as thirty-five, sixteen Dutch, fourteen English, and five Danish. These forts served a three-fold purpose: defence against hostile attack by the natives and from other European powers, as a protection for the trading factories, and as slave barracoons.

We have seen that the Portuguese lost St. George del Mina to the Dutch in 1638, by whom they were finally expelled from the coast some four years later, in 1642. Bosman drily remarks: "The Portuguese served for setting dogs to spring the game, which, as soon as they had done, was seized by others". The Danes in their turn ceded their possessions to the English in 1850, and the Dutch in 1868 and 1872, and many of the old forts are now a mass of ruins and tangled bush. A complete list of the forts will be found at the end of this chapter. The history of the English upon the Gold Coast forms a very interesting study, particularly when regarded with our action of the present day concerning this neglected spot of our great empire.

The first English mercantile transaction recorded is that of Captain Thomas Wyndham, who in 1551 made the first voyage to the coast and sent home a cargo of Malaguetta pepper (Guinea grains) and a large amount of gold dust. It is however stated that the English were acquainted with the coast as early as the reign of Edward the Fourth, but of this there is no authentic record, though the date is fixed at 1556. About the latter end of the reign of Edward the Sixth, some London merchants fitted out the first English ships that ever traded to Guinea, and in the reign of Queen Mary, and for the first ten or twelve years of Queen Elizabeth, sundry other private ships were fitted out for the same parts; but the English, not having as yet any settlements or plantations in the West Indies, and consequently no occasion for negroes, traded in such ships only for gold, elephants' teeth and Malaguetta pepper, and all such voyages were undertaken and performed at the hazard of losing the ships and cargoes if they fell into the hands of the Portuguese, without the least ground to hope for any redress or satisfaction for the same. In the thirtieth year of the reign of Queen Elizabeth, England, being then at war with Spain and Portugal, formed a company for the "better discovering and carrying on of the gum trade, from the northernmost part of the river Senegal, and from and within that river, all along that coast unto the most southern part of the Gambia and within the same". To this company was also granted the sole right to trade, in, to and from the said rivers and countries for a certain term of years, with prohibition to all others to trade to the same places, on pain of forfeiture of ships and goods; and these were the first merchants that ever traded to the coast of West Africa, by and under the authority and protection of the Crown of Great Britain. In the reign of James the First and his successor Charles, and during the time of Cromwell, other persons were encouraged by public authority to trade to other parts of Guinea, and to take such measures for the better carrying on and improving the same as they should judge most proper. The result of this was that one fort was built at Cormantine in 1624 on the Gold Coast, and another on the river Gambia on the North Coast, and these were the only places of consequence which the English possessed on the West Coast at the time of the Restoration.

King Charles the Second, soon after his restoration, was made acquainted with the precarious state to which the trade of his subjects in those parts had been reduced, and having received many complaints touching the interruption to and the depredations committed upon the ships of his nation by the Dutch West India Company on the coast of Africa, it became necessary to consider not only a proper method for protecting and securing the trade for the future, but likewise in what manner reparation might be obtained for damage done. From this arose the first corporation for trade with West Africa, and such subjects of the king as were willing to engage in this trade were granted such powers, privileges and encouragements as the circumstances at that time required. This was done by letters patent under the great seal of England, bearing the date of 10th January, 1662, and the body of English merchants was styled the "Company of Royal Adventurers of England trading to Africa". This power was further augmented in 1672 by charter bearing date of 27th September, granting all the lands, countries, havens, roads, rivers and other places in Africa, from the port of Sallee in South Barbary to the Cape of Good Hope, for the term of 1000 years, with the entire trade and traffic into and from the said countries and places, with prohibition to all others of his subjects to visit or frequent the same without the license of the said Company. Subscriptions were invited from all His Majesty's subjects, but only a sum of £111,000 was obtained, which was largely spent in repairing the existing forts and in hastily building new ones. The small English fort at Cabo Corso was enlarged, and Fredericksborg or Fort Royall near it was purchased from the Danes, forts were also built at Accra, Dixcove, Winnebah, Sekondi, Commendah and Anamaboe, thus placing the English Company on a footing with the Dutch. The fort on the Gambia was lost in 1695, being taken, plundered and destroyed by a squadron of French men-of-war, from which time the French disputed our claims in that territory.

Very little good was done, and it was not until later times that any serious effort at establishment was made, to extend the English trading station and fort established at Cormantine in 1624 between the present Saltpond and Anamaboe. The effort gradually extended itself until, in 1662, we find a company incorporated under the patronage of the Duke of York, afterwards James the Second, when the present James Fort was built in Accra. This was known as the "Royal Company," or the "Company of the Royal Adventurers of England trading to Africa". The life of this venture was of short duration, for from repeated attacks by the Dutch admiral, De Ruyter, it was compelled to surrender its charter to Government in 1667, after a brief existence of five years. The decease of this company was, however, quickly followed by the formation of another, and in 1672 we find fresh powers and privileges granted to "maintain and extend the African trade," under the title of the "Royal African Company". This venture was more successful than its predecessor, and soon some fifteen forts and factories were established along the coast to enjoy a somewhat short and changing prosperity during the time that William Bosman was the chief factor for the Dutch at Elmina, and to whom we are indebted for much of our knowledge of the coast at this time. A strange fatality, however, seemed to follow the formation of the English trading companies. The "Royal African Company" declined, became bankrupt and disappeared from the scene, and to take its place in 1753 the "African Company" was established for free trade on the Gold Coast to all His Majesty's subjects. This company followed in the wake of the others, and in 1821 ceased to exist, and all British possessions on the West Coast of Africa were, by the English Parliament, made mere dependencies of Sierra Leone. This was about the worst thing that could have happened for the prosperity and general welfare of the colony. This was in 1821. Six years later saw another change. Owing to the expenses of Sir Charles McCarthy's Ashanti war, the Government found themselves compelled to deliver the various forts of the Gold Coast over to the merchants, on condition that Cape Coast Castle and James Fort, Accra, should still be administered from Sierra Leone, and that the general affairs should be under the control of three African merchants and a paid secretary, the Home Government contributing £4000 per annum towards the necessary expenses. This arrangement lasted until 1844, when Government again took possession of the Gold Coast, Commander Hill, R.N., being appointed the first Governor. From this period to the present time the various vicissitudes through which the coast has passed will be fully dealt with in succeeding chapters.

According to Bosman, the Gold Coast originally extended for about sixty miles, but this is not at all accurate. He says: "The Gold Coast, being a part of Guinea, is extended about sixty miles, beginning with the *Gold River*, twelve miles above Axim, and ending with the village *Ponni*, seven or eight miles east of Accra". This is so far incorrect, with regard to the distance, that one wonders by what mileage it could have been computed, though it is quite possible the Dutch mile of 9000 yards was the medium of measurement.

From my own actual travelling on the coast, I make the distance from Accra to Cape Coast about eighty-one miles, and from Cape Coast to Axim much the same; add to this the twelve miles between Axim and the Gold River and the seven or eight miles between Accra and the Ponni Village, and we have a distance of about 180 miles English for the extent of the Gold Coast, early in the eighteenth century, between its western and eastern limits as laid down by this old Dutch author.

A glance at the map on page 13 will show to the reader the extent of the coast, with the numerous forts and factories studding the whole coast line, one to every eight or nine miles. Twenty-five are mentioned in his map, of which three were Danish, two belonged to the Brandenburgers, and the remaining twenty to the Dutch and the English.

At Accra the English had but James Fort, while to the west of Accra, or to the windward as it is termed, they held Winnebah, Mumford, Gomoah, Tantum, Cormantine, Anamaboe, Cape Coast Castle, Commendah, Sekondi, Dixcove and Beyin. Intersecting these were the Dutch establishments of Barracoe, Appam, Cormantine, Mouri, Chama, Commendah, Takoradi, Boutri, Acoda, Hollandia, Brandenburg and Axim, while to the east they held Dutch Accra, Labaddi, Pona, Temma and Pram Pram.

In addition to these there were five held by the Danes, *viz.*, Christiansborg, Fredericksborg, Augustenborg, Kongenstein and Prindenstein, all situated between Accra and the Volta River.

The countries included in the Gold Coast numbered eleven, and extended from the Ancobra River to the Ponni Village, each containing two or three towns or villages, situated upon the sea-shore, either under or between the forts of the Europeans; but the largest and most populous towns were found farther inland. These districts were then known by the following names: Axim, Ante, Adom, Jabi, Kommany, Fetu, Saboe, Fantyn, Acron, Agona and Aquambu.

At the present day the Gold Coast consists of a much larger territory than that just described, the coast line having been considerably increased by the addition of the Apollonia country to the west, and the Adangme and Awoonah countries to the east. These last mentioned territories were added to the Protectorate in 1850, when the King of Denmark sold his forts on the Gold Coast to the British Government for £10,000.

Some seventeen years later, in 1867, the Governments of Great Britain and Holland by mutual agreement rearranged their possessions upon the Gold Coast. England transferred all her forts, rights and privileges west of the Sweet Water River as far as Newtown, its western limit, to Holland, and in return the Dutch Government gave over to the English all the forts, rights and privileges previously held by them to the eastward of the same river.

At this period neither Dutch nor English claimed

any land outside their forts, though the former held, near Axim, a very considerable tract of country, watered by the Ancobra, and bounded by the kingdoms of Apollonia, Denkira and Wassaw. A further transfer of territory was made in 1872, when the Dutch Government handed over to the British all its remaining forts and territories held by them at that time, including those that had been previously transferred to them by the English in 1867. Thus, from 1872, the whole coast has been in British hands, with the French for neighbours on the west, and the Germans on the east. The French at this time took but little interest in their possessions to the west, having stations only at Grand Bassam, Assini and Little Bassam, so much so that they let their possessions to Messrs. Swanzy & Co., who opened up a great trade upon the Assini and Tando Rivers, and the lagoons connected with them. Although the French had practically withdrawn, no formal declaration of such was made, and they contented themselves by maintaining a naval connection only with this part of the coast, to be again developed in later years by actual occupation and mercantile activity. Thus ended the rights of the Portuguese, Dutch and Danes upon the Gold Coast of Africa, so that instead of the strip of sixty miles mentioned by Bosman, there is now a seaboard of some 360 miles extending from Newtown, its extreme western limit, to Danoe in the east, bordering upon French Guinea and Togoland respectively. This seaboard is now divided and recognised as consisting of some eight distinct native political divisions, in place of the eleven known in the early part of the eighteenth century, and mentioned by Bosman.

These countries occur in the following order from the west :—
1. Apollonia from Newtown to Axim.
2. Ahanta from Axim to Sekondi.
3. Chama from Sekondi to Chama.
4. Elmina from Chama to Cape Coast.
5. Fanti from Cape Coast to Bereku.
6. Ga or Accra from Bereku to Pram Pram.
7. Adangme from Pram Pram to Ada ; and
8. Awoonah from Ada to Danoe.

Besides this large increase of seaboard, the interior territories have been extended in a most irregular manner, until the whole of the countries from the coast, up to and including the eleventh parallel of N. latitude, are now under British protection, under the comprehensive title of the Gold Coast Colony and Protectorate.

Geographically the coast extends from 3° 2' W. longitude to 1° 3' E. longitude, a distance of some 360 miles from point to point.

The interior territories now include some very important states, the chief of which are :—
1. Aowin and Sefwi.
2. Wassaw.
3. Denkira. } in the west.
4. Tufel.
5. Assin.
6. Akim.
7. Aquapim. } in the east.
8. Krobo.
9. Krepi.

While still farther inland to the north are the important countries of Ashanti, Kwahu, Nkoranza and Dagwumba.

Viewed from the deck of a passing steamer, this coast presents to the eye an almost unbroken line of low, flat, sandy beach, rising at intervals into bold, rocky headlands, projecting in some cases far out to sea. Along this low-lying shore, the great Atlantic rollers break with unceasing violence, causing the beach to be continually fringed with boiling surf, thus making the landing on the coast anything but pleasant, should duty take you there. Upon the Apollonian, Adangme and Awoonah shores, this surf is the most dangerous, and it is only at such places as Axim, Takoradi, Dixcove and Elmina, that landing in an ordinary ship's boat is at all possible, and then often only in exceptionally quiet weather. Navigation along the Gold Coast, and in fact, along the whole coast of the Gulf of Guinea, requires much caution, as the shore is flat and comparatively destitute of any conspicuous landmarks, while the heavy surf, borne in from the whole breadth of the vast Atlantic, breaks continually against the shore. Landing from a steamer is accomplished by a surf-boat. No companion ladder can be used on account of the swell. Men clamber over the side of the ship by a rope ladder of the roughest description into the surf-boat waiting to receive them, while lady passengers are swung between sky and sea in a tub or basket kept for the purpose.

Once in the surf-boat one feels comparatively safe, though to my mind there is more danger attending this last mile and a half of the journey than in the whole 4000 miles' run from Liverpool. Except at the places I have mentioned, great care has to be exercised in the selection of a situation for the anchorage of a ship of any size. As a rule, steamers anchor from one to two miles from the shore in about six to ten fathoms of water. Smaller trading vessels may approach nearer, but as a very heavy swell almost continually sets in, it is necessary not to be too near the breakers. The strength of the current varies along the whole coast, but its average rate may be taken as from one to two miles to the eastward per hour. The surf is supposed to be at its worst at the new and the full moon. The sea-breeze is very regular along the coast and comes up from the south-west. On this account the coast has been divided into windward and leeward districts, the former extending from Cape Apollonia, 2° 35′ west longitude, to the Secoom River, some ten miles west of Accra, and the latter from the same river to the town of Danoe upon the eastern boundary of the colony.

An ordinary surf-boat is manned by a crew of eleven men, ten to paddle and one to steer. Good time is kept in paddling, and the work is somewhat varied by the monotonous droning of a chant in the vernacular, of which the chorus is generally in native English, and runs as follows:—

> "Good old massa come from home,
> Leave him fader, leave him moder,
> Dashee me one hunder pouns,
> Good old massa come from home".

When near the shore a wave is selected; all row for dear life, and, riding in on the crest of the sea, the boat is run upon the sand before the next breaker is able to overtake it. The great danger lies in the boat getting broadside on and turning turtle.

Vegetation in the colony flourishes in many places down to the water's edge, thus causing the spectator, who views this part of the globe for the first time, to think that perhaps, after all, it is a much better land than it has been painted, and giving the country the appearance of being very fertile and extremely well wooded—a character which it most undoubtedly deserves. From the shore, stretching far away into the interior, alternately extend rolling plains and impenetrable bush, gently undulating, rising at last, as far as the eye can carry, to a range of mountains of considerable height, running almost parallel with the coast from southwest to north-east, and branching and extending into the Akim, Kwahu, Aquapim, Krobo and Krepi countries.

In some respects Nature has been most lavish in her gifts to this land, whilst in others, she appears to have been niggardly and selfish. On the one hand, she has given a teeming population, an abundantly well-wooded and fertile country, an unlimited wealth of gold and a fair average of internal water-way; whilst on the other hand, dangerous shoals line the coast, unceasing surf thunders along the shore, the river mouths are locked with sand, where the water surges and boils as though it were the sport of ten thousand giants, and deadly malaria impregnates the air.

The present capital of the colony and the seat of the Government since 1874 is Accra, an anglicised term of the Fanti word "Nkran," meaning an "ant," by which appellation the Akras were once known, and about which I shall have more to say in a subsequent chapter. Accra is situated on the coast near the eastern confines of the colony, and is really composed of three distinct towns under separate native rulers, *viz.:* James Town, Ussher Town and Christiansborg, the whole forming one long, irregular settlement, extending from west to east for a distance of about three miles, there being, however, a considerable stretch of open country between Ussher Town and Christiansborg. James Town and Ussher Town are most irregularly constructed, and contain but few decent streets; narrow alleys and tortuous turnings serving as passages from one part of the town to another. Fortunately, a large portion of this crowded and ill-built section of these towns was completely destroyed by fire in 1894. The area, once thus occupied, is now being cleared; and I believe in the place of the former miscellaneous collection of mud huts and hovels of all shapes and sizes, that Accra will soon be able to boast of a large portion of its area having been laid out in well-planned and symmetrically-arranged streets.

Cape Coast Castle, also on the coast, and about eighty miles to the west of Accra, is the next important town, and was the seat of the Government of the colony until it was removed to the present capital in 1874. *Cabo Corso* was its original name. It is situated on hilly ground, and is, like Accra, most irregularly built, smells horribly and is very hot—native huts and European quarters jostling side by side in all parts of the town. From the sea it looks very picturesque. Other towns of importance on the coast are Elmina and Axim to the west of Cape Coast, Saltpond to the east, and Ada and Kwitta on the eastern shores of the colony.

In the interior are many well-situated towns, at most of which, especially in the eastern part of the colony, are to be found members of the "Basle Mission Society," with their wives and families. Their most important centres are *Aburi* and *Akropong* in the Aquapim country, *Kibbi* or *Kyebi* and *Begoro* in the Akim country, *Abetifi* in the Kwahu country, *Odumase* in the Krobo country, and *Anum* in the Krepi country. *Ada,* at the mouth of the Volta, is also an important " Basle Mission " station. This mission, of which a further account will be given in the later pages of this work, has a two-fold purpose, *viz.*, that of trade allied to civilisation and Christianity. The Wesleyan Mission has also a station at *Aburi* in Aquapim, though the headquarters of this body are at *Cape Coast,* from whence their branch stations extend east and west for the whole extent of the coast, with a few minor interior centres. On the coast, too, are found the stations of the Roman Catholic Mission of " St. Francis de Sales " from Lyons, their most important centres being *Elmina, Cape Coast, Saltpond, Accra* and *Kwitta.*

The population of the Gold Coast Colony is roughly estimated at $1\frac{1}{2}$ millions, mostly the descendants of the negro family, possessing, in the majority of cases, the marked racial physical characteristics of that people, though the close observer might detect slight differences of build and facial expression among the various peoples of the different countries comprising the colony. The wandering Arab of the desert is to be found in every town, and is a stately and well-ordered member of the West African population, though perhaps not quite so clean and sweet-smelling as he might be. The men generally give one the impression of being physically very strong and capable of great endurance; the women are for the most part tall and well-proportioned, and easy in their movements. Maturity in both sexes arrives early, prime of life is of short duration, and senility follows quickly in its wake. The children are active, lithesome little mortals, and, when young, are very precocious and apt to learn. No one, however, in this part of the world seems to work for work's sake. So long as the immediate wants of the present can be satisfied, no one cares to remember the past, or has any ambition for the future. *Man* works to satisfy his most pressing needs, and *woman* works for, and to satisfy, the wants of man.

The whole coast from end to end is dotted with innumerable fishing villages, and the male population in these spend their time in catching enormous quantities of all kinds of fish with which the tropical waters of the Gulf of Guinea abound. The fish is then dried and cured in a peculiar native fashion, which to the European nose is most offensive, packed in loads, and carried by the women and children to the interior towns, to be exchanged for other food products not obtainable near the coast, or to be sold for cash.

Fishing on the Gold Coast was and is still esteemed next to trading, and those who follow it are more numerous than those engaged in other employments. It is now generally followed along the whole coast, and every morning (Tuesday excepted, which is Fetish day or Sunday) hundreds of canoes put out to sea and return about noon with a plentiful harvest, which is dried and sold to the inland inhabitants, who have come down to buy and sell again at the interior towns.

COMPLETE LIST OF FORTS ON THE GOLD COAST.

(A.) DUTCH.

Situation.	Name.	When built.	Present.
Axim	St. Anthony	? Portuguese. (captured by the Dutch in 1642).	Still used.
Montfort	Fredericksborg	1725.	Disused.
Boutri	Bartenstein	,,	,,

FORTS ON THE GOLD COAST.

Situation.	Name.	When built.	Present.
Takoradi	Wilsen	1725	Disused.
Sekondi	Orange	1680	Still used.
Chama	St. Sebastian	1690	,,
Commendah	Vredenburg	1688	Disused.
Elmina	St. Jago	1640	Still used.
Elmina	St. George	1481	,,
Moree	Nassau	1637	Disused.
Cormantine	Amsterdam	1665	,,
Appam	Patience	1697	Still used.
Seniah	Bereku	1667	,,
Cape Coast	Cabo Corso	1624	,,
Dutch Accra	Crevecoeur (Ussher Fort).	1650	,,

(B.) DANISH.

Accra	Christiansborg	1659	Still used.
Teschi	Augustenborg	1700	Disused.
Ningo	Fredensborg	1735	,,
Addah	Kongenstein	1784	Still used.
Quittah	Prindenstein	1784	,,

(C.) BRANDENBURG.

Takrama	Takrama	1674	Disused.
Acoda or Acquidah	Dorothea	1682	,,

(D.) ENGLISH.

Beyin	Apollonia	1690	Disused.
Dixcove	Dixcove	1691	Still used.
Sekondi	Sekondi	1685	,,
Commendah	Commendah	1681	Disused.
Cape Coast	Victoria	1685	,,
,,	William	—	The present lighthouse.
,,	Macarthy	—	Disused.
Cormantine	Cormantine	1624	,,
Tantum	Tantumquerry	—	,,
Gamma	Mumford	—	,,
Winnebah	Winnebah	1694	Still used.
Accra	James Fort	1662	,,
Pram Pram	Vernon	—	,,

CHAPTER II.

The Early Inhabitants of the Gold Coast—Their Traditional Origin—The Dominant Powers—Manners—Customs—Superstitions—Occupations—Religion—Manual Arts—The Aggrey Bead.

AFRICA is supposed to have derived its name from the Punic word signifying "Ears of Corn," and to the ancients was one of the three great divisions of land, of which the world was then supposed to consist. Its western part, covering the whole Gulf of Guinea, and extending southward to the mouth of the Niger, is the home of that portion of mankind known as the Hamitic family, which must have pushed its way westward from the main branch until stopped by the Atlantic Ocean. To trace the origin of the early inhabitants of the Gold Coast is a most difficult task, inasmuch as there remain neither direct traditions nor authenticated accounts, either among the people themselves or from their supposed visitors before the Christian era, or from those who visited it for some centuries after that epoch. By early writers it was supposed that there once existed in this part of the world a most powerful kingdom, whose ruler, by his numerous victories over weaker tribes, subdued the whole of the surrounding country, and formed the so-called mighty kingdom of Guinea, bestowing this name upon the whole coast from Cape Mesurado to Biafra. Other authorities refute this, notable among whom is

Bosman, who says: "How great this mistake is, I hope to evince to you, since the very name of Guinea is not so much as known to the natives here, nor the imaginary Guinea Monarchy yet to be found in the world". The supporters of those who believe in the supposed kingdom of Guinea, attribute to the Phœnicians the first visitation of foreign powers to the west coast of Africa, surmising that Pharaoh Necho, King of Egypt, employed Phœnician mariners to visit the coast some 600 years B.C. After them came the Carthaginians, who are supposed to have explored the greater part of these western shores and even to have settled there.

The Rev. Carl Reindorf in his recently published book, 1895, says: "Hanno the Carthaginian sailed with sixty ships of fifty oars each, some 30,000 men and women and stores and provisions to establish permanent settlements upon the West Coast of Africa, and seems to have reached that particular part now known as the Gold Coast". Coming down, however, to much later times, Mr. F. Romer, the Danish merchant who resided at the present Christiansborg, at the extreme eastern limit of Accra (1735-43), confirms the statements with regard to the early existence of a mighty kingdom. He says: "The Gold Coast was a part of the western division of the empire ruled by the Emperor of Benin, whose territories extended along the coast from Benin to the Gambia, and whose kings were appointed by that emperor". He also quotes the finding of the mosaic or aggrey bead on the Gold Coast and the Slave Coast, as evidences of a trade that must have then existed between West Africa and Egypt, and also mentions that the insignia of the royalty of Accra were the same as those in use in the Benin country, and that many of the religious ceremonies were identical in both countries. Other writers assert that the whole of the tribes now inhabiting the Gold Coast, some nineteen in number, came originally from the interior, being gradually pushed towards the coast by more powerful Arab tribes, who invaded their territories in order to enrol them beneath the banner of the Moslem faith. Foremost among these tribes were the Ashantis and the Fantis, at this period branches of the same family, who are reported to have settled in the countries round the Kong Mountains, a district then known to the Arab traders as Wangara. This migration towards the sea of the present people inhabiting the western part of the Gold Coast from the far interior, appears likely to be perfectly true, but of the tribes to be found in the eastern part of the colony the supposition cannot hold, for according to present local tradition in this part of the country, it is asserted, that the Kings of Lagos came from Benin, and such people as the Akras and the Latès arrived on the coast at different intervals from the East. That the King of Benin once held sway over this eastern part of the Gold Coast, is strengthened by a statement made by the previously mentioned Mr. Romer, *viz.*, that a ruler for the Akim country came with the Akras from the sea.

Another tradition asserts that the Akras and several of the other tribes now inhabiting the eastern portion of the colony came from a country farther east, situated between two large rivers, and crossing the Volta River, distributed themselves over the country, the Akras settling on the sea-shore. There seems no doubt that about the same period that the Ashantis and the Fantis were moving from the interior southward towards the sea, the whole coast line of the present Gold Coast was peopled with the numerous branches of the several tribes, who came from the East by the sea, and occupied distinct and different portions of the country, but divided from each other by a difference of speech, habits, manners, customs and superstitions.

These people from the East seem to have been the aboriginal race along the sea-coast from Assinie to the Volta, at the time when the Ashantis and Fantis were occupying the lowlands of the Kong Mountains, and are now represented by the Akra, Cheripong, Latè, Apollonian, Ahanta and the Adangme tribes. The King of Latè is reported to have had thirty towns under his sway, whilst that of Cheripong ruled over fifty.

To leave this maze of superstition and tradition, and to come down to the descriptions of early writers upon the Gold Coast, we find many of the small aboriginal tribes disappear by the absorption or entire obliteration by their stronger neighbours, and a great part of the coast line, from Chama to Bereku, occupied by the Fantis, who have migrated farther from the interior to the coast, subduing and driving out the peoples they met on their way, and themselves breaking away from their traditional brothers the Ashantis, to found a kingdom of their own. This division of the two great tribes is said to have been the result of a famine, and the origin of the different names is also due to this cause, though more probably, the division was due to the growing power of the one part of the tribe over that of the other.

The common language spoken by the tribes who migrated from the interior towards the coast was then known as *Akan*, which is still spoken by the Ashantis, Akims,

Denkiras, Wassaws, and other peoples of the interior, thus marking the common origin of these various families. Of this mother language, the Fanti of the present day is the most important dialect, a tongue that will carry you throughout a large portion of the colony, but which is more particularly spoken by the Fantis, Elminas and Chamas. This settlement by the Fantis along the shore had the effect of dividing the original inhabitants of the coast into two parts, the newly formed Fanti kingdom being the dividing state. This would account for the relationship still claimed by the Apollonians, Sefwis, Aowins and Ahantas in the west to the Akra and Adangme-speaking people in the east, who still claim to be brothers.

About the same period that saw the removal of the Fanti tribe from their old headquarters, in the interior, towards the coast, witnessed also the first growing power of the Ashantis, and the settlement of such powerful tribes as the Sefwis, Denkiras, Wassaws and Akims to the north of the sea-coast families; until at the end of the seventeenth century, we find, according to Bosman, some eleven different states along the shore in addition to those already existing in the interior.

A full list of these states has already been given in the previous chapter, so no further mention need be made of them here, except to state that the migrating tribes from the interior became from this time, *i.e.*, the seventeenth century, the dominant races upon the West Coast of Africa.

Among the races thus mentioned was a common tradition, that the whole of these people were originally included in twelve tribes or families, according to Bowdich (1817), while the Rev. J. B. Anaman of Cape Coast Castle denies this, and claims only seven great divisions, though the latter authority includes as sub-divisions, several of those mentioned by Bowdich as distinct families. Each of these families contained different branches, which were known by different names in the districts to which they belonged. The families mentioned by Bowdich are: Aquonna, Abrootoo, Abbradi, Essonna, Annona, Yoko, Intchwa, Abadie, Appiadie, Agoona, Tchweedam and Doomina, all of which are given in the Rev. Mr. Anaman's list of seven families and their sub-divisions, though somewhat varied in the orthography.

It would appear that each family name had a distinct significance: thus Aquonna meant buffalo, which was a forbidden animal to that family; Abrootoo was a corn stalk or ear of corn; Abbradi, a plantain; Essonna, a bush-cat; Annona, a parrot; Yoko, red earth: Intchwa, a dog; Appiadie, a servant; Tchweedam, a panther; Agoona, palm oil, or a place where palm oil was collected.

That certain families exist down to the present day is quite true, for I have, in my travels, verified the existence of many of them, in which the natives still class themselves without regard to their national distinctions, and have seen people of quite different tribes at the present day salute as brothers, when each has mentioned the stock family to which he belongs.

Of the families mentioned, perhaps the buffalo, bushcat, panther and dog, are the oldest, marking the people who lived by hunting; while the corn stalk and the plantain represent the beginning of agriculture; the redearth family showing attention to buildings and dwellings; and the palm-oil family denoting the introduction of commerce, in which the natives include the Portuguese, who were among the earliest traders to the coast.

This latter can hardly be possible, for palm oil was not known as an export in the early days, though perhaps the family was named from this commodity being used as food by the natives.

There are, however, natives to be found on the Gold Coast, who assert that the Ashantis were once a water-side people, from which place they migrated to their present inland territory, conquering on their way a very powerful people called the *Intas*, and many small tribes, finally establishing themselves and building Kumasi about the beginning of the eighteenth century.

This conquered nation, the Intas, was supposed to have been rich in barbaric arts, many of which were adopted by their conquerors, in addition to a great portion of their language and their complete system of weights. The headquarters of this ancient Ashanti kingdom were doubtfully placed in the country, behind the present Winnebah, along the banks of the river Ainsu, but the whole theory is not a likely solution of the origin of such a powerful race as the people in question. The ancient history of the kingdom of Ashanti is most uncertain, as it is bound to be, from a people possessing no written language or recognised traditional records; and to make it more difficult, enforcing laws to make it a capital punishment to even mention the particulars about the death of one king or the life of another. This supposed migration of the Ashantis from the coast is assumed to have been conducted by a great leader called Osai Tootoo, who, encouraged by superstitious omens, founded Kumasi, was made king and received the "stool" or native throne from his followers. To conciliate the other chiefs who accompanied and assisted him in the foundation of this barbaric monarchy, he created the aristocracy, and passed a law making the royal family and its descendants exempt from capital punishment.

The foundation of the Ashanti kingdom with Kumasi as its headquarters about this time may be regarded as an absolute fact, but as to whence they came, must still remain an open question. In the Ashanti history, dating from 1700, it will be found that a sister nation, known as the Dwabens, has always played a very important part, and it is generally admitted that the Dwabens became a distinct branch of the Ashantis, under the leadership of a chief Boitinne, a sister's son and cousin to Osai Tootoo, at the same time that the Ashantis were building Kumasi. The town of Dwaben is stated to have already existed, some eight miles east of the site selected for the capital of Ashanti, and it is supposed when the suggested exodus from the coast took place, that the stronger party under Boitinne attacked and captured Dwaben, leaving Osai Tootoo, his weaker companion, to found Kumasi. Although the two parties thus became separate, they still remained the firmest of allies in war, sharing equally in all spoil and conquest. This common interest remained intact for over a century, all other interests becoming subordinate to the one great policy of aggressive increase of territory and acquisition of barbaric power. No earlier authentic records of the Ashantis have been found, either at Cape Coast Castle or Accra, than 1780. The Moors state that the Ashanti kingdom was founded in 1700, and upon this foundation it rests, there being no chronological records in existence to substantiate the statement.

Osai Tootoo appears to have concentrated his energies

upon the consolidation of his newly established kingdom, making Kumasi the headquarters of his military power, and requiring his subordinate chiefs to reside in the various towns that sprang up in the immediate neighbourhood of the capital, bestowing dignity upon them by means of titles. He conciliated his conquered tribes by making them tributary powers, and checked their possible desertion by requiring their constant presence at all political festivities. He held absolute sway over all, while his chiefs and his created aristocracy held all judicial and legislative power, and looked after the common business of the state.

Osai Tootoo was killed by the Atoäs in 1720, on a Saturday, some time before the completion of the building of his capital. The story goes that he declared war against the people of Atoä, inhabiting the district between the Akim and Assin countries. These people, unable to face such an invader in the open field, distributed their small force through the bush, and passing the main body of Osai Tootoo's army, surprised the king and his rearguard of some 200 or 300 followers, killing them all, and shooting Osai Tootoo as he lay in his hammock. This is said to have happened at a place called Cormantee, and on a Saturday, and was the origin of the most solemn oath of the Ashantis for the future, *viz.*, "Miminda Cormantee," *i.e.*, by "Saturday and Cormantee," from which date and circumstance Saturday has always been looked upon as a fatal day by the Ashantis, and upon which no enterprise or important undertaking has since been attempted. So from the beginning of the eighteenth century and on for more than one hundred years we shall find the Ashanti power

MANNERS AND CUSTOMS.

spreading over the whole of the Gold Coast, un[...] the whole country from the Ancobra to the Vo[lta com]pletely under their sway. As a later chapter [deals] with the growth and decay of the Ashanti power, the subject may be dismissed from the present pages.

At the time of which I am writing, the negro tribes inhabiting the Gold Coast were very much alike in their manners, customs, superstitions, religion and occupations.

Their disposition was naturally crafty and cruel, seldom to be trusted, and they lost no opportunity of either cheating the European or one another. In addition they were naturally idle and careless, and possessed none of the finer qualities of mankind that are to be found in other races. Fortune or misfortune concerned them but little, all occasions, whether of grief, pain, joy, or even death, being seized upon as opportunities for feasting, singing and dancing. They lived in the present, speedily forgot the past, and cared not for the future. Of personal adornment they were very fond, while a single cloth worn round the middle was their only clothing, thus leaving the upper portion of the body and the arms and legs quite bare. This cloth was of cotton, silk or velvet, according to the station of the wearer, whilst arms and neck were variously adorned with chains and rings of silver, gold or ivory. A particular vanity of the women was the manipulation of their hair in all manner of grotesque shapes and patterns, which they interspersed with ornaments of gold, coral or the aggrey bead to the value of many pounds sterling.

The bearing and the rearing of children caused but little trouble in a negro household. The women apparently care little about their offspring, the men care less. In some parts of the country the children are named after the day upon which they are born, and in others from the order in which they are born. Thus we get what in English would be Monday boy and Monday girl, and First boy, Second boy, First girl, Second girl, and so on. For the first two or three years the children are nursed by the mother, and then, when able to run, the child goes where it pleases, to the market for food, to the water to swim, with no one to let or hinder.

Male children, as a rule, follow the occupation of their father, and are brought up when very young to his calling, while the female children become the domestic slaves of the house, till ready for sale as a wife to a neighbour.

The ordinary diet of the bulk of the population was, and is at the present time, of a very simple nature. Bosman says that twopence per day was sufficient to diet one of them, and at the present day but threepence is allowed for daily subsistence. Their food consists chiefly of pounded corn, yam or plantain mashed together after boiling, to the consistency of an English dumpling, over which is poured a little palm oil, or a few boiled herbs and peppers, to which they add a little fish. This latter is most offensive to European nostrils, and is deservedly termed "stink-fish". In the interior fish cannot always be obtained, but its place is often supplied with a piece of dried meat of some animal caught in the chase. Of their own native drink, palm wine, they are inordinately fond, and they have also acquired a strong desire for all liquors of an intoxicating nature, but more particularly rum. The old Dutch factor of Axim must have had many opportunities of noticing their predilections in this respect, for he says : " Let the world go how it will, they must have brandy in the morning and palm wine in the afternoon, and he that hath a penny in money, thirsteth after threepenny worth of drink, which is welcome to them night and day ; and we are forced to give strict orders to our men to watch our cellars at night, for they know too well how to get at them. They are so fond of strong drink and tobacco, that you may equally entrust bacon to a cat, as either of them within their power."

I am afraid they have not altered much since Bosman's time, and they are not the only people endowed with such proclivities.

In early times the people were divided into five classes or degrees, foremost among whom were the *Captains*. This title descended in direct line from father to son, and in default of such issue, to the next male in the direct line, being only set aside on account of poverty, or when another branch of the family possessed great wealth. The second were called *Caboceers* or *Caboceros* as Bosman calls them. These were the chiefs or headmen of the town or village, whose duty was the care or welfare of the people, and to settle disputes and any tumults that might arise. The third class included all who had enriched themselves by trade, or who had inherited wealth from their ancestors, upon the amount of which their reputation depended, and of which they made great show upon all available occasions. The fourth class comprehended what would be called the common people, all those who obtained their living by agriculture, fishing or manual work of any kind ; while the fifth and last division was entirely composed of the slaves of the community, who were looked upon and regarded as chattels, and had either been sold by their relations, captured in war, or brought to such a stage by poverty, if such a state existed.

Of time and its divisions they had no idea except what had been learned from the Europeans. The moon to them was their clock, and by it they calculated their times for sowing and reaping. A name for each day of the week is however found in their language, pointing to the fact that the divisions of the week must have been long known to them. The general Sunday on the coast falls on our Tuesday, and that of the Mohammedans on our Friday, though it differs from no other day in the week to them; except that no person may fish, all other kinds of work are perfectly allowable. Many of the interior tribes divide their time into lucky and unlucky periods, with a set time dividing the two. This dividing time between the two fortunate periods lasts seven days, which are observed as a time of idleness, or vacation, and during which they neither travel nor work. The great lucky time lasts nineteen days, then follow the seven days of unlucky time, again followed by the lesser lucky time of seven days. Though this idea is generally prevalent in the interior, the "good" and "evil" days vary in different districts. Why this distinction has been made it is difficult to determine; possibly the result of some important event first settled it, from which it passed into custom, to ultimately become a law. Marriage among the negroes is easily arranged, and the knot once tied, it can be as easily untied should the occasion arise. Among the lower orders the bride brings no fortune, and the bridegroom need have but very little to recommend him. Custom shows that when a young man desires a young girl for his wife, nothing is much more requisite than for him to apply to her father, or mother, or her nearest relations to give her to him. The request is seldom denied, and no feelings of the daughter are allowed to bar the way. The consent of the parents or relations once gained, the wedding is fixed, and all the bridegroom needs is sufficient to pay the expenses of his wedding-day, which consist of some fancy clothes for his bride and presents to her family and relations. These presents often consist of sheep or goats, rum and other drinks, together with a little gold dust or a sum of money. The richer the bridegroom, the more expensive his wedding-day; but, as a rule, a strict account is kept of everything that is presented to the bride or her relations, in order that he may recover their value again should his wife feel inclined to leave him. Should the husband wish to leave the wife, he is free to do so, and the account is then considered closed. For some days before the wedding the bride is dressed in her best, her hair done in the most approved fashion, and if her family be a rich one, she is well bedecked with gold ornaments for the hair, the neck and the arms. These are borrowed for the occasion and returned soon after the marriage. Polygamy is the rule, and a man may keep as many wives as he cares for, who often do all the work and thus keep the husband in idleness. Often in the richer families, one or two of the wives are exempt from the manual labours of the others, their work being solely to manage what household there is, and to keep the rest in order. Bosman declares that as many as twenty wives were sometimes kept, but the common number is from three to ten.

The goods of married people belong separately to each, and the mother just as often sustains the children as the father, upon whom falls the expense of clothing for all—in many cases not a very great one! In the eighteenth century it was the custom, when a man or his wife died, for the relations to come and take away everything that was left; helping in their turn to defray the funeral expenses of the departed.

Should a man have a child by one of his slaves, the child is looked upon as a slave also, unless set free before the death of its father, in accordance with the usual rites and customs necessary to be performed upon such an occasion. If this be properly carried out before the father dies, the child is then treated in every particular as a free person, but should it be neglected, the relations treat the offspring as a mere chattel to be disposed of as they will. The native law of inheritance upon the Gold Coast appears to European ideas a very strange one; the children seldom inheriting property left by their parents. The only exception is, I believe, among the Akras. The eldest son, supposing the father to have been a king, or chief, or captain, succeeds to the title only, together with the arms borne by his deceased parent. Should the father wish to endow his eldest son with worldly goods he must do it during his lifetime, and then it must be done in a very careful manner, for should it be discovered, the relations can demand restoration from the son after his father's death. Instead of the children inheriting the property, when there is any, it descends to the children of the brothers and sisters of the parents. The eldest son is heir to the mother's brother or his sons, and the eldest daughter is heiress to her mother's sister or her daughters.

Thus we find many instances of the native kings and chiefs educating their sister's son as their own, and appointing him as next successor to the throne. This extraordinary rule of succession, excluding all children but those of a sister, is explained in the following manner. The natives say they are more sure that the son of their sister is of their own blood than they are of their own; and that if the wives of the sons are faithless, the blood of the family is entirely lost in the offspring, but if the daughters are faithless to their husbands, the blood is still preserved in part. Not a great tribute to the virtues of the women, certainly!

Superstition is still rife among the natives, particularly among those of the interior. In Ashanti the tradition of the origin of the white and the black man is known to every one, though it differs somewhat from the tradition current on the coast. This forms the source of their religious ideas, and runs as follows: " In the beginning of the world God created three white men and three black men, with the same number of women; he resolved, in order that they might not afterwards complain, to give them their choice of good and evil. A large box or calabash was set on the ground, with a piece of paper, sealed up, on one side of it. God gave the black men the first choice, who took the box, expecting it contained everything, but on opening it, there appeared only a piece of gold, a piece of iron and several other metals of which they did not know the use. The white men opening the paper, it told them everything. God left the blacks in the bush, but conducted the whites to the water-side (for this happened in Africa), communicated with them every night, and taught them to build a small ship, which carried them to another country, whence they returned after a long period, with various merchandise, to barter with the blacks, who might have been the superior people." In some parts of the colony, the people believe that man was created by a great spider called Amanfie, whilst among others the opinion is generally shared that God created two kinds of men, black and white, and offered them two sorts of gifts, *viz.*, gold and knowledge. The blacks had the first choice, and being covetous chose the gold, leaving knowledge to the white man. God gave them their gift, but as a punishment he decreed that the whites should be for ever their masters, and they (the blacks) should be obliged to wait on them as their slaves.

No part of the Gold Coast is without its particular deity, which is known as a "fetish," and is supposed to inhabit particular animals, forests, mountains, trees and rivers. These fetishes are revered in proportion as their predictions (known through the fetish priest and told to the people) are realised. The river Tando was a favourite fetish of the Ashantis, and also the Prah; whilst at Accra the bush-cat was revered, and at Dixcove and other places along the coast the alligator. This last is still worshipped in the present century, and the natives say there is an alligator about twelve feet long in a fresh-water stream near Dixcove, which appears at the call of the fetish man, and receives in payment a white fowl. I was invited to test this by the natives in 1895.

Bosman derives Fetishe to mean false God, which the natives call "Bossum," hence the Bossum or sacred Prah of the Ashantis. The fear of the fetish is deeply implanted in the breast of every negro, particularly those who reside in the interior of the colony. When travelling through the Kwahu district in 1897, I found upon inquiry, that the principal fetish of the district had previously resided in a range of mountains called Atiwa Yaw, supposed to be named after him. He was, from all accounts, a very clever fellow, for he imposed upon the people for years, until, emboldened by his success, he threatened to clear out all the natives in his district who professed Christianity, with a breath. What a sulphurous breath he must have had! A stir was made, a trap laid for him, and he was captured and deported to Accra. When arrested, he refused to go unless accompanied by some Christian natives, to protect him on the way from the violence of his previous dupes and votaries, who were now as greatly incensed against him as they had previously been in fear of him, seeing that he was shown to be human like themselves, and not a spirit. He, however, threatened to return, but never did. Two false "Atiwa Yaws," however, sprang up, both were captured and well flogged by the natives, and many sheep were killed in order to mark the event, the false "Atiwas" being called upon to pay for all the sheep killed.

The Krobo Mountain in the eastern part of the colony, near the river Volta, was once a stronghold of fetishes, and held the whole of the surrounding country in its power, until destroyed by the late Sir W. Brandford Griffith early in 1893.

Every family has its own domestic fetishes, supplied by the priests. These consist of rude wooden figures of people and animals, of the most extraordinary shapes and proportion. They are kept in the house, and upon all customs and festivals are the recipients of good-will offerings and drink.

A string across a road, a branch laid in the path, a bottle hung outside his hut, are sufficient to deter a native from any undertaking, so afraid are they of "fetish".

A FETISH PRIEST.

Upon every occasion his aid is invoked; for trade, for

war, for a journey, for good, for evil, the fetish priest is visited, his verdicts are easily swallowed, and his word never doubted. Happily all this deception is slowly passing away, but in the past every village and town had its appointed grove dedicated to the fetish, where both chief and people frequently visited to make their personal or other offerings. These groves were sacred, and no one was allowed to pluck, cut or break the branches of the trees that formed them, under the most terrible maledictions and punishments.

The fetish priests, or as they are more commonly called, the fetish men, are of two orders, the superior and the inferior classes. The first are generally supposed to actually dwell with the fetish, for whom a small, round house is generally provided a short distance from the town or village, and which no ordinary inhabitant dare approach. The superior classes of fetish men question the spirit upon all matters relating to the future fortune or state of the individual who invokes their aid, convey the answers of the oracle, and call the attention of those spirits to the questions asked by their relations left on earth, who seek advice upon some important point concerning their present welfare. The lower classes of fetish, in addition to their supposed spiritual work, follow their ordinary daily occupation, assisting only in the annual native customs and festivals, and act in general as very ordinary specimens of magicians or sorcerers. This power, however, is quite enough to strongly impress the native mind, and an exhibition of it consists of tying, knotting or dividing a number of cords behind the back, or of plaiting and separating several strips or thongs of leather. There are fetish women as well as fetish men, but these generally confine their attention to medical cures, and are further notorious for their loose ideas of morality.

Every application to the fetish must be accompanied by a gift-offering, which, in gold-bearing areas, is generally preferred by the deity (so says the priest) to be in the shape of a quantity of the precious metal. The kings of Ashanti paid as much as ten ounces of gold, in addition to several slaves, for each invocation of the fetish priest; whilst the poorer inhabitants could invoke his aid for a sum varying according to their circumstances. Bowdich says the Ashantis had no fixed fetish day or Sunday, different families selecting different days of the week, upon which they abstained from work and drink. The former abstention I can quite understand, but not the latter.

Of all their customs, that of the yam is the most important. It occurs annually at the maturity of that vegetable, which, planted in December, is ready for gathering in September, and furnishes the opportunity for the wildest exhibition of native licence and passion. Theft, intrigue and assault are all forgiven during the continuance of this annual feast.

Throughout the whole length of the land, the inhabitants of the coast towns obtained their living by fishing and the making of canoes. These latter vary much in size: the smallest from ten to twelve feet long by two to three feet broad, to the largest size some thirty feet long by six feet broad. In the management of these frail craft they are most expert, and do not appear in the least concerned should they capsize and precipitate their worldly belongings into the sea. The canoe is quickly righted, baled out, and again manned, to be again very soon the victim of a similar fate. In addition to the use of the canoe for fishing, it forms the means for communication and transport of goods from port to port. In them the natives will venture far out to sea, quite out of sight of land, using a large square sail, that bellies out with the wind, and carries the boat through the water at a rapid pace. The canoes carry, according to size, from three to fifteen men, who sit in twos along the sides of the boat, leaving the odd man to steer from the stern. All the larger boats have weather boards in the bow, consisting of planks raised two feet or more to keep out the seas. Instead of oars, paddles are used, which along the Gold Coast are made with a broad spade-like blade, with rather a short handle.

In other parts of the colony plantation work is the general occupation, and in the early days of the colony much rice was grown, particularly in the country round Axim, and carried to all parts of the coast. In other parts the people gave their attention to the cultivation of corn, yams, potatoes, plantain and bananas, and the preparation of palm oil. It would be very difficult to find at the present day a potato grown in the Gold Coast; rice is now very largely imported, but much attention is still given to the cultivation of the yam, cassada and the sweet potato. A large proportion of the people are, and always have been, engaged in trade, acting as the middlemen between the traders on the coast and the people in the far interior. People of all tribes find employment in this capacity, particularly the Ashantis in later years. Head carriage forms almost the only means of transport in the colony, though, where possible, canoes will be found on all the larger water-ways and lagoons. The average native will carry a load of from forty to sixty pounds upon his head for some fifteen miles in a day; though for his own purposes he will carry much more; a private

NATIVE POTTERY AND SILVERWORK OF THE ASHANTIS.

load often weighing as much as 100 pounds. Everything is carried on the head, from an empty bottle to a case of provisions, and it is very seldom that an accident occurs. Through the swamps knee-deep in thick, black mud, up and down the rocky mountain sides, and through the rivers, men, women and children do all the transport work, bringing down the produce of the interior to the coast, and returning to their homes laden with articles of European produce of all descriptions.

In manual arts the colony is not rich, which by Bosman is attributed to the general laziness of the negro. The chief arts to which they turn their attention are the manufacture of wooden and earthen cups, matting, brass or copper ointment boxes, and ornaments of gold, silver and ivory. In the manufacture of gold and silver ornaments they are very adept, particularly when the rude nature of their tools and implements is taken into consideration. Specimens of their work will be found on page 52.

One of their chief handicrafts is smithwork. In past times all their own implements of war (guns excepted) and agricultural tools were made with the aid of a hard stone for an anvil, a pair of tongs, and a pair of bellows with two or three pipes blowing into an open fire. I have not seen any examples of the gold and silver hat bands made for the Dutch in the time of Bosman, of which he says the thread and texture was so fine that he questioned whether European artists would not be much put about to imitate them.

I must not omit to give some description of the weaving of native cloth; an illustration of the loom used will be found on page 54.

Bowdich says that he found the Ashanti loom to be precisely upon the same principle as the English, being worked by strings held between the toes. The web from this loom is never more than four inches broad. They use a spindle for spinning, holding it in one hand, and twisting the thread (which has a weight at one end) between the finger and thumb of the other. In this primitive manner they manufacture cloths of great fine-

NATIVE LOOM FOR WEAVING CLOTH.

ness, variety of pattern, and brilliancy of colour, the pattern running through the cloth, and having the same appearance on both sides. This loom, of which an illustration is given, is not common to the Ashanti country. I have seen them at work in the Awoonah, Akim and Kwahu territories, though very possibly it

NATIVE LOOMS AND CLOTHS.

was introduced into these countries by Ashanti workmen. The cotton from which their native cloth is made is either imported English yarn, dyed with native dyes, or spun from the cotton produced in their own country. They prefer their own dyes, saying that European colours are not fast. Bowdich mentions two dyes only used by the Ashantis, red and yellow, obtained from dye woods, and a third, blue, obtained from the leaves of a plant growing about two feet high, which when mixed with their yellow produces a very fine green.

I have found these myself in the Akim forests and in the Krobo country, and in addition, a fourth, a black dye. This is a climber called Otàtsche, which, when pounded and boiled, gives a rich deep-black dye. The bark and the wood of the Odubeng give the yellow; the leaves of the plant Akásé, or as Bowdich says, Acassie, for blue, and the seeds of the fruit Tsere, a bush growing in Krobo, which yields a red dye called Tchara. Mr. R. Mohr was kind enough to obtain specimens of these for me in 1897, when I was at Begoro in that year inspecting the schools of the Basle Mission at that station.

On another page will be found illustrations of the native pottery of the coast, particularly the pipes. The manufacture of these is not confined to the Ashanti country; most of the specimens I obtained from Osino, in Akim, only one coming from Ashanti. They are of two kinds, black and brown, made of clay, both admitting of a high polish by friction, and decorated with rude patterns, the grooves of which are filled in with a white chalk. A long stem, often of silver, is attached to these pipes, the bowl being allowed to rest on the ground when smoked. Leather is prepared and worked in Ashanti and the countries farther inland, particularly in the Haùsa territory; sandals, cushions, belts, pouches, saddles, cases for native knives and swords, and coverings for bottles being among the chief manufactured articles in this branch of industry. Of their woodwork the Ashanti stool is a fair specimen, which is cut from a solid block and variously ornamented.

Chief among the occupations of the people in the early history of the colony were fishing and hunting. For the latter, the poisoned arrow was largely used to bring down the largest game, including even the elephant. At Labadi and Ponni, villages to the east of Accra, were enclosures, in which was stored the ivory obtained from the slaughter of the elephants, once so numerous, even in the Gold Coast. To the Fantis is attributed the credit of being the first to manufacture nets and hooks for fishing in the sea, and no great improvement in these articles appears to have been made down to the present day.

Next to fishing and hunting, came the manufacture of salt and the washing for gold. The former was carried on at all towns along the coast, that were not engaged in trading with the Europeans who frequented this part of the world, and appears to have been done in the roughest manner. Sea-water was boiled in earthen pots, some ten or twelve in number, arranged in two rows, and cemented together with clay. Under this a fire was kindled and the salt obtained by the evaporation of the water. The Portuguese are supposed to have introduced the use of salt-pits and pans, into which the sea and lagoon waters were allowed to run and spread themselves, to be evaporated by the extreme heat of the sun. In this way the people of the coast towns supplied the tribes of the interior with salt in exchange for slaves and gold.

Washing for gold was carried on in Akim, Denkira, Wassaw and Ashanti, whilst people on the coast throughout Fantiland, at Elmina and Axim, washed for gold on the sea-shore after a heavy fall of rain.

Thus, agriculture, pottery, fishing, hunting, weaving, salt-boiling, gold-washing and gold-work were the original occupations of the people, to which have been added by the Europeans the arts of carpentry, cooperage, masonry, tailoring, boot-making and clerkship.

Native games are few; the chief of them is known as Warri, which, like Bowdich, I have been unable to understand. *It is a game played by young and old, the only requisites being some beans or counters and holes in the ground, or a board upon a stool hollowed with cups into which the counters are played.* It is understood in all parts of the colony; is no doubt of very ancient origin, and is reported to have been played in Syria. Another favourite game is draughts, which is again almost universally played, somewhat resembling the Polish game in its details. The moves and takes are backwards and forwards, and a king moves like a bishop in the game of chess. A third game is played with a board resembling a cribbage board in its perforations, which run in oblique lines in all directions, and each line composed of three holes for pegs. The players have each an equal number of pegs, and begin to play at the same time, and the one who completes a line first, in spite of the play of his adversary, wins a peg from him, and so on until his stock is exhausted and the game won. At Akropong in the Aquapim country, and at several other places, I found the natives gambling for cowries, by spinning beans upon a mat spread on the ground. The native name for this game I was unable to discover, but it was well known by the English name of "marbles". Any number of players can join in the game; sitting in a circle with the mat spread in the centre, a stake is fixed upon, and the winner is the one whose bean knocks out most of the others when all are set spinning. Needless to say, noise, animated discussions and interference by the lookers-on form part of all native games.

I cannot do better than close this chapter with a description of the "Aggrey Bead," one of the few genuine antiquities of the coast. They are reported to be found in the following countries, and are as a rule worth twice their weight in gold: Denkira, Akim, Wassaw, Ahanta and Fanti. The natives say the greater number is found in Denkira, owing to its extra richness in gold. They were originally used as ornaments of dress, and the riches of an individual were computed by the number of these aggrey beads which he possessed, in addition to his wealth in gold. The Rev. Carl Reindorf says: "The mosaic beads known as aggrey beads (Bosman calls them Conte de Terra) found chiefly on the Gold Coast and the Slave Coast must have been brought hither from Egypt". The beads are found in the ground, and native tradition asserts, that the people are directed to dig for them in those spots where a spiral vapour is seen issuing from the ground, and that they are seldom found near the surface. The finder of aggrey beads is said to be assured of future good fortune. They are of two kinds, plain and variegated. The former are of a blue, green, yellow or dull red, while the latter embrace every variety of shade and colour. The Fantis are said to prefer those of the plain yellow colour, whilst the Apollonians prefer the yellow and blue shades. Wherever they came from and whatever their origin, they are of great antiquity, the art of making them, if it was ever known in these parts, being entirely lost, so that it is not improbable, if Egypt ever had any communication with this part of Africa, they may have been imported from that country.

Dr. Leyden says: " The aigris is a stone of a greenish-blue colour, supposed to be a species of jasper, small, perforated pieces of which, valued at their weight in gold, are used as money ". Bowdich never heard of this, and I must say I have never heard of them being used as money. The late Sir R. F. Burton speaks of them as the " Popo Bead," which the above rather describes; though that is semi-transparent, something like carnelian, and said to be found in the same manner as the aggrey bead. Another writer upon the subject, Issert, says: " They are a sort of coral with inlaid work; the art of making the beads is entirely lost, or never was known in these parts, thus pointing to their foreign origin ".

The beads of variegated strata are so firmly united, and so cleverly blended, that they seem superior to manufacture; some resemble mosaic, whilst the surfaces of others are so delicately covered with minute flowers and regular patterns, the shading so softened into one another, and into the shades of the body of the bead, that nothing but the finest painting could equal them. Others show flowers and patterns deep in the body of the bead, with opaque lines of colour running from the centre to the surface. Imitations of the true aggrey bead have certainly been manufactured and imported into the country during more recent times (I have in my possession several such imitations), which the natives called boiled beads, stating that they consist of broken aggrey beads, ground into powder and mixed. They are also heavier than the true aggrey bead. A belief is common among the people that if aggrey beads are buried in the ground, they not only grow, but breed. This probably arose from the practice of burying a number of these beads with the corpse of a deceased person, the number of beads buried varying in proportion to the rank of the departed. Another use for them was to grind a number to powder, and after the body of the deceased had been well greased, to paint the body with the dust of the aggrey beads before its interment.

The burial of the dead in this part of the world is accompanied with many rites and ceremonies, and much drinking of spirits and palm wine. The lamentations are dismal and loud, and respect is supposed to be paid to the departed by the firing of muskets at intervals throughout the days before the funeral. In some parts of the country the corpse is interred under the floor of the dwelling-house, accompanied with many presents of gold and beads for the use of the departed. These buried treasures often form stores of wealth for the family to use hereafter, so that a man, when poor, may dig over his forefather's grave and obtain the wealth there hidden. I have heard a native of Accra state, that he has thus lived for years upon his ancestors! The bodies of kings were often kept above ground for a whole year. Putrefaction was prevented by placing the body upon a wooden bier something like a gridiron, and keeping a very slow fire burning underneath, by which process the body was slowly dried. When this was complete, the body would be richly clothed and placed in the coffin, other rich cloths, gold dust and aggrey beads being also placed with the corpse for use in its future state. The richer the deceased had been, the greater the number of the articles that were buried with him, and the greater their value.

The burying places for the kings were always selected in secluded spots, either in the mountains or away in the depths of the bush. The actual place of interment was carefully concealed, and often the bearers who had carried the corpse to its last resting place were, upon their return to the town, ordered to be put to death by the chiefs, in order to preserve the secret of the burying place. This was a common practice in the Akim country.

CHAPTER III.

The Seasons—Climate—The Harmattan—Productions—Vegetation—Animal Life—Exports—Imports—Habitations—The Slave Trade—Its Rise and Fall—The Labour Question.

SITUATED north of the Equatorial line between the parallels of 4° 45′ and 6° 45′ North, according to the early extent of the colony, the seasons are naturally divided into the wet and the dry periods. The former commences early in April and continues until late in August, and the latter lasts from this latter date until the succeeding April. Although this period is called the "dry" season, it must not be supposed that no rain falls. On the contrary, September, October and November are each interrupted by what are called the "smalls" or the second rains, but from the end of November to the following April fair weather prevails. As in other tropical countries, each change of season is marked by violent atmospheric disturbances in the shape of thunderstorms and tornadoes, those introducing the rainy season being by far the most violent of any that occur on the coast. The rains come, as a rule, from the east, but often veer round to the south, finally settling down to the south-west. It must not be imagined that rain falls uninterruptedly during the rainy season. After the first burst, bright days of sunshine intervene from time to time, but, owing to the extreme amount of moisture to be found everywhere, clouds of vapour rise from the wet earth, and hang about like a white fog. The wind is uncertain, everything is damp, and malaria accumulates from the great pools of water and the rapidly decaying vegetation which everywhere abound. The rains, though severe at all parts of the coast, are more so at and in the neighbourhood of Cape Coast, heavy thunderstorms, continuous downpours, and violent tornadoes, following in succession, with but short spells of sunshine intervening: rivers become torrents, low-lying lands are inundated, and the coast lagoons burst through their banks into the sea. Towards the end of the rainy season the showers become lighter and less frequent; dense masses of vapour gather at night, and are not dispelled till the sun is well up next day; the weather is much colder, particularly the nights, and the period is generally considered to be the most unhealthy time for Europeans on the coast. The fogs that prevail at this time are known as the "smokes". October, November and December particularly are considered to be the hottest months in this part of the world, as September is generally the coldest.

The dry season fairly sets in by October, and with the exception of the "smalls" or lesser rains in November, fair weather remains, with brilliant sunshine, until the following April, when nature again proceeds to usher in the rainy season. In the interior, owing no doubt to the dense vegetation and the elevation of the land, the rains begin earlier in the season, and are more sudden and frequent in their appearance than on the coast line. The land- and sea-breezes alternate very regularly throughout the wet and the dry seasons. The former comes up about sunset from the north-west and the latter from the south-west soon after sunrise every morning. Upon the mountains in the interior it is later, occurring with great regularity about 10 A.M., from sunrise to that time being often a period of stifling heat. So far as I have been able to ascertain, the Fantis are the only people along the coast who divide the year into divisions, according to its climatic conditions, bestowing upon each a distinct and particular name. These divisions are nine in number, commencing with the Harmattan in January, and finishing with the small tornadoes in December.

The Harmattan is a periodical wind which blows at the beginning of the year, varying in its commencement from the middle of January to the middle of February, and which is generally ushered in by a violent tornado. Mr. Zimmerman, an old resident on the coast, describes it as blowing from January to March or April. This wind blows with a peculiar effect, drying and parching the skin and drying up the vegetation. A fine dust comes with it, and during its continuance its progress is marked by the creaking of Madeira chairs and sofas, the cracking of veneered articles, and the curling up of papers and the covers of books. During my last tour (1896-1897) its influence was felt at Aburi, some twenty-seven miles north of Accra, as early as Christmas Day, 1896, and continued throughout January and part of February. The air becomes hot and dry, with very cool mornings and evenings, which to the European are very beneficial, though not so to the natives. Sensible perspiration is sensibly diminished, the action of the kidneys is far more active than at other times, and a sense of dryness is experienced in the nostrils and about the lips. Table salt, which at all ordinary times is in a semi-liquid state, owing to the extreme humidity of the air, becomes solid and hard, and glasses have been known to crack and fall to pieces as they stood upon the table. Its extreme dryness may be indicated by the fact that evaporation proceeds at the rate of several inches per day ($9\frac{1}{2}$), whilst the total evaporation in England is but 36 inches per annum. Much of this extreme dryness is accounted for by the direction from which this wind blows, coming as it does from the great Sahara Desert, from a point a little to the west of due north. To "old coasters" this breeze is very welcome; to new comers it is apt to be a trifle trying. The term Harmattan is of disputed origin. On the Gold Coast it is called by the natives Aharabata or Ahalabata, while the Rev. Mr. Christaller in his book gives it as Haramata, and the Spanish is Harmatan, an Arabic word.

The average range of temperature throughout the Gold Coast is not excessive, though the climate must be described as hot, with some variations during certain seasons of the year. The average shade temperature ranges between 85° and 90° F., falling to 80° during the Harmattan, and of course lower during the tornado season. The extreme humidity of the atmosphere at times gives one the sensation of cold rather than of extreme heat, causing Europeans to wear a much heavier kind of clothing than is usually considered necessary in countries so near the Equator. Woollen garments are the best to wear next the skin, and blankets the most comfortable to sleep under at night. So great is the humidity, particularly along the coast, that all descriptions of wearing apparel rapidly spoil, that which is not destroyed by the ravages of moth and cockroach being quickly attacked by mildew and rust.

Much difference of opinion exists with regard to the general unhealthiness of this part of the world. Sierra Leone was of old known as the "White Man's Grave," and in course of time the same appellation was bestowed upon the Gold Coast and Lagos. That the country has been unhealthy for the continued residence of Europeans admits of no question, and that it will remain for ever so, more or less, while only a narrow strip of low-lying malarious coast line forms the country selected for the habitations of the white traders and officials compelled to reside there, admits of little doubt. In the past, white men were quartered amidst surroundings that were totally unfit for habitation, and in which, in England, people would have hesitated to have located an animal. European quarters were rented side by side with the huts of the natives, round which the accumulated filth of families was allowed to rapidly decompose, and to poison the surrounding air. Little or no system of drainage existed, and consequently every channel and gutter in the street became a sort of open drain when the rains set in, and began to disturb and carry away the stored up dirt of the dry season, spreading disease and sickness among the white population. This sickness gradually disappeared as the rains decreased, and with the advent of the dry season, a more general feeling of safety for the next few months brought relief to the remaining white population of the towns along the coast. This was of annual occurrence for a long period, particularly when Cape Coast Castle was the headquarters of the seat of the Government. After 1874, when a more healthy site was looked for, it was decided to transfer the capital to some other spot. Accra was fixed upon, why I have never been able to discover. It possesses no more natural advantages for commerce than Cape Coast offered, and is situated upon a low-lying tract of sandy soil, bounded both east and west by lagoons. No attempt seems to have been made to secure an elevated spot a short distance from the coast as the seat of Government, and for the residence of Europeans. Many such spots exist, but there was, and is still, no transport to these higher grounds, except upon the heads of the natives by means of a hammock. The hill region of Aquapim lies within twenty miles north by west of Accra; Aburi is but twenty-seven miles from the coast and stands 1400 feet above the sea, where Europeans now go to recuperate after a dose of malarial fever. Why not have faced the difficulty of transport and constructed a railway from the coast to this elevated inland district? But no, Accra was selected, and from Accra no railway could be laid because no railway machinery and plant could be safely landed without first constructing a harbour, and this meant an almost unlimited outlay of money.

So the Gold Coast has gone on from year to year with its death-rate much about the same. Constant change of officers, want of continuity of service and work in the same department, limited occupations, scanty amusements, poor quarters, have all contributed to keep up the bad name of the colony, and to embarrass commercial progress in one of the richest of our tropical possessions.

Within the last few years many improvements both in quarters and sanitation have been effected, but there still exist in many places along the coast habitations that are not fit for the continued residence of Europeans. Until the higher situations are selected, away from the native quarters of the towns, so long will the death-rate continue to be high and violent epidemics occur.

On account of the prevalence of the sea-breeze from the south-west, the western portion of the Gold Coast is called the Windward District. This extends from Half Assini to the mouth of the Secoom River, some twelve miles west of Accra. From this point begins the Leeward District, which extends eastward to the Volta River. Thus, on the coast windward means west, and leeward, east, similar to the West India description, but in East Africa the opposite is the case, for there windward means east.

Bosman found the hottest months to be from October to March, and the coldest to be September, when he says, "We could well endure a fire as in Europe". He also ascribes the unhealthiness of the place to two reasons: First, the extreme heat of the day followed by the coolness of the night, and second, the thick damp or mist that is constantly rising from the low-lying marshy grounds. This latter is made more noxious, he says, "by the negroes' pernicious custom of laying their fish for five or six days to putrefy before they eat it, and to their easing their bodies round their houses and all over their towns". There is no doubt that the great difference between the air in Europe and West Africa has the effect of lowering the constitution, causing one to be the more susceptible to malarial influences, and that, after an attack of fever, the great drawback is the poor quality of the food obtainable. There is little or nothing in the way of food, to be tempting to a weakened digestion. The oxen, sheep and fowls are all lean, dry and tough, requiring an amount of energy, appetite and determination to eat them that a sound man seldom possesses, much less so a man who has just recovered from an attack of malarial fever. Early writers describe the good weather as beginning in September and continuing for the five succeeding months; the bad weather or wet season taking up the remaining six months of the year. The latter season, the rainy one, was further described as containing two rainy, two misty, and two windy months. But then, as now, the seasons altered from year to year, the dry season coming one year earlier than another; the same of which may be said of the winds and the rain.

The productions of the country are largely agricultural, supplying the natives with such a continuous succession of crops, that famine and want of food are absolutely unknown. The whole soil of the country is extremely fertile, providing an abundance of food plants, fruits and useful trees. These may be divided into two classes: those indigenous to the soil, and those that have been introduced into the country. Among those that were cultivated by the early inhabitants, and upon which they lived, were yams, cassada, maize, rice and various kinds of beans, while the arrival of Europeans upon the coast stimulated further cultivation, and led to the introduction of many foreign grains, plants and fruit trees; the Portuguese being credited with the introduction of millet, corn, plantain, banana, orange and apple. There is a tradition in the country that the plantain and the banana belonged to the Gold Coast, and were first discovered in Akim, but it is more than probable that the first roots were taken there from one of the ports on the coast. After the Portuguese, the Danish traders interested themselves in teaching the natives to further cultivate the soil, and introduced coffee and cotton plantations upon the hill lands behind Accra. Since these early times the Basle Mission has worked very hard to teach the native to improve the cultivation of his country, both by example and by the introduction of missionary labour from the West Indies. In 1843, some twenty-four members of the Moravian Mission in Jamaica were brought to the Gold Coast and established at Akropong, a hill station some 1400 feet above the level of the sea, and two days' journey north by east of Accra. The expense of this experiment was borne by the Basle Mission Society, and at the present day there is one of these West Indians still living at Aburi, the Rev. Mr. Clark. By this expedition, the coco, mango, mountain-pear and bread-nut were introduced into the country, and attempts were also made to cultivate tobacco. In addition to the fruits already mentioned, the paw-paw, water-melon, lime, pine-apple, sour-sop and guava grow in different parts of the colony, but they lack many of the fine qualities expected in such fruits, owing to the want of care upon the part of the natives in their cultivation. Rice is grown in Apollonia in the west, and at Quahu in the north, while ground-nuts, beans, onions and tomatoes are found in different parts of the colony. The sugar-cane flourishes in the wet lowlands to the east, and coffee is now very extensively grown in all parts of the colony, particularly by the members of the Basle Mission Society, and Messrs. A. Miller Bros.

A great variety of useful trees is found throughout the land. Along the shore, particularly at its western and eastern limits, cocoa-nut palms grow in great abundance, but little or no use is made of them for the export of copra, coir fibre and coir yarn. In the west, chiefly in Wassaw and Apollonia, the bamboo palm grows freely, supplying at one time a good article of export in the form of fibre, called piassava.

The most important of the palms, however, is the oil palm, which grows most luxuriously and abundantly in many parts of the colony, furnishing the markets of Europe and America with most valuable articles of trade in palm oil and palm kernels. Many kinds of rubber trees and vines are to be found in the extensive forests that stretch across the country from the Ancobra to the Volta, and a large and increasing trade is now being done in mahogany and other timbers of an equally useful nature.

The oil palm, before mentioned, supplies the inhabitants with their native drink, *viz.*, palm wine. Bosman says in his day there were four varieties of this palm known in the colony, and sings high the praises of both the oil and the wine that were obtained from them. The same writer also states that rice was once so plentifully grown, that it was easy to load a ship with it, perfectly cleaned, at one penny or less the pound.

Vegetation in the Gold Coast may be said to flourish down to the water's edge, though near the coast line it is of a bushy and scrubby nature. The coast plains to the east on the right bank of the river Volta are covered with a thick, coarse, rank grass, growing some four to six feet high, and interspersed at intervals with clumps of bushes and shrubs. After the low-lying coast plains are passed, the country becomes elevated and more wooded, the hillsides are covered with timber, and the bush on either side of the path becomes impenetrable, owing to the dense tropical undergrowth that exists on all sides. The forests are full of valuable timber trees. The animal life of the colony has much changed during the last two centuries, and at the present day you may travel through the length and breadth of the land without finding occasion to use your gun.

Through the thick bush nothing is seen and very little heard, while on the plains, an occasional bush deer or a few birds form the only sport to be met with. Up the rivers you may be fortunate enough to have a pot shot at some lazy alligator sleeping in the sun on the muddy bank, but should you miss him, he soon disappears and seeks safety in the depths of the river beneath you. To-day very few tropical animals find shelter in the thick forests, that once formed the hiding-places of elephants, hyenas, leopards, panthers, antelopes, buffaloes, wild hogs, porcupines and squirrels, whilst the trees were alive with gorillas, baboons and black and many other coloured monkeys. At one time a great trade was carried on in monkey skins, but these are now much scarcer throughout the coast, the increasing warfare against these animals having practically exterminated them in the provinces near the shore. As late as 1894 no fewer than 168,045 skins were exported of the value of £41,000, while in 1896 the number fell to 67,660. Add to this the number that annually dies, and it is not far distant when the process of extermination will outstrip that of reproduction.

To find solitary specimens of these animals you must now travel to the remotest and least frequented parts of the colony, and then possibly be rewarded only by disappointment for your energy. Snakes of many varieties, including pythons, horned adders, puff adders and black cobras, though common, are seldom seen in the day time. Many of the smaller kinds are of a most poisonous nature, but the largest are not so dangerous. At Kpong, on the right bank of the Volta, I have seen them as long as twelve and sixteen feet, and as big round as a man's leg. These were generally killed by the watchman at night, when they came from their hiding-places among the palm oil barrels to make their depredations upon the poultry in the yard.

Bosman tells some very good snake stories, of which the following are examples. At Axim, during his time, the natives killed a snake twenty-two feet long, which, when opened, was found to contain the body of a full-grown deer. Another snake, not quite so large, was found near Boutri, in whose body a negro was found. He also relates that his servants when near Mouri found a snake seventeen feet long, engaged in a combat with two porcupines. The men, after witnessing the battle for some time, killed all the combatants, and brought them to Mouri, where they were eaten by their comrades with great relish. While the Dutch fort was in course of construction at the same place, the workmen found a snake of considerable dimensions behind a heap of stones (a common hiding-place), and to dislodge him they removed a great number of the stones, until half of his body was uncovered. One of the natives then seized him by the tail, thinking to dislodge him in this way, but finding this not at all an easy task, he hacked away as much of his body as was visible, and continued to clear away the stones. The snake thus freed, clung round the body of the native, darting his poison into his face, and some entering his eyes, he became temporarily blind, but again recovered his sight. Leopards were once plentiful in the colony, coming down to the trading forts and seizing and carrying off any stray animal to be found within their reach. Bosman calls them tigers, and describes how he assisted in killing one about the size of a common calf, besides being well provided with large teeth and claws. They must have been common along the whole coast, for he also mentions that a boy from their factory at Sekondi was attacked and killed by a tiger. The countries of Axim and Ante were full of these animals, and the capture of one was the occasion for much drinking and enjoyment on the part of the negroes.

Elephants too were once numerous in the Gold Coast, but very few of these animals have been seen of late years. The old Dutch chronicler's account of an elephant shoot is very interesting. "In the year 1700, in December, at six in the morning, an elephant came here to Elmina, walking easily along the shore under the hill of St. Jago. Some natives were so bold as to go against him without anything in their hands, as a sort of welcome to bring him in, when one of our officers belonging to the hill and a native who came down with him, fired on him immediately, the officer's ball hitting him above his eye. This and the following shots which the natives poured on him were so far from provoking him, that they did not move him to mend his pace in the least. He went on, and lastly stepped into our garden, expecting perhaps civiler treatment there. This drew the Director-General and myself into the garden, followed by our people. We found him standing in the garden, breaking down the cocoa-nut trees, either to divert himself or to show us his strength. Whilst he stood here above one hundred shots were fired at him, which made him bleed as if an ox had been killed. During all which he did not stir, except to set up his ears, which were of a prodigious size. But this sport was accompanied with a tragical event, for a native fancying himself able to deal with him, went softly behind him, caught his tail in his hand, intending to cut a piece of it off, but the elephant, being used to wear a tail, would not permit it to be shortened in his life time. Wherefore, after giving the native a stroke with his snout, he drew him to him, and trod upon him two or three times, and, as if that was not sufficient, he bored in his body two holes with his teeth, large enough for a man's fist to enter. Then he let him lie without making any further attempt upon him, and stood still also whilst two natives fetched away the dead body. After the elephant had killed the native, and had been about an hour in the garden, he wheeled about as if he intended to fall on us, so that each endeavoured to secure himself by getting away. We all flew out of the garden by the fore-door, and the elephant took to the back door, which, whether in his way, or too narrow for him to pass, he flung, though a brick and a half thick, a good distance. After which he forced his way through the garden hedge, going softly by Mount St. Jago towards the river, where he bathed, in order to wash off the blood and to cool himself. After a little while in the river, he came out and stood under some trees among our water tubs, which he broke in pieces, and also a canoe which lay by them. While the elephant stood here, the shooting was renewed till at last he fell down, and the natives cut off his snout, which was so hard and tough that it took thirty strokes to separate it, which must be very painful to the elephant since it made him roar, the only noise I heard him make. The elephant was no sooner dead than the natives fell upon him in crowds, each cutting off as much as he could, so that he furnished a great many, black as well as white, with food enough for that day. He was not very large, his teeth only weighing about thirty-four pounds."

Insect life on the Gold Coast is varied and prolific, ranging from the tiny sand fly to the largest of beetles. Butterflies are plentiful, particularly in the months of May and June. They are of gaudy colour, large and small, and in the interior many rare specimens are to be found. Bird life is well represented, and the variety of aquatic and forest birds is very great. Among these may be mentioned kingfishers, ospreys, herons, snipes, cross bills, storks, pelicans, curlews, wild ducks, spur plovers, hawks, crows, vultures, parrots, nightingales, pigeons, bottle birds, doves, wood-peckers and swallows. The plumage is most brilliant, but the birds are for the greater part songless.

The chief domestic animals are the horse, cow, ox, sheep, goat and pig. Of these, horses are only found in Accra, and are not native. They are brought from the far interior, or from the Canary Islands, and do not thrive anywhere on the coast, except in the Accra country, on account, it is said, of the tsetse fly. The tropical waters of the Gulf of Guinea abound in fish, and many varieties of the edible kind are caught by the fishermen along the coast. Some of these are very fine, and include mackerel, skate, bonetta, flying-fish, sole, snapper, barra-couta, eel, mullet and herring. This last forms the staple food of the fisher people, and when dried is carried in enormous quantities to the people of the interior countries, by whom it is esteemed to be a great relish.

In spite of the few improvements that have been made in the colony to render it more habitable to the European, the export and the import trade of the country has very considerably increased during the present century, and though the present trade is said to be

GOLD COAST BEETLES (one-third life size).
"The Goliath." Young Male, Full-grown Male and Female.

dull, no doubt owing to the recent annexation of the Ashanti country, and the present troubles in the hinterland, it will recover and increase so soon as the native mind settles down and recognises the new order of things.

The following information may be of use to some readers :—

Exports.	Imports.
Rubber.	Silk Goods.
Timber.	Cotton Goods.
Kola Nuts.	Woollen Goods.
Coffee.	Hardware.
Copra.	Earthenware.
Skins.	Glass.
Gold Dust.	Metal Work.
Guinea Grains.	Provisions.
Gum.	Drugs.
Ivory.	Furniture.
Kernels.	Oils.
Oil.	Sugar.
Quartz.	Stationery.
Ore.	Books.
Quills.	Beads.
Ground Nuts.	Perfumery.
Fibre.	Wearing Apparel.
Cocoa.	Soap.
	Candles.
	Wines.
	Spirits.
	Building Materials.
	Rice.
	Tobacco.

The revenue of the colony is obtained chiefly from the Import Duties and Spirit Licenses, of which the following are the chief:—

IMPORT DUTIES.

	s.	d.
On wine, ale, porter and beer, gallon or part	1	0
On spirits and liqueurs ,, ,,	2	6
On manufactured tobacco, cigars or snuff, per pound or part thereof	1	0
On unmanufactured tobacco, per pound or part	0	4
On gunpowder ,, ,,	0	6
On lead ,, ,,	0	0½
On firearms (each)	2	0

	s.	d.
On filled cartridges, per hundred	5	0
On unfilled ,, ,, ...	1	0
On percussion caps	1	0

While a 10 per cent. *ad valorem* is charged on the following imported articles:—

Beads.	Timber.
Boats.	Machinery (not mining nor agricultural).
Canoes.	
Brassware.	Perfumery.
Bread.	Provisions.
Biscuits.	Rice.
Building Materials.	Silk.
Cordage.	Soap.
Cottons.	Sugar.
Earthenware.	Apparel.
Flour.	Woollens.
Furniture.	And on all other goods not enumerated and not exempt.
Hardware.	
Kerosene.	
Oils.	

Spirit licenses are a source of great income to the Government. A license to sell spirits not to be consumed on the premises, £5 per annum, and a license to sell spirits which may be consumed on the premises, £5 per annum. These licenses have lately been increased in amount.

On their habitations I am unable to bestow much praise. It is only of late years that two-storied dwellings have been more commonly built by the natives, and then only by the more opulent living in the towns on the coast and in the interior at the large mission stations. It is very rare to find a two-storied dwelling in an interior town. The materials from which their houses are built depend largely upon the natural resources of the neighbourhood.

In the eastern and western parts of the colony, where no swish is to be found, the native huts are entirely of bamboo, laced tightly together with the runners of trees, roofed over with a thatch of palm leaves. In all other parts of the colony the walls are of swish (native mud), and in some isolated cases, of native stone cemented together with swish. In many cases the walls are built after the size of the hut has been laid out in the following manner: Two rows of sticks and wattle-work are placed at a distance apart equal to the intended thickness of the walls of the house. The space between these is then filled up with loose, gravelly clay, mixed with water, and the inside and outside of the framework of the wall smoothly plastered over with swish to give it the appearance of a solid mud wall. The roofs are made with gable ends, to form which, three poles are joined, one from the ridge of the roof, and one from the point to form the sides to the base of the triangle. Over all is spread a framework of bamboo, into which the thatch of leaves is interlaced. This is tied to the poles running from end to end of the gables, and on the inside to the framework of bamboo. Holes are left in the walls for windows, into which rude shutters are fixed at night. At the present day stone buildings with iron roofs are fast becoming more numerous in all the coast towns. The flooring is mostly of the same nature as the walls, sometimes of cement, seldom of wood, and is generally raised from one to two feet above the surface of the ground, the floor being reached by one or two steps of the same material as the walls. The walls of the huts are often washed over either white or red. This latter wash is obtained by making an infusion of red earth found in the neighbour-

TYPICAL NATIVE HUTS.

hood with water, with which the walls are daily coated, the former being ordinary whitewash. The doors are often made of an entire piece of wood, with other pieces, cut and carved, nailed across them. The only fastening is a native Haùsa or a common European lock, often to be used on the inside of the door only. Many huts require no door, the fourth side of the house being entirely open to the winds of heaven. When this is the case, the habitation consists very often of three or four distinct huts enclosing a compound with their open sides turned towards the centre, the whole being enclosed with a palisade of bamboo with a door or gate at one angle. In the centre of this compound the cooking is done, meals are taken, and sheep, goats and fowls roam in and out at will. In many places neither chairs nor tables are to be found, the floor being a substitute for both, and also forming the bed at night, with the addition of a thin bamboo mat spread at night, and rolled up and put away in the morning.

Bosman says the natives build their villages without the least regard to situation or to pleasantness; having no regard for pleasant prospects or walks, nor the valleys and rivers with which their country abounds. This is very true, and they are just as indifferent with regard to the making and the keeping of their roads. A road, which need not be more than two miles in length, is frequently more than three on account of its windings. The native seldom troubles to get over an obstacle in his path, he goes round it like the ant, and the time lost is of not the slightest value to him, and in this respect he is quite at a loss to understand the haste of the European. "One time," or as we should say, "at once," is to him, presently, and soon, in his vocabulary, means any time from one hour to a day or even more. The abundance of time and the climate of the country are the two chief factors against hurry in West Africa. Commercial progress is very slow, and the whole country suffers too much from the literal interpretation of the native saying, "Softly, softly, catch monkey". This may be true of catching monkeys, but I fail to see its universal application to all the improvements so necessary in West Africa.

There is little doubt that slavery has existed in Africa from the earliest times, and the testimony of the ancient writers goes to prove that such early nations as the Phœnicians, Carthaginians, Egyptians, Greeks, Romans and Arabians, all drew their supplies of slaves from the interior of the Dark Continent. Among the inhabitants of Africa, slavery was always the portion of those prisoners of war that were not needed for sacrifice or human food, and so the desire for traffic in human bodies was deeply rooted in the African nature, long before the advent of the Europeans in the fourteenth century. For centuries before this period, the great Mohammedan states of the northern interior were the centres of organised slave-hunting expeditions, by which many of the present tribes inhabiting the Gold Coast were driven farther and farther from the interior towards the sea. For their own defence and safety, family joined with family and tribe with tribe, the increase of numbers bringing increase of power and greater immunity from capture, and possibly leading to the formation and establishment of such extensive tribes as the Ashantis and Fantis of the present day. Slavery existed in the time of Moses, it flourished in the early and middle ages, and assumed its worst form when the slave or pawn became recognised as a transferable article of commerce. The slavery of black to the black and of black to the Arab in these early times was nothing when compared with the slavery of the negro to the white man, that was instituted soon after the discovery of America, and which grew and flourished during the seventeenth and eighteenth centuries until the year 1807. For years before the discovery of the new world slaves were common in Europe, particularly in Spain and Portugal, where it became necessary to legislate to lessen the severity of their lot. These slaves were, however, the result of kidnapping expeditions to the West Coast, and not the result of an exchange for those European commodities that afterwards tempted the eye and incited the wily African to capture his weaker neighbour, or the stranger passing through his country, and at last even his own relation, in order to barter him away for some glittering gew-gaw that had aroused his insatiable cupidity. Though slaves in Africa, they were at home, retaining certain privileges, and able to be freed ; but when once deported to work for the European in the cotton, rice and sugar fields of newly-discovered America, all privileges ceased, and freedom became an impossibility except under most degrading conditions.

It appears from ancient voyages collected by Hackluit, Purchas and others, that it was about fifty years before the discovery of America that the Portuguese attempted to sail round Cape Bojador, and landing on the western coast of Africa, began to make incursions into the country and to seize and carry off the native inhabitants. As early as 1431 Alonzo Gonzales landed on the coast and pursued and attacked the natives, returning six years later and taking the first twelve prisoners, with whom he returned to his vessel and carried them to Portugal.

The traffic in slaves was undoubtedly inaugurated by the Portuguese and the Spaniards early in the sixteenth century, for as early as 1503 we hear of their employment by these nations as miners and field workers in the newly-acquired territories in South America. Some fifteen years later, we find Charles the Fifth granting the exclusive privilege to a favourite Flemish courtier, of annually importing a stated number of slaves into America, which privilege he quickly disposes of to some Genoese merchants; who from this time organise and carry on a regular traffic in slaves, the magnitude of which was soon to be equalled and ultimately surpassed by their rivals, the English. Thus in 1562, in the reign of Elizabeth, we read of the honours bestowed upon Sir John Hawkins, who went as far as Sierra Leone and "got into his possession partly by the sword and partly by other means, to the number of 300 negroes at the least, besides other merchandise". From this time the trade grew and flourished, until the English, copying the example of the Portuguese and the Spaniards, became the leading European nation engaged in this nefarious trade. So, from the middle of the seventeenth to near the end of the eighteenth century, statistics show that nearly $2\frac{1}{4}$ millions of the negroes were deported from their own country by European adventurers to work in the English colonies in the West Indies, the total for given years reaching to no less than 75,000 slaves for a good year's work. From this time until early in the nineteenth century the traffic increased rather than diminished, and after all countries except Spain and Portugal had declared such traffic to be illegal, there is ample evidence to prove that more than 130,000 were still being annually deported from their homes across to America. Educated by European example, the natives throughout the whole coast of Guinea became expert slave raiders themselves, in order to meet the demand of the white man for slaves, and now we wonder why West Africa has made so little progress in the civilisation that has been gradually spreading over the world. The answer is not far to seek. For centuries the tribes inhabiting the coast line had been the means of robbing the interior countries of their best men and women to work in a foreign land; there was no market for old men and children, so they could be left behind and allowed to die in their own country, or more often were killed in the raid that took place, and the wonder is that the previously thickly-populated countries did not more rapidly become changed into more thinly-peopled territories than they did.

To encourage and extend this trade, the coast from Apollonia to Danoe was studded with the forts and trading stations as shown in Bosman's map on page 13, and how eager must have been the competition, is shown by their great number in so small a strip of territory, divided as they were between the British, Dutch, Danish, French and the Brandenburg Companies. To the chiefs and the headmen of the towns where these forts were built, a kind of monthly rent was paid, and upon this slender understanding the tenure of the European was acknowledged in West Africa. Little or nothing was ever done in these early times for the improvement of the native, and the only object in the erection of so many forts, seems to have been to protect the occupiers and to extend the slave trade. No jurisdiction was claimed over the surrounding country, and no interference was attempted in the affairs of the people, except where the squabbles of neighbouring chiefs interfered with the profits of the various companies, by the temporary disorganisation of what was then a very lucrative trade. These squabbles or "palavers" were of very frequent occurrence, often purposely invented by the chiefs and headmen in order to secure an increased monthly payment upon their notes, or to make an extra profit by causing temporary delay in the supply of the cargoes, that were anxiously competed for by the various trading companies.

This was the state of things that reigned for more than two centuries. Popes had granted decrees authorising the slave trade, kings and emperors had given monopolies for pursuing it; and even Acts of Parliament had approved of the continuance of it. All things, however, have an end, and towards the end of the eighteenth century Denmark was the first European Power to forbid the traffic in human flesh and blood. The United States and England soon followed; France partly agreed, and the interests of Portugal and Spain were bought out by the English, by the payment of huge sums of money to the respective nations of those countries, in order to secure their co-operation in putting an end to a trade that had existed for so long. Towards the end of the reign of William the Fourth, the right of search was agreed upon by most of the European powers, and in 1842 the United States and Great Britain agreed to maintain a fleet, for the prevention of the exportation of slaves from the coast of Guinea.

The great question affecting the commercial interests

of the Gold Coast of the present day is the one of labour. Here is a vast country, full of undeveloped mineral wealth (as yet unsurveyed and unexplored), with deep impenetrable forests containing many kinds of valuable trees, only waiting for organisation and discipline with regard to its labourers to cause it to become one of the most important of our West African colonies. The natives in this part of the world appear to work better

A GROUP OF LABOURERS.

out of their own country; thus the Gold Coast is worked by Kru labour, while the best artisans and mechanics from the Gold Coast seek and find employment in the Oil Rivers and the Niger Coast Protectorate farther south. Most of the West African stations, established by the Portuguese for slave trading and captured by the Dutch, who carried on the traffic, fell into the hands of the English, who vigorously pursued the same trade until the middle of the present century. From this date civilisation has been the order of the day—by the aid of the trader—and the old forts became simply centres for the export of palm nuts and oil, ground nuts and gold dust, and for the importation of gaudy articles of European manufacture. Since their emancipation, civilisation and freedom were going to do much for the people, but for years, instead of progressing, they have gradually declined. At the present day a new phase of their existence is opening up; the English are beginning to see their importance, and the Government to wake up to its responsibilities. The same remarks that apply to one of our West African colonies apply alike to them all, Gambia, Sierra Leone, Gold Coast and Lagos, with regard to the labour question. The people, inured for centuries to a system of slavery, resent free labour, and hold agriculture as a degradation to a free man. The women and children perform the field work, the man's ambition is to be idle or at most to become a petty trader. The richest lands are uncultivated and thinly populated, either one or both, and lands once left, soon become an impassable tract of bush. Of the four colonies, the Gold Coast is perhaps the better supplied with population, but labour is scarce, and a strain soon exhausts the supply. A compulsory labour ordinance had to be passed as late as 1896, in order to secure carriers for Government loads for the interior, but even that does not work satisfactorily. Fortunes could be made by the natives by the cultivation of coffee, which grows to perfection, cocoa, rice, cotton, rubber and tobacco for export, and by the cultivation of fruits and vegetables for consumption by the resident Europeans. Hardly any capital need be expended; organised and disciplined labour is all that is required, but even the superior class of native does not seem to be possessed of the necessary energy for the organisation of native labour to carry this out.

The Fantis, Akras and Apollonians will work better than the rest of the tribes, and I firmly believe that much native labour could be organised in the interior, with the assistance of the chiefs of the various towns, to work the gold mines that at present exist, and to open up new ones. Accurate and regular payment for work done, and the establishment and the opening of stores in the interior, would soon create a desire in the native mind for better articles for daily use, and this desire once created, the native would soon work to satisfy his demands.

Until the face of the country is cleared of bush, organised white labour is out of the question, except in a few more favoured parts; the importation of coolie labour would be of no use, as coolies would not stand the climate. The native himself seems to be the only person who can stand the climate, and who should do the work, but the question is, how is he to be induced to do it, in order that it shall be profitable to those who invest their capital? In July, 1897, the late Governor, Sir William Maxwell, caused sixteen Chinese miners to be sent to the Gold Coast. This was to test the climate for Chinese labour, and to see what were the prospects of gold mining in the colony. They returned to England in December last, and spoke exceedingly well of the gold-mining prospects in the Akim and Tarkwa Districts, where they considered alluvial gold was very plentiful, but the climate was in no way suitable to their health. None had died, but most of them had been at times very ill.

CHAPTER IV.

Gold in West Africa—Antiquity of the same—Gold-producing Areas—Present Gold Mines—How Obtained—Gold Work—Gold Weights—The Future of West Africa as a Gold-producing Country.

To obtain a thorough idea of the value of the Gold Coast as a gold-producing area, it is necessary to go back to its early history of the fourteenth century, when the French declare that they imported the precious metal from the present Elmina, just one century before the arrival of the Portuguese. Whether the French claims are good or not, it is certain that the Portuguese, under Gonzales Baldeza, brought gold from the Gold River or Rio de Ouro in 1442, and that in 1470 other navigators brought supplies of it from the neighbourhood of Chama into the European market. About the same period another Portuguese merchant, Fernando Gomez, bought from the King of Lisbon the monopoly of trading in gold dust for five years, at a yearly rental of less than £50, and binding himself in addition to explore some 300 miles of coast line every year. This exploration led to the opening of large and important mines at Commendah, to defend which, it is assumed the castle at Elmina was built, and a flourishing trade was carried on till early in the seventeenth century, when the mines at Commendah were shut down and the digging of gold made fetish by the king, since which time no gold has been worked in this neighbourhood. The rich stores of gold, however, were known to, and used by, the natives long before this period, and it is a very difficult point to settle who were the first navigators to this part of the African continent. Herodotus tells us that the Carthaginians obtained their supplies of gold from black people, who brought it across the great desert from the western shores of the continent, and thus describes the trade that was then carried on. "There is a land in Libya and a nation beyond the Pillars of Hercules which they are wont to visit, where they no sooner arrive but forthwith they break cargo, and having disposed their wares in an orderly way along the beach, leave them, and returning aboard their ships, raise a great smoke. The natives, when they see the smoke, come down to the shore, and laying out to view as much gold as they think the worth of the wares, withdraw themselves afar. The Carthaginians upon this, come ashore and look. If they think the gold sufficient they take it and go their way, but if it does not seem to them sufficient, they go aboard once more and wait patiently. Then the others draw near and add to their gold till the Carthaginians are content. Neither party deals unfairly with the other, for they themselves never touch the gold till it comes up to the worth of their goods, nor do the natives ever carry off the goods till the gold is taken away."

This evidence of the early trade in gold is also supported by other writers upon this part of the world. This trade was continued in gold and slaves for many centuries until Guine or Guinea became the great gold-producing area of the old world, soon after its discovery by the Portuguese. The Portuguese gave way to the Dutch, who held sway over a great part of the coast from 1637 until 1868, but who were interrupted in their turn by the English and the French adventurers, who had heard of this El Dorado of Western Africa, and began to take their share. The first Englishman to bring away the precious metal was Captain Thomas Wyndham, who in 1551 brought to England 150 lb. of gold dust from the Gold Coast. He was quickly followed by many others, among whom were Captain Philips, Richard Thompson and Richard Jobson, but by far the larger share of the gold then produced, fell to the Portuguese and the Dutch traders of that time.

The gold-bearing areas in the vast continent of Africa are three in number, two of which date from the most remote times. The first is found in the north-eastern corner of the continent, including Nubia and Abyssinia; the second extends along the whole of the western shores from Morocco to the Volta, while the third occupies enormous areas in the south-eastern districts. The two first-mentioned areas are of most remote origin, while the third is of comparatively recent date. Tradition on the west coast of Africa points to sensational finds of the precious metal, and the barbaric splendour of some of its past rulers freely justifies such tradition. Ghana, the old name possibly of Guinea, was famous among the ancients for its golden throne: Bontuko, for its golden stool, while Bowdich tells us that the King of Gaman, of which Bontuko was the capital, had steps of solid gold by which he ascended to his bed. The Ashantis were most proficient in the manufacture of ornaments made from gold, but were surpassed by the people of Dagwumba, who inhabited a large territory to the north-east of the Ashanti country, ornaments being made in weight to the extent of more than 1000 ounces.

In fact, the whole of the states north and south of the great range of the Kong Mountains were more or less well supplied with extensive deposits of the precious metal, the source apparently being the Kong range itself, the northern limits being the borders of the Niger. For centuries this vast territory poured into Europe millions of pounds' worth of this precious metal, and coming down to Bosman's time we find six distinct areas in and about the Gold Coast supplying the yellow ore. These were Denkira, including Wassaw, Encasse, Juffer and Commendah, Acanny, Akim, Ashanti, Adansi and lastly Aowin. A reference to the map on page 13 will show the relative positions of these territories. As the old Dutch traders were most assiduous in securing as large a supply as possible of the gold then produced, it may be fairly assumed, that what Bosman says concerning the quantity produced by these countries is correct.

With regard to Denkira, he says: "The first country which produces gold is *Denkira*, which includes the conquered states of Wassaw, Encasse, Juffer, and Commendah". The Denkiras at this period were a very powerful race of people, possessed of vast treasures of gold, partly obtained from their own mines, and from plunder and commerce with the interior tribes. That the countries mentioned produced a vast supply is proved by the fact, that the Denkiras from their own territory and from those in subjection to them, produced enough gold to satisfy the demands of the coast from Axim to Sekondi, a distance of forty miles, containing some eight forts or trading stations. The metal thus supplied by the Denkiras was very pure, though often alloyed with "fetishes," oddly-shaped figures composed of several ingredients. Sometimes these "fetishes" would be mixed from one-third to one-half their value with alloys of earth, silver or copper; those of pure gold being kept by the natives for ornament and seldom parted with. Thus in the early days of his history, the native knew the value of trying to sophisticate his gold for the European.

The second district was *Acanny*, a province not marked in Bosman's map, but lying somewhat north-east of the Axim country between Ashanti and Akim. The people of this country were greater traders than the Denkiras, and bought the gold of Ashanti and Akim, which in addition to their own, they brought down to the forts of Elmina, Cape Coast, Mouri, Anamaboe, Cormantine and Winnebah. The gold brought to the coast by the Acanny people was never mixed with "fetishes," and on this account it was known to the coast natives as " Acanny Sika " or Acanny gold, " Sika " being the native word for the precious metal. These people in turn fell to the power of the Denkiras, who themselves were defeated by the Ashantis, and in after times formed one of the most powerful allies of that rapidly extending state.

The third district was *Akim*, which in Bosman's time produced as large quantities of gold as any land that he knew, and that being also the most valuable and pure of any carried away from the coast. It was easily distinguished by its deep colour. The gold of Akim was brought to Accra unalloyed in any manner whatever. Auriferous Akim, as it has been termed, was generally described as the hill-land, lying an easy journey of a week north by west of Accra, and north of the Aquapim Mountains. The Akims in their turn fell before the superior powers of Ashanti and Aquamu, and were early in the eighteenth century forbidden to dig gold by their conquerors. Eight times they were defeated by the former power, and upon each occasion again purchased their independence by the enormous supplies of gold that their territory produced.

The three countries I have mentioned were esteemed in the time of the Dutch to be the most prolific gold-producing areas of the Gold Coast, though there were others not then thought to be so rich in the precious metal. The principal of these other places were Ashanti, Adansi, or Anansi as Bosman has it, and lastly Aowin. From this it will be seen that the gold-bearing districts in the colony were six in number, and extended from the Tando River in the west to the Volta River in the east, the whole coast well deserving the name that was bestowed upon it.

Bosman gives us but little information concerning two of these last three states owing to their distance from the coast, and we must also remember that in his time the power of the Ashantis was in its infancy. In the time of Bowdich, the Ashantis possessed vast stores of gold obtained from their own mines and as tribute from conquered tribes, and which passed as the currency of the country. Issert, the Danish physician, says, speaking of the King of Ashanti: "This mighty king has a piece of gold, as a charm, more than four men can carry, and slaves are constantly at work for him in the mountains, each of whom must collect or produce two ounces of gold per diem ". The Ashanti pits at Soko were reported to yield from 700 to 2000 ounces of gold per month, and their store was further increased by the daily washings throughout Denkira and the hills between Akim and Assin, then reputed to be very rich in gold. Each chief paid a tax to the King of Ashanti upon the gold ornaments in his possession, and all tributary states contributed annual payments amounting in all to nearly £10,000 per annum in addition to the tribute demanded in slaves, cows, sheep, cotton and silk goods.

Rock or nugget gold had, when found, to be always brought to the king, a third of its value being given to the finder. On stated occasions the market-place in Kumasi was washed, and produced as much as 800 ounces of gold at a time. Gold dropped in the market-place belonged to the king and could not be again picked up on pain of death. The gold thus obtained was stored up by the fetish men against future difficulties, and in times of danger, it is said, was buried in their sacred river the Prah, where I believe much will ultimately be found.

The fifth territory was Adansi or Anansi, the country to the south of Ashanti east of the Tando River and to the east of Denkira, which also furnished large quantities of gold. The sixth and last place was Aowin, the strip of country lying north of Apollonia and to the west of Axim. At one period it supplied vast quantities of the precious metal, which was pure and unalloyed, and the people who brought it to the coast were among the civilest and fairest dealers of all the negroes, with whom the Dutch, according to Bosman, " traded with a deal of pleasure ". The country of Aowin was, however, destined, in its turn, to become tributary to the rising power of Denkira, though not until many battles had been fought. After their defeat, the gold brought down by the Aowins decreased in amount, the inhabitants of the country preferring rather to let it remain in the ground, than to dig it for the benefit of a neighbouring tribe.

The gold obtained by the natives in these early days was of two kinds, dust gold and mountain gold. The former was of the finest nature, often as fine as flour and obtaining the highest price, whilst the latter varied very much both in size and quality. The size of the pieces of mountain gold varied from grains no larger than a pin's head, to others varying in value to twenty or thirty guineas, but these latter were always mixed with a multitude of small stones, which greatly reduced their value. The gold thus found was produced, according to the natives, in three different kinds of places, the exact locality of which was seldom or never divulged to the European, for fear that he should take possession of their mines, and thus rob them of their store of wealth.

The best gold was found in or between particular hills, where the natives dug pits and separated it by washing from the earth thus obtained.

The second place was in, at or about some rivers and waterfalls, where the violence of the water brought down large quantities of earth, bringing the gold with it.

The third place was along the sea-shore, particularly where the streams and rivers emptied their waters along the coast.

This all points to the fact that many of the present hills and mountains in the interior of the Gold Coast must form the sources from which these supplies were then obtained, and that in spite of the enormous quantities that have been obtained in the past, there must still remain in the interior of the country vast stores of the precious metal, waiting to be discovered and worked by European energy and enterprise.

In later times, the known gold-bearing areas became reduced to three, Wassaw, Akim and Ashanti, with its powerful rival, the Gaman country, none of which have ever been properly developed, and which became practically forgotten by the opening up of California and Australia, on account of the gold discoveries in those countries. After the lapse of many years, attention is again being turned towards West Africa as a gold-producing area, and a short account of what really does exist in the Gold Coast will perhaps not be out of place in these pages.

Axim ever was and has continued to be the gold port of the colony, situated as it is to the south of one of the best gold-producing countries, *viz.*, Wassaw, where most of the present gold mines are situated, and many attempts at development are taking place. Tarkwa, the present centre of the mining industry of the colony, is situated in Wassaw, some fifty miles from the coast, travelling by bush and river. The mineral deposits of the Wassaw district may be divided into two classes, *viz.* :—

(1) Gold-bearing quartz, and (2) bedded alluvial deposits, in addition to more recent alluvial deposits.

The first are stated to be found to the west of the Ancobra, while the second are found to the east of the same river. There is no doubt that the present group of Tarkwa mines was one of the places in the Wassaw country, from which the Portuguese and the Dutch were supplied with their gold, though the mines themselves were never held or worked by these early adventurers. Though Bosman may allude to these places as the source of their gold produce, he distinctly says in his sixth letter treating of this part of the world: "There is no small number of men in Europe who believe that the gold mines are in our power, and that we, like the Spaniards in the West Indies, have no more to do than to work them by our slaves; though you perfectly know that we have no manner of access to these treasures; nor do I believe that any of our people have ever seen one of them". That the Wassaw mines were the ones then supplying the gold is further strengthened by his statement at the conclusion of his first letter, for he says: "Several years past we had a fort in the country of Equira (or Eqwira) and drove a very considerable trade there, for besides the afflux of gold thither from all foreign parts, the country itself affords some gold mines, and I remember, when I had the Government of Axim a very rich one was discovered, but we lost our footing there in a very tragical manner, for the commander-in-chief of the negroes, being closely besieged by our men, shot gold instead of bullets, hinting by signs that he was ready to treat and afterwards to trade with the besiegers, but in the midst of the negotiation he blew up himself and all his enemies at once". Bosman marks the Equira country north of Apollonia, to the west of the Ancobra, south of the Aowin country, and Burton and Cameron give it a similar position in their sketch-map of the Gold Coast in 1883, but since that time the name seems to have disappeared from existing maps. The fact is, that all the countries of the present day, Ashanti, Sefwi, Adansi, Denkira, Assin, Wassaw and Ahanta, which form the western part of the Gold Coast, form one of the most promising of the gold-producing areas of the colony, lacking only transport and capital to place their wealth before the European market. Many attempts have been made in this direction, only to meet with failure, because, in the companies formed, adequate preparations were not made, either for the landing or transport of the machinery absolutely necessary for the working of the mines. The top alluvial beds have been worked out, and engineering science is now needed to obtain the gold from the quartz and the lower strata, where it still exists in large quantities. Remains of old Dutch forts are also to be found at Essaman, some twelve miles north-west of Tarkwa, near the main stream of the river Ancobra, and some forty miles from Axim in a straight line, and this is no doubt the place referred to by Bosman, when he says that the gold comes from as far inland, that our servants are commonly five days in going from Elmina to it, and ten days from Axim, not so much on account of the distance, but on account of the difficulties of the road.

In the Apollonian country are to be found remains of old native mines which were visited and described by Burton and Cameron in 1882, and leased through their instrumentality by Mr. R. B. N. Walker, who had first visited the place in 1881. The first was called the Izrah mine, situated within an easy march of the coast from Nanipoli and promising to pay and pay well; the second lay some distance east, a little south from the first at a place called Imyoku, near New Amanta, and could be easily approached from the town of Esiamo on the coast. This mine also gave some wonderful specimens and promised to give a rich reward to the owners. Nothing, however, is heard of it at the present day. A third was situated at Ingotro, a short distance west of the Ancobra River, and was of far larger dimensions than the two previously mentioned. Nothing has been done with this.

ASHANTI GOLD WEIGHTS.

Down to the end of the eighteenth century the mines remained entirely in the hands of the native owners, but in 1825 the Gold Coast Mining and Trading Company, with a capital of £750,000, was formed, for the purpose, among others, of extending the intercourse now subsisting with the native chiefs and princes, and to make arrangements with them to introduce a better method of working the mines and pits in the Denkira, Wassaw, Ahanta and Fanti territories on the Gold Coast. This company, however, left mining alone, and confined its attention to trading. Coming down to still later times, *viz.*, 1874, M. Bonnat, a French trader, drew attention to the possibilities of this part of Africa. He explored the Volta River until stopped by the Ashantis, and was held by them for five years as a prisoner in Kumasi. Released by the Ashanti war of 1873-74 he returned to France, and succeeded in the foundation of the Société des Mines d'Or d'Afrique Occidentale. This was more of a syndicate than a company, and devoted its energies to the acquisition of concessions and demonstrating the practicability of dredging the bed of the Ancobra for gold. The exploration of this syndicate lasted for about three years, when Bonnat again returned to France, and in 1879 he was instrumental in forming the Anglo-French Compagnie Minière de la Côte d'Or d'Afrique, or the African Gold Coast Company. He returned to the coast again in 1881 and died there in July, 1882, being buried at Tarkwa. His name will always be associated with the Tarkwa mines, for he was the first European to call attention to their possibilities, and to visit them. Others have followed, but he was the first. The two French companies joined hands in 1886, and in 1888 the mines were taken over by an English company, who have since that time been quietly opening them up, with promise of great success. Early in 1889 the Tarkwa group of mines was visited and fully reported upon by the late Sir W. Brandford Griffith, the governor of the colony at that period, a full account of which will be found in No. 66 of the series of reports relating to Her Majesty's Colonial Possessions, published in 1889. I cannot omit the closing remarks of this report.

"My visit has impressed me with the following convictions:—

"1st. That the country is rich in gold and that it is merely a matter of the necessary time and scientific application for that gold to pay well for extraction.

"2nd. That earnest and well-considered attempts are now being made to secure success.

"3rd. The country once opened up and cultivated would yield rich returns to capital invested in the economic agriculture of any kind of tropical produce; but

"4th. That the natives of the country cannot, unfortunately, be relied upon to supply the necessary labour, which must come either from the Kru country or from China."

The following is a list of the mines then in existence:—

1. Eassaman Mining Company.
2. Akanko Mine.
3. Swanzy Shaft of the Wassaw, at Adja Bippo.
4. Teberibe Mine.
5. Cinnamon Bippo Mine.
6. Swanzy Estates.
7. Tarkwa Mine.
8. Abosso Mine.
9. Essaman.
10. Gie Appantoo.

In the same report will be found an account of the auriferous lands in the Winnebah district of the Gold Coast, contributed by the request of the Government by Mr. Henry Eyre, a then District Commissioner. Having discussed at some length the mines of the Wassaw country, I will now endeavour to show that other parts of the colony are as rich, and have been so from all antiquity, as those at present known. I refer to the Akim country. Let us see what history has said concerning it. Bosman speaks of it as being the third place of importance for the production of gold, placing Acanny as the second, but neither Acanny nor Akim is to be found upon his map. His information was drawn from intercourse only with the natives, and I am inclined to believe, that the " Acanny Sika " of the seventeenth and eighteenth centuries, the purest gold of any obtained on the coast, was none other than Akim gold, Acanny, according to Dr. Leyden, being another name for Akim. The position of this important country in these early times was very uncertain ; the natives purposely avoided giving its exact location in order to retain in their own hands the enormous supply of precious metal that it furnished.

Bosman says : " Having several times heard that Akim was an extraordinary large country, I took once the opportunity of asking some of the Akimese how many days their country was; they replied, that very few natives knew how far it extended inland towards the Barbary coast, which, according to what they told me, was incredible ".

Again Bowdich says, in quoting Dr. Leyden : " On the west of Aquamboe lies the powerful state of Akim, sometimes denominated Akam, Acham and Acanny, which occupies almost all the interior of the Gold Coast, and

GOLD IN AKIM.

is supposed by the natives to extend to Barbary". This somewhat proves that Akim was the same as Acanny. In Dr. Leyden's map, he places it east of Dahomey, instead of west of the Volta, which is its true situation. In the earliest maps of Africa it is marked *Akim, rich in gold*, and of this fact there is no doubt, for in more modern times it ranks second in importance for the production of the yellow ore, Acanny being lost sight of entirely.

So far as I have been able to ascertain, both from reference and from actual travel through the country, no European attempts at mining have ever yet been made in the Akim country, though the whole territory is largely honeycombed with native pits and women's washings. The abolition of the slave trade and the introduction of rubber into the European market from this part of the world, form no doubt two of the chief reasons for the decline in the working of the gold in the Gold Coast colony. To collect rubber, which abounds in the Akim forests, is far easier than digging and washing for gold, and thus little has been heard of late years of the gold in Akim. It is my firm opinion that the whole of Akim is impregnated with the precious metal, and this opinion has been formed from actual travelling through the country, not once, but ten times. What would be thought of a place, that I can mention, where pieces of quartz, broken off an outcrop in the very street of the town, gave visible gold and assayed sixteen dwts. to the ton? Yet the quartz in this part of the colony has never yet been touched by European machinery, and the whole of Akim is practically unexplored. I will add the testimony of others in addition to my own.

Captain Butler described Western Akim as "a country

teeming with gold," while Captain Glover has stated " that in Eastern Akim gold is as plentiful as potatoes in Ireland, and the paths are honeycombed with gold pits ".

In his *Wanderings in West Africa,* the late Captain R. F. Burton says : " In several countries, especially Akim, the hill region lying north of Accra, the people are still active in digging gold. The pits, from two to three feet in diameter, and from twelve to fifty feet deep, are often so near the roads that loss of life has been the result. ' Shoring-up ' being little known, the miners are not unfrequently buried alive. The stuff is drawn up by ropes in clay pots or calabashes, and thus a workman at the bottom widens the pit to a pyriform shape. Tunnelling is, however, unknown. The excavated earth is carried away to be washed. Besides sinking these holes they pan in the beds of rivers, and in places collect quartz which is roughly pounded." Mr. H. Ponsonby found the natives getting quantities of gold by digging holes eight to ten feet deep on either side of the forest paths. He saw as much as three ounces taken up in half an hour. Around the capital of Eastern Akim, Kyebi or Kibbi, the land is honeycombed with manholes, making night travelling dangerous to the stranger. It requires a sharp eye to detect the deserted pits, two feet in diameter, and sunk straight as if they had been bored by huge augers. The workman descends by footholes, and works with a hoe from four to six inches long by two broad, and when his calabash is filled it is drawn up by his companions.

It is generally acknowledged that the earthquakes, which occurred in and about this part of the Gold Coast in 1862 (April and July), so disturbed the hills in the Akim country, that the natives left their ordinary hole diggings, and went in great numbers to the Atiwa Mountains, where huge landslips had occurred and exposed much nugget gold in the mountain sides. The largest nugget found was reported to have been as large as a child's head. One small village, Adadentum, near Kyebi, was nearly destroyed by a landslip, and report says that so much gold was uncovered, that the natives were enabled to obtain enough mountain gold to fill their calabashes daily.

Another authority, Captain J. S. Hay, stated before the R. G. Society, in 1876, that the entire country of Akim is auriferous in a high degree; the natives, however, are too ignorant and too lazy to work the gold properly, and content themselves with digging circular holes from sixteen to twenty feet deep to obtain it, in the shape of small nuggets and dust, the latter being also found in the rivers and water-courses, where I have myself seen them washing it. The country is honeycombed in some parts with these gold holes, which makes walking a difficult and somewhat dangerous operation. The soil is a heavy, tenacious, red clay, quartz strata and red sandstone cropping up in every direction.

Gold washing is, as a rule, the work of the women throughout the colony. Each woman is furnished with a number of large and small wooden bowls or calabashes, which are filled with the earth and sand obtained by the men from the manholes. This earth is repeatedly washed with fresh water in a most adept manner, the stones and earth being thrown out by a rapid rotary motion of the bowl, till it is cleaned from all the earthy matters. The gold, on account of its weight, sinks to the bottom of the tray. This residue is then passed to a smaller tray and the process repeated until nothing is left but the grains of gold and a little sand, which are again washed and the gold finally extracted. Throughout the whole of Akim, wherever water is available, these washings are carried on, and the farther inland one travels the richer the alluvial deposits become. In some places the quartz is roughly pounded, and generally consists of only those pieces that show visible gold. A slightly hollowed slab of granite is generally used for this purpose, upon which the quartz is pounded with a hand-stone. Often the same stones are used for grinding the quartz, that are used for pounding the corn to make flour.

The Fantis and the Ashantis are the most expert goldsmiths at present in the colony, but in the past each important tribe, in fact each important town, had its goldsmith, who fabricated rough ornaments for the king and chiefs, and the richer portion of the community. These generally took the shape of bangles, rings, studs, bracelets, brooches, chains and charms of all kinds, or fetishes as they were called, ornamented with a common pattern, the "signs of the zodiac," which were no doubt introduced to the country by the first visitors, the Portuguese. The workmen, however, are very skilful in the art of imitation, and can make an article to a set copy, or to any design that may be furnished to them. Articles thus made are sold for the value of their own weight in gold, plus a commission of twenty-five per cent. for workmanship; thus an article weighing one sovereign would be sold for twenty-five shillings. Gold ornaments thus made are very soft, owing to the absence of alloy, which, when it is used, generally consists of a little silver. The natives work in silver as well as gold, charging fifty per cent. of the value for workmanship in the former, owing to the greater difficulty of working the harder metal. The implements at the command of the goldsmith for his work are of a very primitive character. Some bees' wax, a modelling block and stick, melting pots and trays are his chief tools. Their mode of procedure is as follows: Sufficient bees' wax for making the model of the article wanted is worked out upon the modelling block or table by the side of the fire on which stands a pot of water; the modelling stick, a piece of flat, hard wood, is dipped into this, and with this the wax is made of the requisite softness for working; it takes the workman about a quarter of an hour to make the model of a ring. When the model of the article wanted is finished, it is enclosed in a case of wet clay and charcoal, which, being closely pressed round the model, forms a mould. This is then dried in the sun, and has a small cup of the same materials attached to it (in which to put the gold for melting) communicating with the model by a very small aperture. When the whole model is finished, and the gold for the article to be made enclosed safely in the cup, the whole is placed in a charcoal fire with the cup undermost. When the gold has had time to become fused, the cup is turned uppermost, in order that it may run into the place of the melted wax, and take its place in the mould; when cool the clay mould is broken, and the article taken out, which if not perfect is again melted and the whole process gone through again. The stoves for their fires are built of swish or native mud in a circular form and about three or four feet in height, being open for one-fifth part of their circumference. Through the closed part a hole is made on a level with the ground of the fire, through which the nozzle of the bellows is to pass. The bellows are an exact imitation of our own, made with sheepskin tied to the wooden sides with leather thongs, and often two or three pairs of bellows are used to one fire. Should an anvil be wanted, a large stone is generally selected for the purpose, or a piece of iron placed on the ground, and upon this rude surface all hammering work is performed. When the article is completed, it is covered all over with a layer of a kind of red ochre (called Inchuma by the natives), and placed in boiling water mixed with salt and some of the same red earth, boiled for about thirty minutes, and then taken out and finally polished. This process gives a good colour to the gold. In addition to the manufacture of ornaments for the people, the goldsmith is the buyer and seller of the gold dust for the district. He possesses a complete set of weights and scales, the former varying from the value of a farthing to £24 6s. The ackie or one-sixteenth part of an ounce is the unit of value. A native proverb says, " You cannot buy much gold for a farthing," and in this, at least, all Europeans will agree. There are thirty-five weights, each with a distinct value, in use in the Ashanti and Fanti countries, a complete list of which will be found at the end of the chapter. The complete set of weighing apparatus is curious and very complicated, consisting of blowers, sifters, spoons, native scales, and weights of many kinds. The smaller weights are no larger than tiny seeds, whilst the larger consist of brass or copper castings of almost every article, animal, fruit, fish or vegetable with which the people are acquainted. Illustrations of these weights will be found on pages 101 and 113. The King of Ashanti was reported to have scales, blow-pan, boxes and weights all made of the purest gold that could be manufactured. These weights are of great antiquity, and complete sets are very rare. The king's weights are allowed to be one-third heavier than the current weights of the country, and all gold expended in provision is weighed out in the former and expended in the latter, the difference going to enrich the cook and the chief domestic officers of the king's house, as it is thought derogatory for a king to pay his subjects for their services. In the same manner the linguists derive the greater part of their incomes, for all the presents of gold made by the king in the year are weighed out by the royal weights and reweighed by them in the current ones.

Bosman in his day found them to be of sufficient interest to mention them. He says: "I am obliged to say something concerning the gold weights, which are either pounds, marks, ounces, or angels. In Europe twenty angels make an ounce, but on the Gold Coast but sixteen go to one ounce." Thus in the time of the Dutch, one angel was equal to the native ackie of the coast. He also mentions the peso and the bendo, the former being equal to four angels and the latter equal to two ounces. Four bendos made one mark, and two marks one pound of gold, equal in the seventeenth century to 660 guilders. Notwithstanding all this, he goes on to say: "We constantly here reckon three marks of pure gold to be worth 1000 guilders, and consequently judge of the other weights in the proportion which they bear to this quantity. We use here another kind of weights, which are a sort of beans, the least of which are red spotted with black, and are called dambas (equal to twopence), twenty-four of them amounting to an angel, and each of them reckoned two styver weights. The white beans with black spots, or those entirely black, are heavier, and accounted four styver weights; these are usually called tacoes, but there are some which weigh half or a whole guilder. But these are not esteemed certain weights, but are only used at pleasure, and thus often become instruments of fraud! Several have believed that the negroes only used wooden weights, but this is a mistake, all of them having cast weights (see pages 101 and 113), of copper or of tin, which though divided or adjusted in a manner quite different to ours, yet upon reduction agree exactly with them." Since its first discovery by the Europeans, it has been roughly estimated that from 600 to 700 millions sterling of gold have been produced from the Guinea Coast, and in its most flourishing days the town of Elmina alone annually exported £3,000,000 work of the precious metal. Early in the eighteenth century Bosman computed that twenty-three tuns of gold were annually brought by the natives to the forts along the coast, a tun of gold in Holland at that date being reckoned at 100,000 guilders, or about £10,000. He made the total output 7000 marks, and estimated it in the following manner:—

The Dutch West India Company . .	1500 Marks.
The English African Company . . .	1200 ,,
The Zealand Interlopers . . .	1500 ,,
The English Interlopers . . .	1000 ,,
The Brandenburgers and Danes . .	1000 ,,
The Portuguese and French . . .	800 ,,
Making a total of . .	7000 ,,

Early in the nineteenth century the export became reduced to slightly under £500,000 sterling, about 120,000 ounces, and averaged this amount for nearly

ASHANTI GOLD WEIGHTS.

half a century. Early in the sixties this export fell to under 50,000 ounces, constantly varying between that and the 120,000 ounces of the earlier part of the century.

This became again reduced in the seventies and the eighties of the present century to an annual average of about £120,000 sterling, which is about the output at the present time.

With the decline of the slave trade began also the decline in the gold-mining industry, though the discovery of new gold-bearing areas in more healthy parts of the world, must also have had its effect upon the output of the Gold Coast. Another reason for the decline is that the natives always wash and dig for years in the same place after the rains. They seldom or never follow the gold to the hills from whence it is carried by the torrents, but rest content with the head waters of the various rivers that flow from them, where the rapidity of the stream has already cleared much of the sand and clay away for them. As a rule, the richest deposits are found after the rains, near the foot of some hill where gold has been previously seen. According to the natives, the most likely places in which to find gold, are those that contain a foundation of reddish sand mixed with small particles of black matter, like fine gunpowder, and called by the natives "sana mira". The same style of washing and panning is common throughout the Gold Coast, and apparently there is an art even in this simple process, for some women will find gold where others cannot. No mercury is ever used, and consequently much fine gold must be lost in the primitive process of washing. In some places nugget gold is again buried, in order that a more bountiful supply may be obtained in the future, and tradition has it, that in some places the presence of a thin white smoke or vapour leads to a rich deposit, while the finding of white gold (silver) invariably leads to the abandonment of that particular place. The presence of ferns is also regarded as a sign of ground rich in the precious metal. Fetish too plays an important part in West African gold finding. Accidents were common in the native shafts owing to the inability of the natives to shore-up the walls, and these caving in often caused loss of life, and led to the closing of that particular place. This is particularly true of the country round Winnebah, near Mankwadi, or the Devil's Hill, and near the right bank of the Volta, where there are supposed to be some very rich deposits.

Generally speaking the gold deposits are stated to extend in more or less quantity from the French boundary on the west to the Volta River in the east, a direct distance of some 240 geographical miles, and inland to a distance of about 100 miles. They may extend east of the Volta, but that they extend for more than 100 miles inland, I am sure, for the country near the town of Obo in Qwahu, where the river Prah has its source, is honeycombed with native shafts, and when there early in 1897, I was offered twenty-seven pounds' worth of gold dust by the natives in exchange for small English silver, which is much wanted in these interior provinces.

Very little, however, will be done in the way of mining in the Gold Coast, particularly in these interior provinces, until some comprehensive scheme of roads and transport has been devised, in order that the interior may be reached in less time and with greater ease than at present. What development can be expected in a country where head carriage forms the only means of transport, and it takes ten days for a parcel of sixty pounds' weight to reach Kumasi from the coast, at a minimum cost of 12s. 6d. for carriage, a rate equal to nearly £25 for a ton? No mining scheme for the Gold Coast will ever succeed, that does not include provision for a means of transport and the construction of better roads than at present exist. A Roads Department is wanted in this country, with travelling road commissioners, who should report from actual inspection upon the state of the roads. Narrow paths are of no use; they soon become overgrown with bush and practically useless for all transport purposes. A minimum width of sixteen feet should be cleared, well banked in the centre, ditched on either side, stones being used wherever obtainable for the edges of the roads. Timber exists in abundance for bridges, and soft places could be corduroyed with the trunks of the smaller trees. A Roads Department was created in 1894 by one governor to be abolished by another in 1896, when it was merged into the Public Works Department, before it had had time to prove its worth or uselessness. All departments in the colony suffer alike from this want of continuity of purpose. In the height of their power the Ashantis knew too well the value of roads, for they caused to be kept open and maintained, no less than nine good roads that led from their capital to the other most important parts of the Gold Coast. These roads were to Dwaben, Akim, Assini, Wassaw, Sauree, Gaman, Soko, Daboia and Salaga. The chief Kumasi-Accra roads were two in number, both passing through the Akim country; one took fifteen days and the other seventeen. This latter passed near Lake Bosomshwi and covered a distance of 230 miles in a south-easterly direction (see page 291).

The future of the Gold Coast lies in its commercial prosperity, and this can only be increased by greater attention to the mining capabilities of the colony, and the production of timber and rubber. Good roads once established, the introduction of wheeled traffic will soon follow, though the matter of animals for draught purposes will still be somewhat of a difficulty. Horses do not thrive, oxen have never been tried, elephants would be too expensive, but I think mules from Canary could be used to great advantage. These last are now being tried by the Government in the Works Department.

Before much introduction of these animals takes place, large areas in the mining districts of Wassaw and Akim should be cleared of vegetation, and "hydraulicked" for the gold that they contain. This should produce enough gold to pay for the railways necessary for the transport of heavy machinery, in order to work the reefs that would be laid bare by the process previously referred to. Before any railway can be laid, a port on the coast is wanted where a breakwater could be easily constructed, and railway plant securely landed. Under existing circumstances everything is transferred to a surf-boat for landing, and more often than not the goods are landed in the last breaker on the shore, instead of upon dry land. Much damage and loss is the result, in addition to a great waste of time, which to a white man often means loss of money.

Every coast line, however bad, has somewhere in its length a natural coign of vantage, where engineering artifice could easily step in and make the necessary improvements. This natural advantage in the coast line is to be found, along this surf-beaten shore, between Dixcove and Sekondi in the western part of the colony, somewhat nearer to the latter place than the former. At Takoradi is a bay large enough to contain a fleet at anchor, with deep and comparatively still water, and at Apoassi, or Sekondi, is a natural point, which could be extended into the sea without much difficulty, and formed into a breakwater, along which vessels could moor and discharge their cargoes, undisturbed by the long Atlantic swell for ever breaking on this coast. This point should be made the chief port of entry for the colony, a coast railway should be constructed west to Akim and Apollonia, and east to Cape Coast, Saltpond and Accra, with branches to Tarkwa, Insuaim, Kumasi, Kyebi and Abetifi.

The Tarkwa line could run direct from Sekondi; the Insuaim-Kumasi line from Saltpond, and the Kyebi-Abetifi line from Winnebah or Accra. The capital required to construct a harbour at any other point along this coast would be sufficient to lay the greater part of the much-needed coast railway. If Apoassi were made the chief port of entry for the colony, I am aware that it would necessitate the establishment of a Customs station and the European officials at or near that point. So much the better; Accra is not a desirable place for headquarters. There are many places in the west far better suited for the residence of Europeans. Boutri is one of these, Dixcove and Sekondi are others, all situated in what was known as the Ante country in the days of the Dutch and the Portuguese, and where the former traded considerably for a large quantity of gold.

Boutri is situated about one and a half miles east of Dixcove and originally possessed a fort built upon a very high hill, strengthened with two batteries of eight small guns. The Dutch name for this place was Bartenstein (barte meaning profit), though Bosman humorously remarks it should have been called Schadenstein (schade meaning loss) on account of the decline of the trade in the place during the latter years of his sojourn on the coast. In the next chapter I will attempt to justify my selection of this place as a habitation for Europeans, and cannot do better than close the present one by a short description of the false gold manufactured by the natives in many of the gold-producing parts of the colony, particularly by those inhabiting the Dixcove or Infuma country.

In the palmy days of the gold export from Guinea, the natives were very adept artists in the sophisticating of gold, neatly counterfeiting and falsifying both the gold dust and the mountain gold, so as to deceive even experienced traders who came to the coast. Nugget gold was made, with the outside of the thickness of a blade of a knife of the purest gold, while the space within was filled with copper or iron filings. Other nuggets were made of a mixture of silver and gold, or copper and gold, highly coloured to improve upon the deception practised. Dust gold was sophisticated by the introduction of copper or coral dust, the whole being highly coloured in order to complete the fraud. To such an extent was this carried on that Bosman describes the natives of the Dixcove country to be so intractable, fraudulent, villainous and obstinate that the English could not trade with them, but were compelled by the natives at last to jointly agree to cheat all the ships that came to trade there, by putting this sophisticated gold upon them. The old Dutch factor was very strong upon them, having no doubt been bitten in his turn, and quotes a case where the masters of two small

English ships received false gold for the whole of their cargoes, of which they disposed, one to the value of £1700. Bosman says they complained to the English governor at the time, but that to complain to him was as good as going to the devil to be confessed, and the trade in false gold so prospered that open business was done in it at the rate of one dollar for two pounds' value sterling of false, until this part of the country became known as the false mint of Guinea.

TABLE OF GOLD WEIGHTS AND THEIR VALUES IN ENGLISH MONEY USED IN THE GOLD COAST COLONY.

Weight.	Value.			Weight.	Value.		
	£	s.	d.		£	s.	d.
Puwa	0	0	0¼	Akau-dwuasru	0	15	0
Pesiwa	0	0	1	Abau-dwuasru	0	18	0
Damba	0	0	2	Suru	1	0	3
Simpuwa	0	0	3	Piresuru	1	2	6
Kokuwa	0	0	4	Asia	1	7	6
Akau Taku	0	0	6	Kandwua	1	11	6
Taku	0	0	9	Anamfi-sur	1	13	9
Ntaku-mmiensa	0	2	3	Abau-dwua	1	16	0
Suwa-fa	0	3	4½	Osua	2	0	6
Dumba-fa	0	4	0	Ndwua-mmien	3	12	0
Agyiratwi-fa	0	4	6	Ndwua-mmiensa	5	8	0
Suwa	0	6	9	Asuanu	4	1	0
Ntaku-akum	0	6	9	Asuasa	6	1	6
Dumba	0	8	0	Benda	7	4	0
Agyiratwi	0	9	0	Pireguan	8	2	0
Nsuwa-nsa	0	10	1½	Ntanu	16	4	0
Bodombu	0	11	3	Ntansa	24	6	0
Nsau	0	13	6				

I will conclude this chapter by endorsing the remarks of Bosman written nearly two centuries ago, but which are nevertheless true of to-day. "I would refer to any intelligent metallist whether a vast deal of ore must not of necessity be lost here, from which a great deal of gold might be separated, for want of skill in the metallic art; and not only so, but I firmly believe that large quantities of pure gold are left behind, for the negroes only ignorantly dig at random, without the least knowledge of the veins of the mine. And I doubt not but if this country belonged to the Europeans, they would soon find it to produce much richer treasures than the negroes obtain from it."

Note.—Since this chapter was written, a copy of the *Atlas Maritime de l'Asie et de l'Afrique* (1764) has come into my possession. In map 106, " La Coste d'Or," the two divisions of the Akim country are marked as follows : Western Akim as " Pays d'Akanni, autrefois très puissant et riche en or," and Eastern Akim as " Pays d'Akim ou Grand Akanni, très étendu et riche en or ". This proves that "Acanny Sika" was the same as Akim Gold. See pp. 104 and 105.

CHAPTER V.

Half Assini to Axim—Apollonia—The Lake Village—Axim and its Neighbourhood—The Ante Country—Cape Three Points—Chama and the Prah—The Kingdoms of Wassaw, Denkira and Sefwi.

THE lower course of the Tano or Tando River forms the western boundary of the Gold Coast colony, though the coast extends in a strip some two or more miles wide farther west to Newtown, a short distance beyond the Assini Hills, where it joins the territory known as French Guinea, the old Ivory Coast. Here the French have two important trading stations, Grand Bassam and Assini, or as the latter was once called, Fort Joinville, from which port large quantities of timber are now exported. The whole of the Apollonian coast, from Newtown to the mouth of the Ancobra River near Axim, is a low stretch of sand, studded with no less than forty fishing towns and villages between the two points I have mentioned, in a distance of some sixty odd miles.

Immediately behind Newtown, extend the Tano and the Eyi Lagoons, into which are discharged the waters of the river bearing the former name, after a course of some miles from the ancient town of Takima, some distance north of Kumasi, whence the Fantis are supposed to have originally come. The most important towns along this western seaboard are Newtown, Half Assini, Beyin,

Attuabu, Esiamo and Kikam, which become at times special ports of entry for steamers when the need arises.

Landing along this coast is at all times most dangerous, the breakers rolling in upon the rapidly shallowing shore from seven to ten deep. You may land safely, but seldom if ever with a dry skin. Travelling along these sixty miles of sand is monotonous in the extreme, and gives one the idea that it is a part of the coast that has been long forgotten. No elevations break the regular coast line, and during the whole history of the colony but one fort has ever been built in this part of the country. This was built by the English at Beyin, and called Fort Apollonia, for which an annual ground-rent was paid to the king, and where a large trade in gold dust was carried on until about the middle of the present century. In past times Newtown was also famous for owning a fine alluvial gold deposit, some distance north of the lagoon that borders the town, and the traveller can still, or could as recently as 1896, purchase nugget gold from the native traders in this town. The English fort is now a mass of ruins and overgrown with bush, though repaired and occupied as a store by Swanzy's early in the eighties. If I remember rightly part of it is still so used, but little or no trade is done in the place.

Beyin, the headquarters of the kings of the country, who once ruled the whole coast from Assini to Axim, was the scene of a fight in 1848, when Captain William Winniett, who succeeded Commander Hill, R.N., as governor, 1846-50, attacked the then King of Apollonia, Quaw Attah, and took him prisoner for having killed the French Commandant at Assini.

The western boundary of the colony proceeds from

Newtown into the interior in a most irregular manner, and at the present day is not at all well defined. In the map published by Stanford in 1895 a note states that, "The boundary between the English and French possessions has been taken from the text of the agreement between Great Britain and France of 12th July, 1893, and the map attached thereto, but has not been demarcated on the ground, and the line must therefore be regarded as only approximately correct".

This approximate line of demarcation runs east from Newtown for some twenty-five miles, and turns north to follow the Tano River for about the same distance. It then leaves the Tano, still going north, trends north-west until the same longitude as Newtown is again reached, and then north again for about 100 miles, to turn off again towards the east. Thus the whole of the upper waters of the Tano are in English territory, and the lagoons into which its waters are emptied remain in French Guinea. The result of this is, that the French port of Assini has become the centre of the mahogany trade that comes down the Tano River, which is in English territory. A canal should be cut from the lagoon behind Half Assini to the shore, and an English timber port established at this latter place. The inland territories to the north of Apollonia contain the kingdoms of Wassaw, Sefwi and Denkira, which will be separately treated in this chapter. This coast received its name of Apollonia from the Portuguese, who named it from the saint bearing that name, the presiding saint of the day upon which it was first discovered, *viz.*, 9th February. There is also an Apollonias of 5th March.

In the old days the Kings of Apollonia were held to

be important personages, and much human sacrifice was practised upon all great occasions. Meredith in his *Account of the Gold Coast* says that when a king died, twenty men were sacrificed every Saturday for the following six months, when the "great custom" took place, while the journal of an African cruiser, published in 1848, mentions the royal residence of the Apollonian kings as being most gorgeously furnished in imitation of European style, and containing vast stores of riches. The death of a king was the occasion for the sacrifice of sixty men to attend their lord to his next realm, each being buried with knife, plate, cup, sword, gun and cloth for use in the unknown land, while the corpse of the king was well oiled and powdered with gold dust.

In the early history of these savage people, many strange devices were resorted to in order to escape falling into the hands of their enemies, many preferring death by their own hands to torture and death from the hands of the victors. One illustration will be sufficient as an example of a practice once common throughout the colony. About the year 1785, the King of Apollonia died, and two competitors appeared and claimed the "stool," one of whom was called Suikee. To test their right each collected his slaves and adherents and fought. Suikee was defeated in the engagement, fled and hid himself in the bush. In the meantime his opponent was duly made king, but the people being dissatisfied with the conqueror, Suikee reappeared against his old enemy and besieged his capital. The king, his rival, reduced this time beyond all hope, threw all his gold, which filled several jars, into the lake, and collecting his wives and the different branches of his family, took them to a remote part of the bush, cut all their throats with the exception of one son, who assisted him to bury the bodies. He then made fetish, and caused his son to swear upon it that he would kill and bury him, and never disclose the place of the burial of the bodies. The son did this and returned to Apollonia, and was for a time lost sight of. Suikee, now seated firmly on the throne, by some means discovered the burial place. He caused all the bodies to be dug up, carried to Beyin and ranged them in a sitting position upon the beach, with stakes supporting their arms and heads. There this horrid spectacle remained until even the bones had perished, and Suikee had thus gratified his revenge upon the dead bodies of his adversaries. Many instances of similar barbarities could be given.

The country immediately to the north of Apollonia was known as Amanahea. Both were once under the sway of the Ashantis, who extorted gold from them in various quantities, though no annual tribute was fixed. The Apollonians are a branch no doubt of the once great Akan family, all speaking the same language, and related to the Akra, Cheripong, Latè, Ahanta and Adangme tribes, and include the people of Axim, who are Apollonians. Their speech differs somewhat from the Fanti, but each is intelligible to the other. Fishing is their chief occupation, though the Apollonian men make good hammock men and carriers. They are fond of drink, somewhat noisy, easily pleased, and clean as regards the washing of their bodies. Fowls, goats, cattle and sheep thrive throughout the country, the sheep being among the best in the colony. The women are much the same as all others in the colony, though a trifle taller, and perhaps a little more graceful in their movements, with here and there a cast of countenance more resembling the Moor than the true negro. The children are noisy and precocious when young, learn easily, and as easily forget what they learn. The Wesleyan Missionary Society have some seven or eight inspected schools along this seaboard. The people take an interest in learning English, the chiefs setting the example to their people by giving an annual donation to the schools. The King of Beyin gives £20. Whenever I have visited this part of the colony I have been most hospitably treated; king, chiefs and elders attending the examination of the scholars, the schools and their approaches being gaily decorated with palms and flags in honour of the visit of the " white big-book man," as they were pleased to call me.

Many of the Apollonians find occupation at the Tarkwa or the French mines, where they are said to have a good reputation, and work well under European discipline. Gold too is to be found in Apollonia, and would no doubt pay for mining were proper facilities afforded. The native mines at Izrah, Inyoko and Ingotra have already been described in the previous chapter, so that a mention of them here will suffice. No proper survey either geological or geographical has ever been made of this country, but when it is, I confidently expect that it will be found worthy of European capital and enterprise. Bitumen has been obtained some distance inland from Newtown, and petroleum has recently been discovered in the neighbourhood of Half Assini, though the latter has been found to be more of a lubricant than an illuminant, and is mixed with sand.

Until quite recently, big game and elephants were to be found within a two days' journey in the grassy lands above Beyin, but it is very seldom now that a tooth is ever brought in, though quite close to the old Ivory or Tooth Coast, belonging to the Côte d'or of the French. I cannot leave the Apollonian country without giving a short description of the lake village that is to be found a short distance inland from Beyin, and which has been visited by very few Europeans. In Meredith's *Account of the Gold Coast* (1812) it is thus described : " About three miles from the fort inland, there is a very fine lake of fresh water that forms the boundary of the plain, and may be computed at six miles in circumference. It is deep, for no bottom was found about the centre with a line of thirty fathoms. There is a variety of fish here : the crocodile or alligator inhabits it, and a large species of snake has been discovered on its banks. A small village is erected on this lake ; the houses are formed on wooden piles ; they are separated from each other so that every house is insulated. The inhabitants form a communication by means of canoes, which are generally paddled by women.

" The original inhabitants of this village are said to have been composed of disaffected and ill-disposed persons, who emigrated from their native country Chama, a small state some distance eastward of Apollonia and where the Dutch had a fort. It is reported that the King of Apollonia at first refused them any indulgence, and desired them to depart from his kingdom ; they, however, entreated him with much importunity, and informed him that they were willing to undergo the meanest office if he would permit them to settle in any part of his country. At length the king allotted to them a small spot of ground adjoining to the lake, but told them they must not build upon it but endeavour to erect houses in the lake, so as to be secluded from his subjects. Necessity thus obliged them to exert all the ingenuity and art they were masters of; and after much labour they succeeded in forming comfortable and secure houses of wood, chiefly of the bamboo cane. The inhabitants of this village are careful in retaining their primitive language, and have no further intercourse with the Apollonians than a trifling trade will admit of, which only consists of the fish caught in the lake, and for which they get corn and rice in exchange. Whatever may have been their character and disposition, they appear to live peaceably and happily. Their situation is favourable to tranquillity, as no part of a family can move abroad without some difficulty, which affords no opportunity of using malpractices, and fearful of incurring the displeasure of the king, they must be strict in their behaviour and conduct."

This village is of great antiquity, and is situated a short distance to the east of the town Nuba or Niba, which can be approached either from Beyin or by a long waterway running parallel to the coast from the fishing village of Eku Enunu Ebomesu at the mouth of the river, some sixteen miles to the east of Beyin. The locality of this peculiar village is not shown on any ordnance map before 1887, and an interesting account of a journey there, made by the then District Commissioner of Axim, Mr. C. A. O'Brien, appeared in *Black and White* in January, 1897, of which the following is an extract:—

"The lake village is situated in Apollonia, the most western part of the Gold Coast Colony, some miles from Beyin town and five or six from the coast; yet its existence is virtually unknown to Europeans, close as it is to the coast line. Doubtless this is owing to the fact that the white population in that portion of the colony resides at Axim, some thirty-five miles away. Till after 1887 no trace of such a village could be found in the maps prepared by the Intelligence Department of the War Office. Burton and Cameron were both at Axim for a time, and explored the country and its vicinity. Still they make no mention of this extraordinary village, which they certainly would have done had they seen it." The writer here is so far correct in stating that Burton and Cameron never saw it, but that no mention is made of it by them is a mistake, and I am sure he will forgive me for pointing it out. In the map prefacing volume i., *To the Gold Coast for Gold*, by Burton and Cameron, 1883, the lake village is distinctly marked, as also the waterway leading to it, but not the town of Nuba, while on pages 148-151, volume ii. of the same work, is to be found a full description of the lake village and its surroundings, which I shall have pleasure in quoting later on.

Mr. O'Brien continues: "I had occasion to travel to Nuba, lake village and some other places by a route other than the ordinary one—that is, not by Beyin, on the coast line. It became necessary to travel through dense bush or forest to several villages unknown to white men save by name, and thence by a series of lagoons; some of them, though dignified by this title by the natives, were naught but evil-smelling drains, sometimes not three feet wide, and often with no more than six inches of water in them. Completely covered in by trees, they were even in the daytime dark tunnels, while at night the blackness became awful in its intensity. Having been through several of them by day, I determined to push on to Nuba by night. So my party embarked in canoes and entered the most evil-smelling waterway imaginable. The lanterns at the head of the canoes merely rendered the darkness more palpable, and shortly after the start progress became well-nigh impossible, owing to the water being insufficient to float the craft. In this emergency the four canoe-men in each boat were obliged to get out and drag the frail craft over the slimy mud. Whenever the water was sufficient, they resumed paddling, only to jump out again to pull the canoe over some fallen log that barred the way. This, with the accompanying danger of snakes dropping from the trees, and of being upset into the slime, made this night travelling anything but pleasant. At length the Nuba was reached about midnight, and a halt was called till next morning. Daylight, however, seemed to change the outlook considerably. Presently bright daylight was admitted, with shade sufficient to protect us from the sun. Time and inclination to look about were now afforded, and I noticed on each side tiny waterways just large enough to admit the smallest description of canoe, which occasionally glided as though from the land into the now ten-foot wide lagoon that was by-and-by covered with water lilies. Indeed, it assumed a close resemblance to the backwater of some English stream.

"Paddling gaily along for some time, we suddenly burst into an exquisite lake some two miles square with this extraordinary village built in the water opposite to us. It is hard to describe the splendour of the morning when we emerged from the lagoon-tunnel into this lovely expanse of water that mirrored the palm-trees and other tropical foliage on its banks. It affected even the canoe-men, who challenged one another to race. The five canoes were ranged in line, and then started for the lake village. While this two-mile struggle was in progress, I had time to notice the peculiar village we were approaching. It is built on piles and is surrounded by water, while each house, placed on a kind of platform, supported by these stakes, seemed to be distinct from its neighbour, and to have its own rough ladder leading to the water. The only means of communication is by boat, there being no connection with the land at the back. If a native desires to visit another three or four houses off, he has to go down his ladder, enter his canoe and paddle to the house. The population numbers about 300, and I should say there are sixty or seventy houses in all. I tried to discover the reason for building the village in this manner, but could get no satisfactory explanation. One said that the method adopted was convenient for fishing; and another, that the place was once used as a place of confinement for persons troublesome to former kings of Beyin. The present inhabitants, at least, are not prisoners in any sense, as their canoes have free access everywhere. Like other natives on the coast, they live by fishing and trading." [1]

The account given by Burton and Cameron of this extraordinary village is not from their own pen, but from an excursion made to the place by Mr. Edward L. McCarthy, in August, 1881. I will give the account in his own words, and the reader can judge for himself how the two accounts agree. Mr. McCarthy says: "Accompanied by Prince John Coffee, heir to

[1] By the kind permission of the publishers of *Black and White*.

King Blay, three other chiefs, their servants, and my own party of Krɔɔ men, we left the town of Béin, Apollonia, to go up to the village in the bush called Esuá-ti. Half a mile from the town we found canoes awaiting us, and in these we were poled along for over half an hour over what in the dry season is a native path, but now a narrow channel of water, winding about in a dense jungle of reeds. . . . Emerging from these reeds, one broad sheet of water presented itself to the eye, encircled by a low shore fringed with canes, bush and palm trees. The lagoon receives several small streams and empties itself into the sea by the Ebomesu River, its mouth being about half-way between Béin and the Ancobra. The length of the lagoon appears to be about three to four miles, and about one to one and a half in breadth. Twenty minutes' paddling brought us round the point of a small headland, where we came in sight of a pretty lake village, built upon piles, at some little distance from the shore, the whole forming a most picturesque and animated scene.

"From house to house canoes laden with people, plantains, etc., were passing to and fro; groups of villagers, some standing, others sitting, upon the raised bamboo platforms outside their houses, were busy bartering fish for plantains, while the children played around, apparently unconscious of any danger from falling into the water. The settlement consisted of over forty houses, mostly of bamboo, a few of swish, forming one long irregular line, and three or four standing away from the rest, round a corner of land, after the Fanti custom. These houses were built on a bamboo platform supported by piles, and raised above the water some three and a half feet. One half of the platform is covered by the house; the other half, left free, is used to fish from, for the children to play about on, and for receptions when palavers are held. The distance from the shore varies with the overflow of the lake, at the time of my visit about thirty or forty yards, though for miles beyond this the ground was saturated with water, whose depth varied from three and a half to nine feet. I closely questioned the natives as to why they had built their village upon the lake, and they invariably gave as their reason that they chiefly fished at night; and, as the water often overflowed, they would have to build their houses too far away to come and go during the night; whereas, 'now,' they said, 'we are close to where we catch our fish, and we often catch them even from our houses'. Underneath each house were tied from one to five and sometimes more canoes. These were much lighter, more rounded off in the keel, stem and stern than the beach canoes."[1]

"Three white men, they told me, had visited their village, Captain Dudley in 1876, judging from the age of a child that was born at the time of his visit; Captain Grant and Mr. Gillett in 1878, I afterwards learnt were the other two."

Thus, except for the visit of Mr. McCarthy, who wrote the above account, I believe Mr. O'Brien is the first white man to visit this interesting spot since that time.

The port of Axim lies as near as possible in latitude 5° N. and 2° 14′ 45″ W. longitude. Its appearance from the sea is most picturesque, and the first impressions of the place are far from dispiriting, and upon the whole, the health of the Europeans stationed there is decidedly good. Two bays are visible from the sea, a larger and a

[1] *To the Gold Coast for Gold.* Burton and Cameron (1883).

smaller. The former stretches from Akromasi Point to Pépré Point, and includes the latter, which contains the bay of Axim. Vegetation flourishes down to the water's edge, backed with a dense forest of enormous trees, which stretches away inland as far as the eye can reach. Landing here is comparatively easy, and it is one of the few places along the coast where it can be accomplished in a ship's boat. Opposite the landing-place is the island called Bobowusua, or more commonly called "pigeon island," the native haunt of many kinds of birds, from the turkey-buzzard to the pigeon. In olden times Axim was a country, and embraced that region marked in some maps as Hollandia, with the town of Axim as its port. It suffered much at the hands of the Apollonians, but on account of its position has always recovered from its greatest disasters, and became and still remains the chief gold and timber port of the western part of the colony.

Old authorities state that Axim was once, according to the notion of power in this part of the world, a powerful monarchy, but that the arrival of the Brandenburgers in the seventeenth century, divided the inhabitants into two factions, one part putting themselves under the protection of their new masters, and the other part remaining faithful to their old. The country of Axim extended in those days for some twenty or more miles from the Rio Cobre or Ancobra River to the town of Bushua, then called Boesua, three miles to the west of the Dutch fort at Boutri.

The inhabitants at this time were very rich, driving a great trade with the Europeans for gold, and being otherwise engaged in trade, fishing or agriculture. This last included the cultivation of rice, which then grew in this part of the colony in such abundance that it was carried to all other parts of the coast and exchanged for millet, yams, potatoes and palm oil (then used for food), which were not to be obtained in any quantities in the Axim district.

The Ancobra, or Snake River, called so on account of its windings, is the Rio Cobre of Bosman, and is now navigated in steam launches for some eighty or ninety miles. "It was," says the same author, "a waterway too

FORT ST. ANTHONY, AXIM.

pleasant to be lightly passed over, its mouth being some distance to the west of Fort St. Anthony." It possesses a wide, shallow estuary, sand-locked like all other rivers in this part of Africa, over the bar of which the great Atlantic rollers thunder with unceasing roar, that makes it impassable to ordinary vessels; while a short distance inland, it grows deeper and narrower for some miles of its course, and becomes a useful stream. In the early part of the eighteenth century, a small three days' voyage upon it was considered a great undertaking, and afforded a pleasant trip. In those days the banks down to the water's edge were adorned with lofty trees, affording the most agreeable shade to the voyager, while the trees were enlivened with troops of monkeys and varieties of birds of the most variegated plumage. The lower reaches of the river are very tortuous, and many towns and villages are scattered upon its banks. For some years the Dutch held a fort at the village of Equira, some miles from the mouth of the river. This district was then the centre of a large gold-mining industry, and the people did a very considerable trade in the precious metal derived from the mines then in existence in the neighbourhood, as well as from the great amount of gold brought in from the surrounding country. Burton and Cameron must have passed near to the source of this wealth when on their way to the Ingotra mine described in the last chapter, though I am of opinion that this mine is one of the old native workings of that date, included in this district of Equira. In my copy of Bosman's *Guinea* (1705) no mention is made of the name of the fort at this place. Burton calls it " Fort Equira," while Bosman speaks of it as " the country of Equira ". Some authorities, among whom are Bowdich and Meredith, place Elisa Carthago at this spot, while others, including Bosman, Lieutenant Jeekel (Royal Dutch Navy) and Burton and Cameron, place Elisa Carthago upon Akromasi Point, near the mouth of the Ancobra River.

The account of the destruction of the fort is mentioned by most authors, but the difficulty remains as to whether it was Fort Equira or Fort Elisa Carthago. The latter place was built by the Portuguese, sometime before 1700, and captured by the French, who held it for a considerable time, did a great trade in gold, and were finally driven out by the Dutch. These last possessors did not enjoy it for long. The following account of its destruction is by Bosman: " I remember when I had the government of Axim, a very rich one (mine) was discovered, but we lost our footing there in a very tragical manner, for the commander-in-chief of the negroes being closely besieged by our men (so fame reports) shot gold instead of bullets, showing by signs that he was ready to treat and afterwards to trade, but in the midst of their negotiations he blew up himself and all his enemies at once, as unfortunately as bravely putting an end to our siege and to his own life, and, like Samson, revenging his death upon his enemies. To encompass his design he had encouraged a slave, by promise of new cloths, to stand ready with a match, with which he was to touch the powder when he saw him stamp with his foot, which the silly wretch but too punctually performed, undiscovered by any one but one of our company's slaves, who, observing it, withdrew as silently as timely, being only left alive to tell us the news ; and since we could get no better account, we were obliged to believe this, it being too certain that our fort, to the cost of our director and some of our enemies, was blown up."

The Axim of the present day and the immediate country surrounding presents a very different appearance to what it did in these early times. The old Dutch fort has seen several masters and undergone many changes. Originally built by the Portuguese about 1515, in the days of Don Manuel, and named Santo Antonio, it fell into the hands of the Dutch in 1642 and became St. Anthony. It was captured by the English in 1782 under Captain Shirley, restored to its Dutch owners three years later, to again come into English hands in 1872, by the convention at the Hague. It is now the headquarters for the district, and in the upper rooms of the old fort resides the District Commissioner, and until quite recently, an assistant colonial surgeon; while the lower rooms furnish the necessary accommodation for Commissioners' Court, Post and Telegraph Offices and Customs and Police. The basement is occupied by numerous darksome, evil-looking cells for the detention of prisoners. A long, straggling path leads from the beach road through the principal street of the town up to the fort, which commands Axim Bay. A short distance to the east of the present fort once stood the chief settlement of the Brandenburgers, Fort Brandenburg or Fredericksborg, called after the Elector of that name, which fell into the hands of the Dutch soon after the capture of Santo Antonio. The Brandenburgers finally left the coast in 1720. For many years prior to this they maintained several important stations in the neighbourhood of Axim, the chief of which was Fredericksborg, and which were the source of no little trouble to the Dutch. Speaking of this chief station Bosman says: " Their principal fortress is not above three (Dutch) miles east of ours of St. Anthony, situated on a hill Mamfro, and is handsome and reasonably large, strengthened with four large batteries furnished with forty-six pieces of ordnance, but too light and small. The gate of this fort is the most beautiful on all the coast, but proportionally much too large for the structure, so that the garrison seems to have an equal right with the burghers of Minde to the advice, that they should keep their gate shut for fear the fort should run away!"

This was called Fredericksborg and was near to the town of Princes at the mouth of the Princes or St. John's River. Only the great double doorway now remains.

Some ten miles farther to the east was another Brandenburger fort called Dorothea, which appears to have been given by the Dutch to the Brandenburgers, who considerably enlarged and improved it. It was flat-roofed, contained two small batteries, and was furnished with a number of rooms and conveniences slightly built and somewhat crowded. A third place of importance belonging to these interlopers, as they were styled, was a small fort-house between the Mamfro Hill and Fort Dorothea, built on the middle tongue of Cape Three Points, at the village of Takrama, in 1674.

At the end of the seventeenth century these places were the centre of a thriving gold trade; at the present time they have disappeared and their sites are almost forgotten. The Brandenburgers were not successful in their dealings with the natives, who treated many of the directors and officers of the company with the utmost contempt, finally breaking their power and becoming masters over them, until they were compelled to leave the coast through the stagnation of their trade.

Axim is now an important trading station, and has yet a great fortune in store as the entrance port to the valuable Tarkwa mining districts, and to the timber forests to be found on either bank of the Ancobra River. The amount of gold still shipped annually from this port amounts to £6000, whilst thousands of fine mahogany trees are felled every year, and towed down the Ancobra, to be squared upon the beach and exported to Europe. Rubber and skins are also brought from the interior to this port in large quantities. The surrounding country is hilly and well wooded. Water is plentiful and the whole district is very rich in gold. Transport is the one thing wanted to transform this comparatively healthy

SQUARING MAHOGANY ON THE BEACH, AXIM.

part of the Gold Coast into a busy centre of mining industry and trade, which is at present crippled by a transport costing some £25 per ton from Axim to Tarkwa.

Axim is variously written Axem, Atzyn and Achen, while the natives called it Essim. It must not be confounded with Akim in the eastern part of the colony to the north of Accra.

The country of Ante or Hante, the present Ahanta upon modern maps, was continuous with the Axim territory, and extended from Bushua or Acoda in the west to Sekondi, a distance of some twenty-five miles. For many years the Ante country included Axim, which was known as Upper Ante. It was a populous and powerful state, inhabited by a war-like people, who gave much trouble to the Dutch, and were constantly at war with their neighbours, more particularly with those to the north of their own territory, in the Adom country, and who finally broke their power. At Dixcove, or Dick's Cove, the Dikjeschoft of the Dutch, in the Infuma country, a little to the west of the village of Bushua, the English established themselves and built a fort in 1691, after several struggles with the Brandenburgers, who disputed this territory with them. This took six years to complete, and became the headquarters of the trade in sophisticated gold mentioned in the previous chapter. Burton says it was built in 1681 and finished in 1688. At the present day it has a territory quite distinct from the Ahanta country, extending along the shore to Achowa Point, and for some twenty miles inland.

Three miles to the east of this settlement were Boutri Village and Fort. The small river running into the sea at Boutri rises in the Adom country, which is said to abound in gold. Amanfee also abounds in very fine gold, which is generally found in quartz, and is ground upon stones arranged under large sheds for the purpose. The former remains, but the latter has been long in ruins, while sixteen miles farther to the east was Sekondi, where the Dutch had a small station called Orange Fort, below which the Ante country ended. I trust I may be excused for treating of this part of the coast in so minute a manner, but my excuse must be, that I believe it will become in the near future a part that will be found more suitable for European residence than many other spots on the coast, and will ultimately be, on account of this and its natural facilities and richness, the great centre of future trade, and contain the chief entrance port for the Gold Coast colony.

The coast line contains the one natural harbour, where a landing stage could be easily constructed, and from which the railways of the colony could run, and deep water is to be found up to the very shore. The Ahanta country is extremely well wooded, rich, fertile and well watered, and could be made to produce an almost unlimited supply of grain, fruits and vegetables of all descriptions. The hill lands, which are abundant, contain, I believe, many quartz formations, and I have myself brought home specimens of gold-bearing rock which yielded on assay, no less than 1 oz. 12 dwts. 5 grs. of gold to the ton of ore, in addition to 5 dwts. of silver. These specimens were obtained within an easy distance of the sea-shore. In past times it was a land that yielded its cultivators as plentiful a crop as could be wished, and was well furnished with all kinds of tame and wild animals, particularly at the end of the seventeenth century. The English (1615) and the Dutch (1680) possessed forts at Sekondi, where they were rivals for many years, much to the detriment of both companies. During Bosman's time the English fort was destroyed by the people of Ante, thus leaving the Dutch masters of the field, where they traded very considerably for a large quantity of gold. The English made several attempts to rebuild their fort, but met, upon each occasion, with much opposition from the natives, the town of Sekondi itself falling at last before the ravages of the people of Adom. Sekondi is also described as being one of the healthiest places on the coast for the residence of Europeans. The country round is diversified and very fertile.

Some four miles west of Sekondi are Takoradi Bay and Fort, the latter now in ruins and overgrown with bush. The fort was built sometime before the middle of the seventeenth century, and has had many European masters, the English, Dutch, Brandenburgers, Swedes and the Danes each having had possession in turn. De Ruyter took it from the English in 1665, during the Dutch wars in the reign of Charles the Second, and after many years of prosperity the town gradually declined, to be at last destroyed by the people of Adom. Takoradi was the scene of the murder of the Dutch military commandant of Boutri and his assistant in 1837, and an encounter between the Dutch troops and Bousu, the chief of the Ahantas.

The whole country appears to have been at the height of its prosperity at the end of the seventeenth century, when it contained numerous villages, well populated, a plentiful harvest, and abundance of cattle, so much so, that the Dutch soldiers, who could hardly live on their pay elsewhere, could here live well upon half. Bosman declares Boutri to be healthier than other places along the coast, for during his stay there he observed, that fewer people died there in proportion to the number of people and time than anywhere else, and that if the whole coast were like it, it would soon lose its deadly name.

About midway between the village of Boutri and

Takoradi Fort is the small town of Adjuah. This place, though not very large or populous, is a port of entry, and is provided with customs, post and telegraph offices. It is reported that large beds of slate are to be found in this neighbourhood, which may in time prove of value. The mosquitoes at this town at certain times of the year render life to the European almost unbearable.

The Ante country was finally subdued about 1692 by the Adom people, who were governed by five or six principal men without a king, and who were a terror to all the tribes around. Their country extended north of Ante from the Ancobra to the Prah, a distance of more than fifty miles, and for about the same distance inland. Their leader in war was a native called Anquah, whose name was a terror to all the tribes around, on account of the atrocious manner in which he treated his prisoners.

Cape Three Points stands about midway between Axim and Dixcove, upon the middle point of which stands the present lighthouse. This was the old Cape Tres Puntos of early days, forming an excellent landmark for mariners, the capes being respectively fifty, forty-five and forty miles west of Cape Coast. About four miles to the east of the cape are the remains of another Dutch ruin, now called Acquidah, the Acoda of the seventeenth century, one of the stations of the Brandenburgers, built about 1680 and named Dorothea, which I have previously described. Good oysters abound here.

The next town of interest along the coast is Chama, situated at the mouth of the Prah River, between which point and the town of Sekondi extends a strip of country known by the same name. Chama is also written Chumah and Essama, pronounced by the people Nshama.

It is continuous with the Ahanta country, and resembles it in point of fertility. The town itself is fairly large and well populated, but is very hot, and on the whole not so healthy as the country farther west. The present fort, overlooking the town, was built by the Portuguese in 1680, and captured from them by the Dutch. It is very small, containing four batteries, and is known as

INTERIOR OF WESLEYAN SCHOOL, CHAMA.

Saint Sebastian. It furnishes miserable offices for the District Commissioners who reside at Elmina, and quarters for an assistant Colonial Surgeon in addition to the usual rooms for customs, post and telegraph requirements. In the Dutch wars with England it was almost completely destroyed, but was restored by the Dutch, in whose hands it remained until the whole coast was finally handed over to the English. The country round Chama produces the finest oranges of any part of the colony. The skin of this fruit, when perfectly ripe, is of a deep green colour, and contains much essential oil. A short distance to the east of the town the river Prah empties its waters, twenty-five miles west of Cape Coast Castle. By the Ashantis and the Fantis it is called the Busum Prah, which means the sacred river, and in time past human sacrifices were made to it at its source. This is to be found in a rugged mountain near the town of Obo, a little to the south of the Kwahu country, nearly 200 miles from the coast. It runs in a south-west direction to Prahsu, where it soon bends south and falls into the sea at Chama. The total length of this river, with its windings, cannot be less than 400 miles. At the mouth is a dangerous bar, with water from two to five feet deep, which makes the river useless for navigation, though small crafts can proceed up it for a three days' journey, until stopped by the rapids and waterfalls. From the town of Prahsu, for some sixty miles to the north-east, this river formed, until the last Ashanti war, the boundary between the Ashanti country and the Gold Coast. At this town it flows between steep banks varying from forty to sixty feet in height, and runs with a current at the rate of three or four miles per hour. The Dah and the Ofin are its chief tributaries on its right bank, the former rising near the old town of Kwaben north-east of Kumasi, and emptying its waters into the Ofin, which carries the two waters into the Prah, at a distance of some two days' journey west of Prahsu, while on the left bank it receives the waters of the Birrim, which joins it at a point about one day's journey north-east of the same town. The whole of the upper courses of the Prah and the Birrim flow through a rich auriferous country, Eastern and Western Akim, which I hope will be opened up in the near future to European development.

The kingdoms of Wassaw, Sefwi and Denkira lie directly to the north of the Apollonian, Ahanta and Chama countries on the coast. The largest of the three is Wassaw, which was governed in the past by four chiefs, whose relation and power were exercised independently of each other. Sefwi and Denkira form the northern boundaries of this country, which is generally given to extend from 100 to 120 miles east to west and some sixty miles from north to south, the eastern portion of the country coming down to the sea at Sekondi. The Ancobra flows through the centre of the country, and the Tano upon its western border, almost dividing it from Assini in French Guinea. The Tarkwa and most of the present well-known mines are situated in Wassaw, and most of the timber exported from Axim is obtained from the same territory. The chief towns are Akropong, Awudwa and Tarkwa. It is very thinly populated in proportion to its size, and was once a strong tributary power to the Ashantis, paying an indefinite yearly tax, based upon the number of towns and villages found in the country.

Sefwi lies due north of Wassaw, having Aowin for its western boundary and Ashanti on its north. Very little is known about the country and its inhabitants even at the present day, this part of the colony having been visited by very few Europeans, and consequently but little explored. Like Wassaw, the country is well wooded and is watered by the upper courses of the same rivers. In some maps this country is included in the Ashanti territory, and the people were no doubt tributary at one time to the dominant power of this race. The chief town in the Sefwi country is Wiawusu, near the northern border of Wassaw. Sefwi is also written Sawee and Sahue.

Denkira is the third of these inland states, lying northeast between Wassaw and Ashanti, and is the smallest of the three territories. Its capital bears the same name and is situated a little to the west of the Ofin River, which passes through the centre of the country. Osai Tootoo, the first King of Kumasi of whom mention is made, conquered Denkira, notwithstanding that the latter country received help from the Europeans at Elmina, in the form of cannon, about 1720. These cannon were captured by the Ashantis and carried as trophies to their capital. Before this time the Dutch governor of the coast paid a monthly sum to the King of Denkira for Elmina Castle, which, by his conquest by Osai Tootoo, became the spoil of the victor, whose ancestors enjoyed it for many years afterwards. These monthly payments were called "Notes," and many stations along the coast were held by the Europeans in the same way. The brother Apokoo, and successor to Osai Tootoo, completed the conquest of Akim, and secured from the people of that district the paynotes that the Akims held for the English, Dutch and Danish forts at Accra and for those farther to leeward. These paynotes had been originally held by the chiefs of Accra, who lost them to the Akims when seeking help from them against their enemies, the Aquamboes, a Volta River people.

Judging from their language the Wassaws, Sefwis and Denkiras all speak dialects of the same tongue, which would induce to the belief that they have sprung from the same source, being only different branches of the same family, and related to the Fanti, Akim and Ashanti people.

Before leaving this part of the coast, I must mention one other station belonging to the Dutch, some five miles west of Chama. It was then called Aboary, the Aboaddi of our modern maps, and forms a small point of rocks jutting for some distance out to sea. For several years during the early part of the eighteenth century, a Dutch lodge was maintained at this place, but as it appeared to bring more profit into the pockets of the officers residing there than into the coffers of the old Dutch Company, it was closed as being unnecessary, the first principle in Dutch trading being, "That you must trade with advantage to yourself or not trade at all".

CHAPTER VI.

Chama to Elmina—Commendah, British and Dutch—Cape Coast Castle—Landing—The Town in General—The Lighthouse—The Resting-Place of " L. E. L."—A Memoir—The Road to Kumasi—Mouri and Fort Nassau—Anamaboe and Saltpond—The Tufel and Assin Countries.

PROCEEDING eastward from the mouth of the Prah, the coast preserves much the same character until Elmina is reached, and no very important places are passed on the way. Some ten or a dozen fishing villages dot the coast, and ruins of a past commercial rivalry are to be found at Commendah, which is situated about half-way between Chama and Elmina. This strip of shore was known in early days as Kommany, but now more generally called the Commendah and Elmina countries, extending eastward from the mouth of the Prah for some twenty miles, and bordered upon the inland side by the Adom and Jabi territories. Bosman says: "The country of Kommany extends itself five (Dutch) miles long by the seaside, reckoning from the river of Chama (the Prah) to Mina; and it is about as broad as it is long. In the middle of it, on the strand, at Little Kommany, or Ekki-Tokki as the natives call it, we have an indifferent large fort, built by Mr. Lwertz in the year 1688, called Vredenburg, and a musket shot or two from thence the English have a very large fort of which more hereafter."

The old Dutch fort thus mentioned was a square building, strengthened with large and roomy batteries, on which was accommodation for no less than thirty-two guns, each gun having its separate port in the breast-work, and garrison-room for sixty men. It was seldom, however, that the full complement of guns and men was found necessary to defend the place against the attacks of the natives. In 1695 the place was besieged by the surrounding tribes, and sustained a vigorous attack, of which the following is the Dutch account:—

"Our enemies attacked us by night, when I had but a very sorry garrison, not full twenty men, half of whom were not capable of service, and yet I forced them to retire with loss, after a fight of five hours. 'Twas wonderful that we lost but two men in this action, for we had no doors to most of our gun-holes, and the natives poured small shot on us as thick as hail; insomuch, that those few doors which were left to some gun-holes were become like a target, which had been shot at for a mark, and the very staff which our flag was fastened on, though it took up so little room, did not escape shot-free. You may imagine what case we were in when one of them began to hack our very doors with an axe, but this undertaker being killed, the rest sheered off. The general to whom I had represented my weak condition, advised two ships to anchor before our fort, in order to supply me with men and ammunition. Peter Hinken, the captain of one of these vessels (the day before I was attacked), sent his boat full of men with orders to come to me, but they were no sooner on the land than the natives fell upon them so furiously, even under our cannon, that they killed several of them, which though I saw, I could not

A STREET SCENE IN ELMINA.

prevent, for attempting to fire upon the enemy with the cannon, I found them all nailed, of which piece of villainy, my own gunner was to all appearances the actor. For this reason I was forced to be an idle spectator of the miserable slaughter of our men, not being able to lend them the least assistance, and if the natives had at that instant stormed us, we were in no posture of resistance. But they going to eat, gave me time to prepare for the entertainment I afterwards gave them. I cannot help relating a comical incident which happened. Going to visit the posts of our forts, to see whether everybody was at his duty, one of the soldiers quitting his post told me that the natives, well knowing that he had but one hat in the world, had maliciously shot away the crown, which he would revenge if I would give him a few grenadoes. I had no sooner ordered him two than he called out to the natives from the breastwork in their own language, telling them he would present them with something to eat, and kindling his grenadoes, immediately threw them down amongst them; they, observing them to burn, crowded about them, and were at first very agreeably diverted, but when they burst, they so galled them that they had no great stomach for such another meal."

The quarrel of the natives with the Dutch came about over the supply of the precious metal, and this disagreement allowed the English to firmly settle themselves at Commendah as rivals to the old Dutch traders. The Dutch were settled on the western bank of the little river Susu, and the English, under the "Royal African Company of England," built their fort upon the eastern bank of the river, each having their own native town under the walls of their forts. The rivalry between the two companies existed for many years, and at the present day Commendah is divided into two factions, English and Dutch, though the forts and trading factories have long since disappeared from the scene.

The Dutch fort was destroyed during the American War, and time and climate have destroyed that of the English. When approached from the west Commendah is backed by a high hill, an insulated elevation known as the Gold Hill, the source of the native dispute with the Dutch, which is related as follows: Large quantities of gold were exported from this part of the coast, and the Dutch were naturally anxious to become possessed of the source of these supplies, supposed to be the Gold Hill. Arrangements had been made with the natives, and in 1694 the Dutch caused four miners to be sent from Europe to prospect the country for gold. They were ordered to assay the hill in question, which was situated in the Kommany country, about two miles from the Dutch fort Vredenburg, which seemed to be well placed for the purpose, and promised to reward them well for their pains. As was often the case with the natives of the coast, this hill was at this time a fetish, and dedicated to one of their many gods, and thus considered sacred. The Dutch miners went to work, but in a few days they were assaulted, ill-treated and robbed by the natives, and even taken prisoners. The Dutch complained to the king, but in the usual shifty fashion he placed the blame on somebody else, and the war began between the Dutch and the natives which led to the firm establishment of the English, as before mentioned, on the ruins of the old fort they had previously possessed. Commendah has been variously written Commenda and

Kommany, and is called by the natives Ekki-Tokki or Akatay Ki, and sometimes Akatay Kin. The English were said to be well fortified at this place, so well so that Bosman said it would be impossible to move them except in time of war, and even then they would have a nice bone to pick. The fort was large and possessed four batteries, in addition to a turret that could also be used for guns, and seriously incommode the Dutch, as well as having more and larger cannon than their rivals. Commendah is one of the towns mentioned by Barbot to which the Rouen and Dieppe traders sent their fleet of three vessels as early as 1383, one of which, called *La Vierge*, touched at Komenda or Komani one hundred years before the arrival of the Portuguese.

Some ten or twelve miles to the east of Commendah stands the present important town of Elmina, with its two forts of St. Jago and St. George d'Elmina, famous as being the first European establishment on the Gold Coast. The castle of St. George is supposed to have been built by the French in 1383, rebuilt by the Portuguese in 1481, captured by the Dutch about 1638, and handed to the English by the last owners in 1867, and is one of the largest and finest castles remaining upon the Gold Coast at the present day, standing as an example of the patience, skill and industry bestowed by the Portuguese and Dutch upon their colonial possessions. The native name for the town is Oddena, Addina or Edina, and why the Portuguese named it Ora del Mina or mouth of the mines, it is difficult to say, for no mines are now found in the immediate neighbourhood, though it was famed for centuries as the port from which the greatest output of gold came, probably drawn from all parts of the coast, and which reached its zenith early in the eighteenth century, with an annual export of nearly £3,000,000 of the precious metal.

The castle is one of strength and beauty, built square with very high walls, and four batteries within and another on the outworks of the castle, all well furnished with brass and iron guns (of course now obsolete), and providing garrison accommodation for 200 men, in addition to the officers' quarters. On the land side it was supplied with two canals or moats, cut in the rock on which the castle stands, in order to provide enough fresh water for the garrison and the ships frequenting the port. Above it, a short distance inland, stands Fort St. Jago or St. James, called by the Dutch Conradsburg, on a hill bearing the same name, which completely commands the other fort of St. George, and is a large rectangular fort with one square tower, the whole being now used as a jail. St. Jago was built by the Dutch in 1640, and it was from this hill, before the fort was built, that they directed their guns and compelled the surrender of the Portuguese in Fort St. George in 1638, the one completely commanding the other. Directly under the fort of St. George is situated the native town, long and irregularly built, the houses being mostly of stone, which is very plentiful in the neighbourhood, and contrasting very much with the ordinary mud houses of the coast towns. A short distance east of Elmina the Sweet River runs into the sea, possibly called so because it brings down so much fresh water in the rainy season that its waters are quite fresh, while in the dry season the opposite is the case. This river rises in the Denkira country, and in early times formed the boundary between

CAPE COAST CASTLE.

the kingdoms of Kommany and Fetu, its near neighbour. Its course is very swift.

The present castle of Elmina is now the residence of the District Commissioner, an Assistant Colonial Surgeon, the Officer Commanding, and some few Hausà troops, besides providing the necessary accommodation for the various departmental officers. Prempeh was detained here after his capture in 1896. The country round Elmina is diversified, and gives evidence of having been worked for gold. The town itself is unhealthy; the natives suffer from small-pox and Europeans from the dreaded malaria so prevalent along the coast.

A three hours' journey, the distance being about eight miles, along rather a good road, brings us to Cape Coast Castle, the Ooegwa of Bosman and Cabocors or Cabo Corso of the Portuguese. The castle, next to that of Elmina, is the largest and best on the coast.

On approaching Cape Coast from the west three elevations are seen, two forts and the castle. The most westerly is Fort Victoria, once called Fort Royall, and also Phipps Tower, and the early Fredericksborg of the Danes, built in 1659, bought by the English in 1685, and consisting of a huge round martello tower, unoccupied and commanding both the town and the castle. The second is Fort William, once known as Smith's Tower, built by President Maclean about 1830, another martello, circular below and square above, mounted with twelve guns and also commanding the castle. It is now the lighthouse for the port, and stands nearly 200 feet above the sea level.

Cape Coast Castle itself stands upon a narrow spit of rocks with the native town clustering behind it. Fort Cabo Corso is supposed to have been built by the Portuguese in 1624, though the Rev. Mr. Reindorf states that it was built by the Swedes in 1652, by whom it was named Carolusborg or Charles's Fort, and that in 1658 it fell into the hands of the Danes, through the instrumentality of one of their servants. In 1659 the Danes surrendered it to the Dutch, from whom the natives of Fetu captured it in 1660. From these the Swedes are supposed to have taken it, in whose hands it remained for three years, when it again fell into the possession of the Fetus, who voluntarily surrendered it to the Dutch in 1663. In the next year, 1664, Admiral Holmes captured it for the English, in whose hands it has since remained, though several times besieged; by De Ruyter in 1665, and by a French squadron in 1757. The author of *British Battles* places its capture by Admiral Holmes in 1661, and this is borne out by another authority, the Rev. J. B. Anaman, who states that the English enlarged it in 1662. However this may be, Cabo Corso was the finest fort in the hands of the English during the eighteenth century, containing well-built quarters for its officers. It was strengthened with five batteries and a turret, all well supplied with guns, commanding both the land and the sea, which made it almost invincible to attack from either side.

The Cape Coast of to-day is a large and irregularly built town of some 12,000 inhabitants, European quarters and native huts being in close proximity, much to the detriment of the health of the inhabitants of the former. Next to the castle the chief buildings of importance are Gothic House, the residence and offices of the District Commissioner, the Colonial Hospital, the English, Roman Catholic and Wesleyan places of worship and their respective schools, and the houses of the merchants and the richer natives. The streets are very rocky and hilly, and the town is surrounded with high lands on the north and east, with a large lagoon upon its western side. These are generally said to contribute to the unhealthiness of the town, though I believe it is more attributable to the general want of sanitation, and the dirt that is allowed to be thrown into the streets. The town is very hot, the light glaring, and it seems an impossibility to secure shade and breeze. The town is of great political importance, being the gateway of the coast through Prahsu to the Ashanti country, and was the chief seat of the Government until 1874, when it was removed to Accra. A very considerable trade is done at Cape Coast with the interior tribes, the most important exports being rubber, gold dust and monkey skins, in exchange for articles of general European character.

A little to the north-east of the town lies Connor's Hill, the present site of the Government schools, once the military barracks, and the location of the Army Hospital during the 1895-96 Ashanti campaign. This should be the site for the future residence of the Government officials, and many of their present quarters in the town should be burnt. It is the best site in Cape Coast, but would involve a short morning and evening walk from the Government offices. Excellent school buildings are in progress at Cape Coast to the west of the town for the Government scholars, and the present site is, or soon will be, available for building purposes, if not already allotted for an official bungalow for the governor. The officials at Cape Coast are much worse housed than those at Accra. The best quarters are, of course, to be found in the castle, but this has been, and will remain, in military hands for some time to come. The result is that other officers have to live where they can, there bei. g little other provision for their accommodation.

Landing at Cape Coast is at times very unpleasant, but during the Harmattan season in December, January and February the sea is fairly calm, and landing is effected

THE LIGHTHOUSE (FORT WILLIAM), CAPE COAST.

without the least danger, while between May and August the surf is often so bad that boats cannot work for days together. The principal landing-place is a small bay just under the north-east of the castle, partly protected by a reef jutting out from the rock on which the castle is built. Near the landing-place are a number of cannon (lately piled to extend the breakwater) lying near the beach, landed no one knows when, and left there ever since to rust away. Cape Coast is not the only town along this shore where now obsolete cannon ornament the beach, a tribute to the lack of energy of bygone days. The whole coast is an example of the undoing by one Governor of the doings of his predecessor.

There has been in the past little or no continuity, and this perhaps is to be accounted for by the fact that each new-comer, knowing his stay will be brief, is anxious to carve out fame for himself as quickly as possible, by pursuing a plan that brings the individual into prominence, but sometimes to the detriment of the general welfare of the colony. West Africa is a country where great haste is injurious, and the native motto "Softly, softly, catch monkey," is a very true one. The motto of one governor was "Festina lente". It was erased from the place where it was inscribed by his successor. Both are now dead and gone, but the fact points a valuable lesson nevertheless.

In the triangular courtyard of Cape Coast Castle lie the mortal remains of Mr. and Mrs. Maclean, the last resting-place of the poetess "L. E. L." and her husband, President Maclean. The local practice of inter-mural sepulture was here followed, and the floors of the surgery, the kitchen and the store-rooms of the colonial hospital have all been used for the same purpose. The graves are marked in the following manner, and a neat tablet on the wall near by, bears record of the death of the poetess, and the survivor's grief.

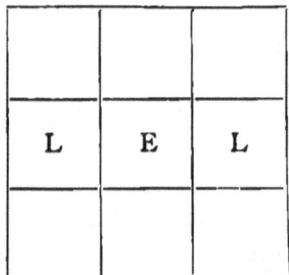 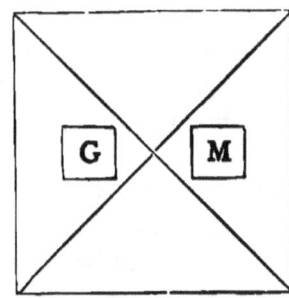

Mr. and Mrs. Maclean landed at Cape Coast in August, 1838. The poetess died on the 15th of October, and her husband followed her in May, 1847, to the great regret of the whole population. The story of her tragic death need not be retold in these pages, but a short account of her life may be of interest to many readers.

Laetitia Elizabeth Landon was descended from a Herefordshire family, which held landed property in the county. Her grandfather was the Rev. John Landon, Rector of Tedstone. This living, together with Tedstone Court and estate, was sold in his lifetime, and the family was left with very slender means. At an early age his eldest son, Miss Landon's father, went to sea; but some years later he settled in London, where he became an assistant and finally a partner in the house of Adairs, army agents. Soon afterwards he married a Welsh lady of the name of Bishop, and took up his residence in Han's Place, Chelsea, where in 1802 his eldest child, Laetitia Elizabeth, was born. In her sixth year she was sent for a few months to a boarding school, almost next door to her father's house; but Mr. Landon having taken a farm on the borders of Herefordshire, which he confided to the superintendence of one of his brothers, thither the whole family removed. Here her cousin became her governess. But she would learn nothing that was not in accordance with her own inclination, though books were her early and almost sole delight. Many years afterwards, when on a visit to the family of her uncle, she thus playfully wrote in reference to her want of accomplishments :—

"When I first arrived, Julia and Isabel began to cross-question me. 'Can you play?' 'No!' 'Can you sing?' 'No!' 'Can you speak Italian?' 'No!' 'Can you draw?' 'No!' At last they came down to 'Can you read and write?' Here I was able to answer, to their great relief, 'Yes, a little'. I believe Julia, in the first warmth of cousinly affection, was going to offer to teach me the alphabet." The date of her first literary composition is not known. In 1815, when Laetitia was about fourteen, her family returned to London and settled in Brompton, where they chanced to have for a neighbour Mr. Jerdan, the editor of the *Literary Gazette*. Her literary tastes had grown with her growth, and like most persons similarly situated, she wrote or rather scribbled incessantly, until the encouraging "not so bad" gradually rose to "very clever, indeed," and inspired the longing desire to appear in print. Mr. Jerdan was consulted: his fiat was favourable, and the destiny of the youthful aspirant was fixed for life. From this period her "Poetical Sketches," to which the magic letters "L. E. L." were appended, appeared regularly in the *Literary Gazette*, until the initials emerged into a popular and celebrated name. In 1824 appeared the *Improvisatrice*, the success of which was unequivocal. "L. E. L.'s" vocation was now confirmed; for with fame came fortune, which the straitened circumstances of her family made doubly welcome. Shortly after the publication of the *Improvisatrice*, which, though far from being her best, was her most popular work, Miss Landon lost her father, to whom she was deeply attached. In 1825 she published a volume containing "The Troubadour"; "Poetical Sketches of Modern Pictures"; and "Historical Sketches". The next production of her muse was *The Golden Violet* in 1826, followed by *The Venetian Bracelet* in 1829. Miss Landon might now have gracefully reposed upon her well-earned poetic laurels. But she resolved to enter the lists with the novelists of the day, and to struggle in a new arena for the wreath of fame. Her first venture in this new and perilous field was *Romance and Reality*, published in 1831, followed by two others, *Francesca Carrara* and *Ethel Churchill*.

From her childhood " L. E. L. " might be said to have lived upon the same spot, and with the same people. Soon after her father's death she became an inmate of the family of the Misses Lance, who had occupied the house in Han's Place, in which she had for a brief time gone to school, and which was for many years a temple of tuition, and could boast of many gifted scholars, among others, Miss Mitford and Lady Caroline Lamb. Her attachment to London was intense. She paid a visit now and then to her relations in the country; but we find from her correspondence that her heart was always in London. In the summer of 1834 she joined Sir A. Farquhar and his daughter in an excursion to Paris. She does not appear, however, to have been so deeply impressed with the novelty, gaiety and picturesqueness of the French metropolis as might have been expected from her lively and susceptible imagination. On her return to London she resumed her literary pursuits with even greater zest than before.

In the spring of 1836 the friends of "L. E. L." were apprised that she was about to form a matrimonial alliance with a gentleman whose friendship she had long enjoyed. Circumstances, however, induced her to break off this engagement, and in 1838 she gave her hand to Mr. George Maclean, Governor of Cape Coast Castle, who had been for some time on a visit to England. A fortnight after her marriage she sailed for her home on the shores of Africa, full of plans for the continuation of her literary pursuits. But all her anticipations of the future were doomed to disappointment. The same vessel that brought to her friends and relatives so many pleasing hopes and reminiscences, conveyed also the stern announcement that "L. E. L." was no more, for early on the morning of the 15th of October, 1838, she was found dead in her room, lying close to the door.

A little to the north of the castle stands Fort Macarthy upon an isolated eminence, while about one mile to the north-west lies a large lagoon, known as the Saltpond, the scene of a skirmish with the Ashantis in 1816, and approached by the Saltpond Road. Women have frequently washed gold from the sands to the west of the castle, and the land at the east side of the town is studded with gold-diggers' pits, now become receptacles for all the refuse that can be found to be thrown into them; evidences of the richness of the soil in former days.

About one mile to the east of Cape Coast Castle is the small fishing village of Manful or Amanful, the scene of an Ashanti attack early in the present century.

One of the best roads in the colony extends from Cape Coast to Prahsu, until recently the boundary of the Ashanti country, a distance of some seventy-nine miles almost due north from the castle. This road was constructed in 1873 by Sir Garnet Wolseley for the transport of the troops to Ashanti, and has been kept in good repair since that date. This road has now been carried across the Prah, through the Adansi country to Kumasi, and telegraphic communication is now established the whole way. The total distance from Cape Coast Castle to Kumasi is about 180 miles, but in a direct line not more than 125.

The country for the first few miles along the road to the Prah is covered with rather stunted bush, giving way at last to taller trees and the denser growth that extends through the country from east to west for about fifty miles north of Kumasi, this in its turn giving way to the vast grassy plains that roll away to the foot of the Kong Mountains. From the river Prah to the Adansi Hills, which are about forty miles away, the country is more open and a little less wooded—thinly peopled by scattered villages of not more than 500 people. After the Adansi Hills are crossed the real Ashanti country is entered, and the villages on the road are more numerous and more thickly populated.

The Adansi Hills constitute the most serious physical difficulty to be overcome between Cape Coast and Kumasi. They cross the Prah road some forty miles from Prahsu, and are supposed to be connected with the Akim and Aquapim ranges in the east. The ascent on the south side is very rugged and steep, rising to 1600 feet, where a small plateau extends for a short distance to lead down on the other side by a much more favourable path.

There are other roads across this range of hills known only to the natives of the country. Immediately to the north of the old Fetu country in which Cape Coast is situated, and to the king of which an annual rent was once paid for the ground on which the castle now stands, are the countries of Tufel and Assin, extending for some fifty miles into the interior until the southern limits of the Adansi country are reached. The lower reaches of the Prah water the Tufel country, and the main road from Cape Coast to Prahsu passes through the middle of Assin. The nations inhabiting these territories became each in their turn tributary to the old Ashanti power, once dominant from the Ancobra to the Volta. The whole country is well watered and covered with dense forests, supplying the natives with abundance of palm oil and rubber, which they bring down to the ports on the coast. Transport is only needed to bring down the fine timber with which the forests abound. Mampong, near the Prah, is the most important town in the Tufel country, and Mansu and Prahsu the chief centres of the Assin territory. The main road from Kumasi to Wassaw and Apollonia passed through the Tufel country, and that to Cape Coast and Elmina through the Adansi and Assin territories. These means of communication to the centre capital had to be kept open by the tributary states, and in this way the subdued tribes were made to prepare a path for their conquerors, available for use by the Ashantis upon the appearance of the slightest apprehension of revolt on the part of their weaker neighbours.

Bosman describes the strip of shore extending from Cape Coast Castle to within a short distance of Mouri as the kingdom of Saboe, though in his map of the

Guinea Coast he marks Saboe as an inland country. Saboe, he says, begins at the bottom of the hill and ends about half a mile below Mouri, being in its whole extent along the shore about two miles (Dutch) and about twice as broad. From the Danish mount, *i.e.*, Fort Victoria, it is about half a mile (Dutch) to Congo, where the Dutch formerly had a fine stone house, divided and situated upon two small hills, upon which their flag was planted in order to keep out other Europeans who might have been tempted to trade there, and thus have considerably interfered with the trade done at Mouri. The Congo of which he speaks I am unable to find any mention of, and the site seems to have disappeared from the maps, if it was ever marked.

Saboe was about equal in power with Kommany, and its people were as great villains, but the country produced an abundance of corn, yams and potatoes, and from Mouri about 100 canoes were daily laden with palm oil for Axim and Accra.

The Dutch fort at Mouri was called Nassaw, and was built by them in the seventeenth century, being their chief place of residence when the Portuguese held Elmina. It was a large fort, almost square, with the front somewhat broader than the other sides, provided with four batteries supplied with no less than eighteen pieces of ordnance, the walls of the fort being higher than those of any other fort along the coast, Elmina excepted. The curtain on the seaside contained two batteries, almost as spacious and convenient as those at Cape Coast, while at each angle of the fort was a spacious tower. This place was once garrisoned by seventy men for defence against the natives and the attacks of other

European powers. The village of Mouri was situated close to the fort. It was not so large as Elmina but contained more people, who were chiefly engaged in fishing. The Dutch exacted a toll upon this town, as also upon Axim, Chama and Elmina, of every fifth fish that was caught by the natives, which was paid every day to the factor who governed the town. From Mouri alone some 400 or 500 canoes would go out to fish daily,

INTERIOR COURTYARD OF CAPE COAST CASTLE.

so that the garrison must have been well supplied with this useful article of food. No other Europeans on the coast ever exercised such a prerogative as this over the natives. Near Mouri is the Iron Hill, an elevation about a quarter of a mile long, covered with the thickest bush. From the fort on this hill the Fanti country stretches away to the east, a description of which must be reserved for the next chapter. The true Fanti country commences at the foot of the Iron Hill and extends along the sea-board for some thirty-five miles, and into the interior for some ten or a dozen. In early times the English held four stations in this territory—one fort and three lodges, and the Dutch had one fort also.

The first English settlement was at the present Anishan, some eight miles east of Cape Coast, where, according to Bosman, "the entire garrison consisted of one whole Englishman, who lies there". Some hours' journey to the east of this lodge is Anamaboe, where in early times we had a small compact fort, which was the centre of a very considerable trade, English vessels being always in the roads, much to the chagrin and annoyance of their Dutch competitors.

Anamaboe Fort was built by the English in 1753, but the natives were so troublesome that they often confined the English garrison within the walls of the fort, and held generally such power over the traders that, when a governor was sent to the fort to superintend the trade there, and in any way displeased them, they returned him in a canoe again to Cape Coast. Peace was constantly bought with them by presents, and the oftener this was done the more troublesome they became. As a native town Anamaboe was the strongest on the coast, on account of the number of armed natives that it contained: the whole land round was well populated, besides being very rich in gold, slaves and corn, this last being sold to the English vessels in great quantities. The present town of Anamaboe was once the flourishing centre of a very important trade, which has of late years been considerably diminished owing to the rise of the neighbouring town of Saltpond. In the year 1807 the town was the scene of a very determined attack by the Ashantis, which was repulsed by the garrison of the fort. The town was once the headquarters of the Wesleyan Mission on the coast, and still possesses a very handsome chapel, but the large houses of the town, once inhabited by the prosperous merchants, are now mostly in ruins, and give one a most depressing idea of its present state. It contains about 2000 inhabitants.

The Fantis in this part of the coast owned allegiance to no king, but the reins of power were vested in the hands of a chief commander or leader, who was termed " Braffo," and who administered the affairs of the country, under the advice of a council composed of the elders of the community. The inhabitants of the coast towns gained their living by fishing and trading with any vessel that might come into port there, in direct opposition to their arrangements to trade with the English and Dutch vessels only. The people of the interior towns and villages were mostly occupied in agriculture and in the drawing of a particularly good kind of palm wine, called "Quaker," which possessed extraordinary exhilarating properties, and was eagerly sought after by the natives on the coast, though sold at double the price of the ordinary wine of the country.

A very short distance from Anamaboe Fort was a smaller post occupied by the English, but I am not able to trace the date of its construction. According to the old Dutch authority, it was called Adja, and originally belonged to them, till they lost it by the so-called treachery of the English. It would appear that the two garrisons, Dutch and English, jointly occupied it, and that with our usual ambition to be sole masters or not at all, we pushed out our enterprising rivals, much to their disgust. The remains of an old fort are still to be found here, and the latest map of the Intelligence Department of the War Office marks the place "Etsin". This was probably the site of the Dutch Adja, and the cause of the commercial rivalry early in the eighteenth century.

Not far away stood the village called Little Cormantine, where the Dutch held the fortress called Amsterdam, which was the chief residence of the English traders in Fantiland until 1665, when the Dutch admiral De Ruyter drove them out. The fort was built by the English in 1624, was of fairly large dimensions and contained one large and three small batteries, mounted with twenty pieces of cannon, and in the time of the Dutch governed by a chief factor, as at Mouri.

Near Little Cormantine, upon another hill about a cannon shot from Fort Amsterdam, stood a large and very populous town called Great Cormantine, the inhabitants of which, besides being traders, were fishermen to the number of 1000. Nothing but ruins are now left of Fort Amsterdam, and the towns of Cormantine are of the most wretched description.

The original Fanti kingdom ended at Mumfort or Mumford, and between Cormantine and this place were two more English establishments, Tantum or Tantumquerry and Mumford, the former place being known as Tuam. Both these forts were built by the English, after much opposition on the part of the natives, towards the end of the seventeenth century. The buildings have long since disappeared and their sites are almost forgotten. The country in which these two towns are situated was once known as Gomoah or Gomoor, and was situated on the east of Fanti and to the south of Akim. The district itself was well populated, all the inland towns being quite surrounded by the densest forests, where the people long maintained their barbarous practices. The people now inhabiting the coast towns are almost entirely engaged in fishing. The Fanti natives in those early days gave much trouble to all the traders, and their character is best shown by the following extract :—

"The English and the Dutch possess in Fanti an equal power, that is, none at all, for when these villainous people are inclined to it, they shut up all the passes so close that not one merchant can possibly come from the inland countries to trade with us; and sometimes not content with this, they prevent the bringing of provisions to us till we have made peace with them. They have a hank upon us, we having formerly contracted to give them a good sum of ready money, besides 300 guilders, for every one of the company's ships which for the future should bring any goods hither, in consideration of their aid in taking Fort Amsterdam and other auxiliary assistance; but in this contract it was particularly stipulated that slave ships should be excepted from paying anything, notwithstanding which they are now become so unreasonable that they will make no difference between slave ships and others, obliging us equally to pay for all, and all our remonstrances that it is contrary to the treaty are wholly ineffectual, for if we will live at quiet, we are always obliged to humour them."

In later times Fanti included all the countries from the Sweet River, Elmina to Mumford, and comprised Cape Coast, Anamaboe, Abracrampah, Dunquah, Dominassi, Mankassim and Adjumako, all of which and many other smaller towns are governed by separate kings and chiefs. At the present time Fanti is the most confused part of the Gold Coast with regard to political divisions. In every croom or village there is a king or chief, though his land often does not extend for a mile round his so-called capital. Fanti is, however, the most civilised portion of the western division of the Gold Coast.

At Cape Coast and Anamaboe are some good, strong, substantial buildings of native-made bricks and stone, but in the majority of the towns the houses are of simple mud and sticks. The towns are quite devoid of properly laid out streets, the native huts being jumbled together in a confused mass, many presenting a very unfinished appearance to European eyes. About one in a hundred of the Fantis can read and write, and ninety-nine of a hundred still dress in the native fashion. Gold is found all through the Fanti country in small quantities below the surface soil, which is washed by the women; the men consider it beneath their dignity to do such work, and spend the greater part of their time sitting lazily about under the shade of the trees.

Domestic slavery exists in all its various forms. The women are the hard-working portion of the community, tilling the ground and bringing its produce to the markets for sale, which is exchanged for either gold or silver Yams, plantains, cassada, corn and a large quantity of vegetables are grown in the country within a few miles of the sea coast, but very little or nothing of native growth is exported from this fertile part of the colony. Domestic slavery and the plurality of wives enervate the energies of the male population, so that even the produc-

THE TOWN OF SALTPOND.

tions for home consumption are often not sufficient for the wants of the people.

The currency of the country is gold dust and silver, but in some of the towns to the east of Cape Coast cowry shells are still used as money. Gold, monkey skins and a little ivory are brought down from the interior, and palm oil from the districts round Saltpond.

The Saltpond of the present day is a town of comparatively modern growth. It is situated some two miles east of Cormantine, and possesses no fort like most other towns on the coast. The Government House, the residence of the District Commissioner, is situated on the beach, and contains the usual departmental post, telegraph and treasury offices. The custom office is situated in an adjacent building. The main street of Saltpond runs almost north and south, and a fairly good road runs out of the town through the Adjumako and Essecumah districts to the capital of Western Akim, and from this point there is a good road to Kumasi.

The town is a rising and prosperous one, contains rather more than 4000 inhabitants, and is rapidly increasing in size and importance. Compared with other towns in the colony the streets are wide and well drained, and the houses of the more prosperous traders are large and substantial. There is a large lagoon at the eastern extremity of the town, which undoubtedly contributes greatly to its unhealthiness.

The surf at Saltpond is one of the most dangerous on the coast. The nature of the country is undulating, fertile, and well wooded, the more inland parts being exceedingly rich in the oil palm, and an enormous quantity of palm oil and palm kernels are annually exported from this town, in addition to large quantities of rubber and monkey skins. As a port, Saltpond ranks third in importance on the Gold Coast. The interior country is well watered by the rivers Amissa and Narkwa. The former is a stream of considerable breadth, though shallow and unsuitable for navigation, and flows, after a course of nearly fifty miles, into the sea at a distance of five miles east of Saltpond. The river Narkwa rises near Insuaim, the capital of Western Akim, and after a course of some sixty miles empties itself into the sea near the town of Narkwa, some ten miles away. The schools in the town of Saltpond are among the best in the colony, and are under the management of the Roman Catholic and Wesleyan Missionary bodies. They are well attended, and new and substantial school premises have lately been provided to meet the wants of the population in this respect, which is fast awakening to the value of a sound elementary education for its children.

Tufel and Assin are two small states lying immediately to the north of Elmina and Fanti, and to the south of Ashanti, by which power they were conquered under Osai Tootoo. Very little is known about the former country, except that it is remarkably well wooded and is watered by the middle courses of the river Prah, and was possibly once a part of the great kingdom of Denkira, before that power became tributary to the Ashantis.

Assin is situated to the south-east of Denkira, and was also once a powerful province of Ashanti. It was originally bounded on the north by that country, south by Fanti, west by Denkira and east by Akim. It was politically divided into two divisions, each of which had

VIEW OF THE TOWN OF CAPE COAST.

its own king, one of whom lived at Mansu and the other at Yancoomasie. They were not very powerful monarchs, nor are their successors at the present day, whose chief occupation is sitting all day on a large stool, surrounded by their chiefs and headmen, who sing and dance to amuse their kings and join in drinking their rum.

The kings settle all disputes, inflict heavy fines which go to provide more drink, and they are reported to run away on the approach of an enemy. The country of Assin is by no means well peopled; it contains the main road from Cape Coast to Kumasi, along which its principal towns are situated, with a few scattered villages on either side. The whole surface of the country is covered with a thick, dense forest, with very few hills and no mountains. The soil is fertile but is very little cultivated, and the people are generally very poor, almost barbarians, and lazy. A small quantity of gold is said to be found in this country, towards the Denkira boundary, but there are no known gold mines of any importance.

CHAPTER VII.

Appam—The Devil's Mount—Winnebah—Bereku—Accra or Akra —The Akra People—Manners and Customs—The Adangme Tribe—Names—The Present Town—Christiansborg—Meridian Rock.

OF the coast countries known to the early visitors to this part, there are now but three left to describe. These are marked in old maps as Acron, Agonna and Aquamboe. The first extended over the present Winnebah country; the second lay to the north a little inland and is marked as Agoona on recent maps: while the third was a small strip of country situated beyond the Aquamboe Mountains in the district of the same name. It is at present called the Akwamu country, the people speaking the Akra and the Adangme languages. The first point of interest in the old Acron country was the then village (now a town of considerable size) of Appam, where in 1697 the Dutch began to build the present fort, or rather house, which was subsequently fortified with two batteries. The fort stands upon a considerable eminence, and has of late years been repaired, and accommodation provided for any European travelling through the place, though there is no European resident at present at Appam.

By the Dutch this fort was called Leydstambeyd or Patience, on account of the manner in which their virtue was tried in this respect by the natives, when they were building the fort. At the present day it is more generally known as Appam Fort. On the two batteries were mounted eight pieces of cannon, and a fine turret commanded most extensive land and sea views. The whole of the Winnebah district is extremely well wooded, often being called " The Forest Country," and comprises a series of undulating rocky hills, rising apparently to about 300 feet, with well-clothed valleys between, watered with innumerable small streams that flow on all sides.

From the elevation midway between Appam and the town of Winnebah, is the Devil's Mount or Monte da Diable, about which many a native legend exists, and which is fetish to the inhabitants. It is supposed to have derived its name from the sailors of the old sailing vessels that frequented the coast, from the fact that being very high and close to the shore they could see it at a long distance and yet could not reach it, for the wind is very contrary in this direction. The hill itself is over 600 feet high, and is now known as Mankwadi Hill, forming the most important landmark between Appam and Accra. The district is supposed to be gold-bearing, and the hill is reported to be rich in gold. It has never been properly prospected, though it is affirmed that after violent storms of rain the natives of the locality always find a considerable amount of gold round its base. Early in the present century a Mr. Baggs was sent out by the directors of the African Company, with all necessary apparatus, to test the ore from this hill, but he unfortunately died on his way at Cape Coast Castle. Since this date no serious effort has been made, and the fact of a white man dying, when on such an expedition, has only tended to strengthen the opinion of the natives that the mountain itself is a very strong fetish. While on the subject of gold in this locality, I may as well give what evidence there is of its existence, and for this purpose will quote from a report on gold mines, made in 1889 to the Secretary of State for the Colonies by the late Sir William Brandford Griffith, the governor of the colony at that date. A Mr. Eyre, District Commissioner, was sent to the Winnebah district for this purpose in 1888. He reports as follows:—

"In the afternoon (24th July, 1888) I examined the rocks cropping out along the sea-coast immediately in front of Winnebah and extending up the coast for about a quarter of a mile. These rocks are principally ironstone with quartz veins running through them, though here and there the quartz reef itself also crops out. The quartz varies much in colour, from dirty red to pure crystal and opaque white, but does not show any indication of being auriferous, at least not at the surface, though I believe that below the surface there are auriferous veins running through the quartz, especially the quartz veins running through the ironstone, but as I had no tools with me sufficiently powerful for breaking through the surface-stone, I was unable to ascertain the fact. The land immediately around Winnebah is of a light, sandy nature, with either clay, dark-coloured earth, or quartz or ironstone below it. The quartz crops out every here and there, and is principally of a dirty red colour; but white opaque and clear crystal quartz also crop up at times, but none of them show any traces of gold, at least not at the surface. The natives state that they obtain gold here near the sea-beach by washing, after the rains, the dirt taken from the tracks of the water-flows. They sink holes till they arrive at a black

sand (almost pure iron ore) mixed with a rubble
and small broken quartz and lying generally on a clay
bottom. By reducing this dirt containing the black sand
by washing, until only the black sand and the gold dust
are left, they obtain by degrees a quantity of this black
sand mixed with gold dust. This they dry in the
sun, and then get rid of the sand by fanning and so obtain the pure gold. The quantity of gold dust obtainable by this means in a single day is generally very
small, though the natives state that at times they obtain
nuggets of varying sizes, but more frequently small
particles of gold the size of grains of sand.

"On 27th July I left Winnebah about 6·30 A.M. and
proceeded to the town of Pomadi, about eight miles from
Winnebah and situated at the foot of a small range of
hills lying at the back of Winnebah (evidently the Mankwadi range). All this neighbourhood is worked by the
natives for gold. At Pomadi I got a guide to take me
to the hills at the back, and to show me where the
natives were in the habit of washing for gold. About
three miles from Pomadi we came to a dry water-course,
which the guide pointed out as being one of the chief
spots where they obtained gold. The whole of the bed
of the stream was composed of fragments of quartz and
ironstone with quartz veins through it, the stones varying
in size from large boulders of several tons' weight down
to small broken quartz the size of gravel. I examined
very many of these stones, but I could not find any trace
of gold in them, and at the time was unable to follow
the stream up to its source from want of time. All the
slope of the range was strewn with fragments of quartz
and ironstone, and the guide said that the people and

their forefathers obtained gold almost anywhere along the foot of this range of hills by sinking holes and washing as described, and that sometimes nuggets were found. From the nature of the country, and the evident fact that the natives do obtain gold here, I should say that if the base of this range of hills was properly prospected, in all probability alluvial deposits bearing gold in payable quantities would be found, and the reef from which they come could subsequently be traced. Wherever there is a flow of water on the hill-side during the rainy season the quartz reef has been laid bare in places.

"Tuesday the 31st I left Appam about seven in the morning with Mr. Williams, the native proprietor of the hotel, who wanted to show me the various spots where he himself had obtained gold. After proceeding about three miles along the Akim road, we came to the bed of an almost dry water-course. Here Mr. Williams showed me various holes along the track of the stream, and about fifteen to twenty feet from it, where the natives had been or were still procuring gold by washing. I took away some of the earth from these holes, and on our return had it washed, and obtained specks of fine gold dust mixed with the fine black sand already mentioned. After examining the holes and procuring some of the dirt, Mr. Williams took me to several places where the quartz reef crops out, and where he had tried to sink holes to see whether there was gold or not in the lower strata. From one of these holes he found a small nugget lying in the soil. He then took me to where an outcrop of ironstone veined with quartz occurs, and where he had sunk a hole about ten feet deep through the ironstone,

Here, wherever the quartz veins traverse the ironstone, specks of gold are most distinctly visible to the naked eye, and even through the ironstone itself specks of gold are to be seen, but very few. Another metal is traceable in this stone, resembling silver in colour, but very brittle, but with which I am not acquainted. August 2nd I left Appam for Mankwadi. I stopped on the way at the small town of Moeyans, where there are very extensive gold diggings, one hole being about twenty yards in diameter and eight or nine feet deep and full of water. All around this central excavation are innumerable smaller holes, all of which have been sunk for gold. I tried dirt from several of these smaller holes and in each case obtained specks of fine gold dust, and also larger particles the size of fine sand. Here the natives inform me that nuggets are by no means unfrequent and that grains of gold like sand are common. This spot is by far the best I have examined yet for alluvial working, and seems from all accounts of the natives to be fairly rich in places. The native gold holes here are many of them sunk to a considerable depth, till they reach the clay bottom on which the gold rests. Gold washing seems to be very extensively carried on here, the holes dug by the natives lying in every direction. These holes are all sunk at hazard and consequently are no guide to the direction taken by the gold. The formation continues from the town of Moeyans to the town of Mankwadi, and is about a quarter of a mile in width. In conclusion I will add that I believe there is a considerable quantity of gold in the district, and that in places it would probably pay Europeans to work it; but until the direction it takes has been fully determined and the richness of the deposits practically ascertained nothing is likely to come of it."

I must now return to the town of Appam, which in early times was but a mere fishing village, poorly inhabited, lying just under the walls of the fort. It was well situated for trade and soon developed, being for some time a populous and important town. The country was governed by a king and was under the protection of its more powerful neighbours, the Fantis, and on this account, was very seldom engaged in war, so that the natives of this part of the coast had a comparatively quiet time of it and were able to devote all their energies to the cultivation of the soil. Deer, hares, partridges, pheasants, wild fowl and quadrupeds were found in great abundance. The following chase of a hare is told by Bosman as being very uncommon, in which I think all my readers will agree.

"Behind our fort, which is built on a hill, is a vale which is about a mile square, where there were abundance of haycocks; here about twilight we met a young hare that, being pursued by my dog, took refuge in a haycock, in which, though we made a diligent search, we could not find him, till at last, burning the haycock, to our mighty surprise we found the hare sitting under the ashes of the hay, unhurt, and we carried her alive with us to Elmina."

The small territory of Gomoah or Gomoor is situated south of Akim and north of Fanti. The Acron country was divided into Little and Great Acron, the former being the country I have just described. Great Acron lay farther inland, its government being a kind of republic, or rather anarchy, and these two divisions, though they had no

VIEW OF THE BEACH AT CAPE COAST.

dependence on each other, were in perfect amity for many years. A small river empties itself into the sea near Appam, the waters of which are always more or less salt, and which in some maps is named the Salt River.

The Devil's Hill, previously mentioned, was the commencement of the Agoona country, which was reported in the seventeenth and eighteenth centuries to have been governed by a woman, who showed as much spirit and courage in the conduct of affairs as many of the male rulers. She was indeed sufficiently wise to remain unmarried, in order to retain the government of her kingdom in her own hands, though report had it that she did not completely remain a stranger to the soft passion, but satisfied her desires with amours with the best of her slaves, upon whom she bestowed her favours without fear or scandal. About the middle of the Agoona country the English built a fort in 1694, which took its name from the adjacent village of Wimba or Simpa, and is now called Winnebah. This fort had a flat roof and was supplied with four batteries, so large, says Bosman, "that a man could leap over them without a stick"! The guns too were of a proportionate size, one of them discharging a half-pound ball! The Agoona district was of twice the area of its neighbour Acron, possessing too more power and riches, though equal in general fertility and pleasantness, the coast being well supplied with all kinds of fish and oysters, while the country inland was plentifully supplied with all sorts of apes.

The Winnebah of the present day is the name of both the old Agoona district and the present town, bounded on the west by Saltpond and on the east by the Sekoom or Humo River, a distance of some forty miles from west to east. The sea-board is level, but the interior is diversified with several ranges of hills, of which the Mankwadi Range is the most important. The district is well watered by the river Anisu, and its tributary the Akora, the former rising in the Akim country and emptying its waters some two miles east of Winnebah after a course of about forty miles. The productions of the district are kernels, palm oil and rubber, to which, in the past, might be added gold dust, the gathering of these products and fishing forming the chief occupation of the people, who number some 4000 in Winnebah alone. In addition the people are great agriculturists, the inland plantations producing large supplies of ground-nuts, plantains and bananas for home consumption. Native canoes are also made here in large numbers, which are used as far down the coast as Benin, and are much sought after. The forest lands contain hard and valuable woods, the odom, mahogany and African cedar being among the best, but little export trade is done in these on account of the want of transport. The quarters in the old fort are very damp and most unsuitable for the residence of Europeans. The Colonial Hospital, a good, substantial building, is about a mile from the fort. The last station of importance along this coast is Bereku, some twelve miles from Winnebah and about twenty-one miles from Accra. The Dutch had a fort at Bereku, of which but little mention is made. The fort is now converted into a rest-house for travelling officers, and but little trade is done in the town. Bereku Point is a well-known landmark, on which the native town is situated.

This brings us to the last division of the Gold Coast, the Aquamboe country, which in the seventeenth and eighteenth centuries absorbed and included the present Akra or Accra. It is reported that Accra was the original name of the country until it was conquered by the Aquamboes, when its inhabitants were forced to retire to Little Popo, one hundred and seventy miles east of Accra, from whence they returned in later times. The territory extended from the mouth of the Sekoom River to the Ponni Village, the most eastern point of the Gold Coast, where, at the end of the seventeenth century, the Dutch commenced to build a fort which was never finished. Accra was at this time an important town in the Aquamboe country, where English, Dutch and Danes each possessed trading stations, for which an annual rent was paid to the natives. The first or most western fort was James Fort, situated at English Accra or James Town, built by the English in 1662 by the British African Company, and named after James, Duke of York. Captain Brakenbury says (1873) that James Fort, British Accra, was the first English fort ever built on the Gold Coast and that it was built by "The Company of Adventurers of England trading to Africa". This could hardly be so, for Cormantine was built by the English in 1640. This was a square well-built fort, with four batteries, the walls being very high and thick, particularly on the eastern side, that next the Dutch. The fort was furnished with twenty-five pieces of cannon, though not of much account nor so heavy as those of their near neighbours. In the time of the Dutch it was meanly garrisoned, the English companies seemingly being content to build forts and furnish them with guns and provisions but with very few men. Within a cannon shot to the east of James Fort was the Dutch fort of Crevecoeur, now known as Ussher Fort, after a governor of that name, which was built a few years before the English fort. The Dutch fort was much larger and better furnished with guns than the English, though of about equal strength, with the exception of the walls, which were thinner, and consequently less able to stand a siege. Some two miles farther east was the Danish fort of Christiansborg, built in 1659, and taken from them by the natives in 1693, who held it for a considerable time. This fort was far stronger and better than either that of the English or the Dutch, and more than a match, with regard to the number of the garrison, for the combined forces of the other two. The date upon its walls is 1694, but this, I think, must refer to its restoration in that year, after the natives had captured it in 1693, and stripped it of everything, leaving only the walls standing.

This misfortune was caused by the death of several of the Danish garrison, the remainder being ill-treated and plundered by the natives, under one Assameni, who dressed himself in the governor's clothes, and caused himself to be saluted by his name, wasting the powder in the castle by thundering salutes to every vessel that passed, until the arrival of two Danish vessels at Accra, when he was induced to give up possession. The fort was square in shape, with four batteries furnished with twenty good guns available for use at all points, the roof being entirely flat. One account says, the castle was built by the Portuguese during the seventeenth century, in what year cannot be accurately laid down. It was a small fortification, and resembled a block-house more than a fort. The Swedes expelled the Portuguese; and in the year 1657 his Danish majesty Frederick III. sent an expedition to the coast of Africa under the direction and command of Sir Henry Carlof, who conquered the Swedish forts Carolusborg (now Cape Coast), Taccarary, Anamaboe, and Ursu Lodge (now Christiansborg). At this period the Danes erected a fort near Cape Coast and named it Fredericksborg (which was afterwards purchased by the Royal African Company and destroyed). The governor of this fort enlarged Ursu Lodge, and gave it the name of Christiansborg. The Danes remained uninterrupted masters of this place until the year 1679, when it was treacherously sold to the Portuguese by a man named Peter Bolt. In 1683 it was restored by order of the King of Portugal, and ten years after, the Aquamboes, who then lived but a short distance from Accra, took possession of it, at the instigation of the Ursu Caboceer, in the following manner. They brought down a number of slaves and a large quantity of gold and ivory, in exchange for which they would take nothing but guns and powder. This was agreed to by the governor, who also consented that the guns and powder should be proved before they were taken out of the fort. Having now charged a number of their muskets, they loaded them with bullets which they had concealed, and in a moment seized the unguarded garrison, as also every white person in the fort. There was but little resistance made, no lives were lost, and the fort was plundered but not injured. The Ursu Caboceer was proclaimed governor, and compelled both English and Dutch whites who had occasion to pass the forts to pay their obeisance to him; after which he generally treated them civilly, and frequently honoured them with a salute from the great guns. He often indulged himself with a salute, sometimes at midnight. The next year it was delivered up, through the intercession of the Dutch nation, and on a large sum being paid by the Danish Government. The town of Christiansborg was situated immediately under its walls. Although the English, Dutch and the Danes possessed forts at Accra, the power of each was very limited, and authority existed within the

CHRISTIANSBORG CASTLE, ACCRA, RESIDENCE OF THE GOVERNOR.

walls only for their own defence. One might suppose from the presence of three important trading companies in the one place, that competition would have limited the trade then done, but it seems that the contrary was the case, for such was the supply of slaves and gold in these early times that no one was in danger of losing a share. At Accra alone, the amount of gold received was often more than that from all other places on the coast put together. The bulk of this gold came from Akim, and could easily have been increased, but for the wars between that country and Aquamboe.

The three forts thus described still exist, though put to a very different purpose at the present than in the past. James Fort is the signal station, lighthouse, sheriff office and jail of Accra. Ussher Fort is in possession of the Hausà Forces, and Christiansborg Castle was until the present year the official residence of the governor of the colony.

The true Gá or Accra country extended from the mouth of the Sekoom River near the Cook's Loaf to the town of Temma, some seven miles west of Ponni Village, the boundary fixed by the Dutch, and contained a sea-board of about thirty miles. The southern boundary is the sea, and the northern the Aquapim Mountains. Much doubt exists as to the origin of the name Akra (wrongly written Accra). It is generally supposed to be derived from the Fanti word Nkran, meaning an ant, and was bestowed upon them by the Fantis, either when the Akras returned from Little Popo, or when they first came from the east and settled in that part of the country, on account of the numbers in which they came. Some people hold that the Akras did not come from this direction at all, but had their origin in a small village at the back of Winnebah, called Nkran at the present day. The Akra name for themselves is Gá, which duplicated into Gaga means a species of black ant, which bites severely and is the enemy of the white ant, and these ants are called Nkran by both the Tshi and Fanti peoples. If such be the case, and the name has any designation, they must have been a very numerous and powerful people, who easily subdued the original inhabitants of the country they now occupy. According to their own traditions, their largest towns were situated some distance inland, before the present coast town of Accra had any existence, and occupied most of the eminences south of the Aquapim country. Fourteen such towns existed inland from Accra, and many others in the neighbourhood of the present towns of Ningo, Labadi and Temma, whilst such states as Adangme, Akwamu and Aquapim were at one time tributary to them. That they are a distinct race from the other tribes on the coast admits of no doubt, the difference of language, manners and customs being most strongly marked.

Upon this leeward part of the coast, two principal languages are spoken, the true Gá, and its mother tongue, the Adangme. The true Gá or Gá Akpa is spoken in all the coast towns from the Sekoom to Teshi, a village five miles east of Christiansborg, and once the site of fort and station Augustenborg of the Danes, built in 1700 but now completely in ruins, while the Adangme language is the tongue from Teshi to the Volta River, the Krobo country and several towns at the foot of the Aquapim Mountains. The Akras, Krobos, Krepis, Awoonahs and Addahs differ greatly from the branches of the Akan family in physique. As a rule the men are taller and stronger, and the women remarkably well formed, with complexions not quite so black as those descended from the Tshi-speaking race. They are expert fisher- and boatmen, and make excellent carriers.

Unlike the people of the other tribes on the coast, they

name their children according to the number, and not from the day of the week upon which they are born. Thus there are the first male, second male, first female, second female, and so on. Appended are the Akra names:—

	Male.	Female.
First	Teti	Dede
Second	Tete	Koko
Third	Mesa	Mansa
Fourth	Anan	Tsotso
Fifth	Anum	Manum
Sixth	Nsia	Sasa

while the seventh, eighth, ninth and tenth are Ason, Botfe, Akron and Badu respectively for both male and female.

Most of these names have been taken from the Tshi numerals, and Europeans are generally named from the day upon which they land in the colony. In many places, however, in addition to this nomenclature, the children are named after their parents or grandparents, the name of the latter preceding that of the former, while in all the pure Akra names of male and female children, the name of the father precedes that of the child. Thus Ayi Dede would mean the first daughter of Ayi.

In manner the Akras are quiet and unassuming, though somewhat difficult to govern, and when thoroughly roused hard to conquer. In the country districts the European is made welcome, a house is cleared on his arrival, and whatever the place affords is soon brought in for his use. The chief fetish of the Akras is water, to which it was usual for them to make an annual sacrifice. Every year a girl of twelve years of age was sacrificed to the sea, and at the present time it is their custom to visit the chief rivers and streams, to make their offering in the shape of food to the god that inhabits the water. The food is prepared on the banks, part thrown in and part eaten. Many of their customs strike the European as being very strange, found as they are in a land far from any other, where such rites are performed. In their early historical times the Akras were forbidden by their priests to touch human blood, and when blood was spilt by accident or design, the king and elders of the people made sacrifice by way of atonement for it, and the people causing it were fined in proportion. A kind of rude baptism of their children is also observed. A week after the birth of a child, when it is to receive its name, the father sends the best of his relations or friends into the house where the child and the mother are to bring it into the open, where his friends are assembled. The father then proceeds to throw some water over and upon the roof of the principal room of the family house, which is again caught in a calabash or dish used for the purpose, and thrown three times on the child, when it receives its name. Another universal practice among the Akras is that of circumcision, which is practised by all the Gá and Adangme-speaking tribes. By the natives this rite is called Keteafo, or shortening, which every male child from the age of six to ten years is made to undergo. Slaves are also subject to the same operation, and no uncircumcised person, from the king downwards, is allowed to enter the inner yard of the fetish priest's house, to witness any ceremony that is there being performed by him. Some people think, from this practice, that the Akra race obtained the rite from the Jews, but we must remember that these people derived the custom from Egypt, and that Egypt is in Africa, where the rite had perhaps been practised for centuries before the Jews went to Egypt. At the annual custom called the Homowo, corresponding to our harvest home, the door-posts are smeared with red clay, and all the differences between members of the family are amicably settled.

The following tradition is told of the origin of the Adangme or mother tribe of the Gá. It is said that the people of this tribe came from a country near the Niger called Sarne, situated between the two rivers Efa and Kpola, and were driven from their habitations by the continued hostility of their neighbours. These people, travelling southward past Dahomey, reached the river Volta at a point where it was easily fordable. Here they found a huge crocodile lying across the river fast asleep, which they used as a bridge, and which was made on this account a sacred animal by their fetish. After crossing the Volta the tribe divided; one part left for the coast and settling there formed the present Adangme country, while the remainder formed their habitations at the foot of the Krobo Mountain. The crocodile, leopard and hyena are sacred animals to these people to this day, neither are they allowed to touch gold or ivory, nor to have anything to do with human blood. Should a leopard, hyena, or crocodile be by accident killed, the same custom must be made as for a dead man.

The great festival of the Akras is the Yam custom, called by the Europeans the native or black Christmas. This is generally celebrated at the end of August or the beginning of September, from which time they date the commencement of their New Year. Before the first yam is eaten many ceremonies are performed; and then the feast begins. The fetish is the first to eat, followed by the king and his chiefs, and lastly the people. This custom is called in the native tongue Yereyelo. After the first custom follows the Homowo, when the yams are gathered, which means literally the "mocking of hunger," and which is the thanksgiving for the harvest. Each of these ceremonies furnishes the occasion for much gun-firing, music, dancing, singing, eating and drinking, but at Accra the excesses are not so great as in many towns in the interior. The Akras do not recognise a personal deity, attributing their highest power, which they call Nyonmo, to many events. The word means Almighty, but it is also used for the sky, rain, thunder and lightning. Throughout the whole of the Gold Coast, however, among the Tshi and Gá races there exists a belief in the transmigration of life, which takes the form of a spirit and animates all the actions of the individual. This spirit is known as the Okla or Okra of a person. It instigates him to actions (good or bad) while alive, and is supposed to inhabit another body after the first is dead. Every person is supposed to be attended during life by two such Oklas, a male and a female, the former for bad and the latter for good deeds. The word Okla means literally a sanctified boy, and many of the people of higher rank possessed a number of such boys, who attended them during life, and were sacrificed at their master's death, to be his companions in his next state. When a King of Ashanti died, his Oklas, to the number of 100 or more, were murdered on his tomb. During their master's life these attendants are distinguished by a large circle of gold suspended from the neck : many of them are favourite slaves, raised from the common people to this distinction, all of whom are glad to stake, as it were, their lives upon that of their master, during which time they are free from all palavers and supported by his bounty, to be sacrificed upon his tomb when he dies.

Children born with supernumerary fingers or toes were often strangled or burnt alive, and when several children had been lost by a family, the body of the last that died was often cast into the bush, and any deformity possessed by a subsequent child, whose body they believed to be the same as the one cast into the bush, was attributed to the bodily injuries that the dead child had received from the wild animals of the forest.

From the sea the town of Accra has a very imposing appearance, stretching along the sea-front from east to west for a distance of nearly three miles from the landing-place to Christiansborg Castle. The town itself is not continuous for the whole distance; James Town is first with its fort and signal station; Ussher Town, with its Dutch fort and its suburb, Victoriaborg, adjoins it, and then comes a stretch of green level country for a mile along the sea-shore, intervening between Victoriaborg and the castle and town of Christiansborg. Landing from the steamer is generally accomplished at the west of the town, near the Custom House, except in very bad weather, when a point farther east is generally selected, under the walls of James Fort. It is generally accomplished with ease compared to other parts of the coast: half an hour's paddling from the side of the steamer to the breakers, a rush through the breakers, generally on the crest of a wave, and the surf-boat touches the sand. Paddles are thrown overboard, the boys spring out, and carry the passengers pick-a-back to dry land. This costs a "dash" of five shillings, which is well laid out, for should there be any delay, the next wave generally swamps the boat. July, August and September are generally supposed to be the worst months for landing at Accra, but in most cases there is little more to risk than a wet jacket, unless the boatmen are at all careless, when danger may easily arise. A fairly steep bank of reddish earth or clay leads from the beach up to the Custom House and Post Office, and the visitor is in the main road of Accra. The impression from this point is not encouraging, the place giving one the idea of general bankruptcy. To the west of the landing-place and close to the edge of the cliff are the Postal and Telegraph Offices, with the Queen's Warehouse and the Public Works Yard hard by, whilst on the opposite side of the road are the old Treasury Buildings and the Custom House Offices. Behind these buildings lies James Town, a motley collection of native huts of all sizes, interspersed with the old ruins of many a past dwelling, and mixed indiscriminately with the newer stone buildings of modern times, that belong to the richer natives and traders. To the right or east of the landing-place the road widens and leads past the fort, leaving the large rectangular Wesleyan Chapel on the left, behind which are the present Government Schools accommodating about 1000 scholars, once the site of a French factory. Behind this are the Wesleyan Mission House and School, once the property of old Mr. Bannerman. From this point the main thoroughfare of the town is entered, which leads in a direct run of over two miles to Christiansborg. This is known as Otoo Street, the high street of the capital, along which are situated some of the principal trading houses of the town. Yates Brothers' well-known " Blue Front Store " is situated at the corner on the right, and tells the nationality of the hospitable and enterprising owners; the premises of Messrs. Chase & Nash are hard by, while innumerable native stores of F. & A. Swanzy, Alexander Miller & Co., and other well-known commercial houses line the street on either side.

Nearing Ussher Fort the road widens considerably, sloping down on the left hand to Ussher Town and the extensive market of Accra, known as Salaga Market, which is well supplied with native beef, mutton, fruits and vegetables. In this respect Accra is the best provisioned town on the coast. Continuing along this road almost due east, the recently opened premises of the Bank of British West Africa are upon the left, and almost opposite on the right, the store of the African Association. Next come the trading premises of the Basle Mission; the headquarters of the native police; Swanzy's house; and a two-storied structure, known as the "birdcage," supported by iron columns, and belonging to the African Direct Telegraph Company, which brings us to the eastern extremity of Ussher Town, and the commencement of its suburb, Victoriaborg. Between the Basle Mission premises and the above-mentioned "birdcage" is the beautiful English Church, built by the authority of the late Sir W. Brandford Griffith in 1895, under the able superintendence of Mr. Gubb, a gentleman sent from England to carry out the design and to superintend its construction. It is built entirely of stone quarried in the neighbourhood, and will stand as a lasting memorial of what can be accomplished by native labour in West Africa, when superintended by European patience, skill and industry. Almost opposite the church, but standing back a little from the main road, are the headquarters of the African Direct Telegraph Company, roomy and commodious premises standing in their own grounds. Victoriaborg is now entered; the native Haùsà quarters and parade ground are on the one side, and the Haùsà Native and European Hospitals on the other. The newly constructed Accra Club House and the Colonial Secretary's residence are next passed, one on either side of the road; the former sanctioned as a place of recreation for resident Europeans, by the Right Honourable the Secretary of State for the Colonies, in 1897, and the latter erected in the same year, as private quarters for the residential Colonial Secretary, F. M. Hodgson, Esq., C.M.G., now the Governor. To the left is the Secretariat, once European quarters, but now devoted to the official accommodation required by the various heads of departments in the service of the colony, while a branch Post Office, the new Treasury Buildings, the Government Printing Office and the new Bungalows, complete the chief places of interest in what is known as Victoriaborg. This part of Accra is now the principal residence of the officials of the town, some twenty bungalows having been erected at various spots in this locality during the past five years, to take the place of the previous quarters that were provided in the native parts of the town. It is impossible to over-estimate the benefits that have accrued from this change of residence, with regard to the health of the Government officials at Accra. Malaria still exists, but many of its most pernicious effects have disappeared. A walk or drive of rather more than a mile upon a good road brings us to Christiansborg, the late residence of the Governor and the headquarters of the Inspector-General of the Hausà Forces and his staff. On the road, lying back some distance to the left, is the cemetery, where many a European has found his final resting-place. It is now a well-ordered and well-kept enclosure, with double gateway and porch, over which is the somewhat ambiguous and mutilated scriptural quotation : " Here the wicked cease from troubling and the weary are at rest ". Why the first word is " Here " instead of

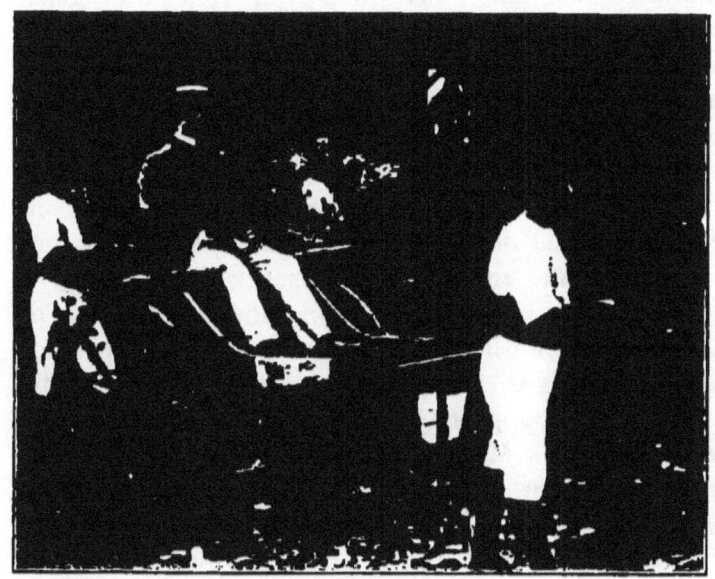

TOWN TRAVELLING IN ACCRA.

" Where " no one seems to know, except that from inspection, it seems there was not enough room for another letter, and the person who carved it possibly thought, that the omission of a letter would not much matter.

At the eastern extremity of Christiansborg, and at the

western end of Accra, are the usual lagoons so often found skirting the towns along the coast, and which contribute to their general unhealthiness. Christiansborg is the coast headquarters of the Basle Mission Society, where they have chapels, schools and workshops, in addition to spacious quarters for the residence of the European members of the Mission. The road from the port of Accra to Christiansborg is broad and hard, fit for wheeled traffic, and is continued from the latter place to Abokobi and Aburi, some fifteen and twenty-seven miles north from the coast. The country behind the capital is rolling grass land, rather thinly wooded and sparingly watered, stretching away to the horizon in a line of thin fading blue hills, the highlands of Aquapim and Akim, reaching to 2000 feet above the sea level. Herds of cattle now feed upon these grass lands, but birds and game are scarce. Horses, which die after a few months at other points along the coast, thrive at Accra, but do not live long when taken into the interior, possibly owing to the presence of the fatal tsetse fly, which, though supposed to exist, has not definitely been found to do so. Mules and asses would, I think, thrive in this neighbourhood, if the necessary care and attention could be ensured for them, from the hands of their native attendants, who ride them furiously at all times and seldom or never think of keeping them clean. The usual mode of travelling in Accra is by what is termed a "Go-cart," an illustration of which appears on page 201. These are entirely drawn by Kru boys.

Many Europeans and natives keep horses in Accra, and driving or riding is a common recreation after 5 P.M. An annual two days' race meeting is held just outside the town on the race course at Victoriaborg, and the only impediment to a good gallop over the open country round, is the presence of holes and the general unevenness of the ground. Tennis, polo, cricket and golf are also played from 5 to 6·30 every evening, and social life in Accra is made as enjoyable as possible.

The salt lagoon at the western end of the town runs far into the interior, but flows only during the rainy

A GROUP OF OFFICIALS AND MERCHANTS, AFTER WORK.

season, taking its rise not far from the historic battlefield of Dodowah. Its bed and banks are composed of fetid mud, the haunt of sand flies and mosquitoes, and though at one time a frequent promenade for residents of Accra, it is now deserted, except for the natives, who bathe *coram publico* in its muddy waters.

The native streets—alleys they should be called—are generally very dirty, containing the garbage thrown out from the huts, which crowd together on all sides; while dogs of very doubtful pedigree are common everywhere. Fortunately, the greater part of the native quarter of James Town and Ussher Town was destroyed by fire in 1895, and in the place of the previous overcrowded and ill-kept streets, spacious thoroughfares are now being provided, with properly constructed drains to carry off the water, well lighted with oil lamps, and with roads fit for wheeled traffic. In 1893 Otoo Street was about twelve feet wide, it is now as many yards.

Many of the Akras and also the Elminas are exceptionally good cooks, the men being much better than the women, which is often the case in uncivilised races. Some of the native dishes are particularly palatable, and far preferable to many of the badly cooked European foods that have been introduced. "Kankie" takes the place of bread, and is made from the flour of native corn, undergoing many operations before being boiled or roasted in plantain leaves and fit to eat. Many people prefer it to the sour English bread that is made on the coast, though this has considerably improved of late years. "Fou-fou" is a tenacious mass composed of yam, plantain or cassada, which is peeled, boiled and pounded and then made into large balls, to be served up with the various kinds of native soups, in place of the European potato. It is much like boiled batter pudding, but more tenacious, and is very savoury. Freshly baked flour cakes seasoned with the oil of the palm kernel are much relished by the natives, but are far too rich for the visitor. Fish and stews are well prepared, and turtle is good and plentiful during the Harmattan season, but not after March. The fish mostly eaten by the native is a kind of herring, which abounds in the Guinea Gulf in immense numbers, and which, when cured, is carried far into the interior beyond Ashanti. When these fish are opened, cleaned, stuffed with green pepper and fried in the freshest and purest palm oil, it is called "Kinnau," and forms an admirable food. "Palm-oil chop" is another favourite dish on the West Coast of Africa from Sierra Leone to the Congo, some Europeans being very fond of it. The ingredients are freshly made palm oil, meat or fowl, well peppered and served up in a native pot with freshly boiled yam or "fou-fou" or rice. It is the curry of Africa, but is too rich a dish for many people. A liqueur of cognac after such a meal generally prevents a recurrence of its flavour. "Ground-nut soup" is a general favourite with most people on the coast, which is prepared in much the same way and with the same ingredients as "palm-oil chop," but with finely-pounded ground-nuts instead of palm oil as the basis. Last, but not least, is the native "kickie," a compound of finely-minced fowls or fish, high flavoured, and served up with "fou-fou" in the Accra-made pots of black porous earth into which the pepper thoroughly sinks. It is somewhat like the West Indian "pepper pot," and is very tasty to the palate. The Accra fowls are poor and stringy, but good ducks and turkeys are supplied from Ada and Jella Kofi, near Kwitta. Mutton and beef are poor, but are improving in quality, and could be made very good if some enterprising native would only breed the animals, and feed them in a proper manner upon the grass lands at the back of the town. But such an undertaking requires too much energy from the hands of a native, though a fortune would soon be made from supplying the town and the numerous vessels that call here with good fresh meat. Fruits are plentiful; oranges, limes, bananas, pine-apples, mangoes, guavas, are always obtainable. The topical rains at Accra are light compared with those at Freetown, Sierra Leone. The annual average is about eighty inches. The best season for travelling into the interior is during the Harmattan, when it is very pleasant, but it is attended with little danger from November till the end of April or May.

Rude native gold work is done at Accra, which chiefly finds its outlet in the manufacture of the zodiac ring, which is worn by almost every one. Studs, brooches, watch chains and bracelets are also made from copied patterns, but the natives possess but little artistic merit of their own.

Accra possesses with Christiansborg some 20,000 inhabitants, and the whole Gá country some 100,000. The majority are engaged in fishing, though good carpenters and masons are to be found, while many are employed in petty trading. Education is making rapid strides, and there is no lack of native clerks for mercantile and official work. Though the seat of the headquarters of the Government, the trade of the town is not increasing; the chief imports are rum, gin, tobacco, cottons, provisions and building materials, while rubber, palm oil and kernels, gold dust and kola nuts form the bulk of the exports. Gold dust is exported in but small amounts from Accra, and comes from the Aquapim, Akim and Ashanti countries. Many tribes in the interior and on the sea-coast of this part of the colony regard gold as fetish property, which if they keep, would kill them. They will not, therefore, on any account, keep gold dust or even gold coin, or touch it. If they do, they immediately wipe their hands. They receive all gold coin in pieces of paper or cloth. This is particularly observable in the Krobo and Adangme countries.

The town of Christiansborg was bombarded in 1854 by H.M.S. *Scourge*, followed by an attack with a force of six English vessels to disperse a mutinous rising among the natives. Some four or five miles to the east of Teshi, the eastern boundary of the Gá country, stands a small black boulder on the beach, known as the Greenwich or Meridian Rock, marking the same meridian of longitude as that of Greenwich. Time in Accra is the same as in London, though there is a difference of 46° in the latitude.

CHAPTER VIII.

The Akim and Kwahu Countries—Begoro—Kyebi—Abetifi—The Akim Forests—The Tshi People—Manners and Customs—The Future of Akim—Native Traditions—Akwamu or Aquamboe.

THE Akim and Kwahu countries of the Gold Coast lie between 6° and 8° north latitude, and nearly 1° west longitude. Akim being the more important of the two, and situated nearer the coast, I shall describe that first. It is bounded on the north by the Kwahu (sometimes Okwahu) and the Kanaki countries, on the east by Krobo, on the west by Adansi and Ashanti, and on the south by Aquapim. It is often described as the hill land lying north-west of Accra, and the whole surface is occupied with a series of mountain ranges, in some places as high as 2000 feet, with the exception of a small portion in the south-east and in the west where the land is low. The Akim country is divided into Eastern and Western, the former having Kyebi or Kibbi, and the latter Insuaim, for its capital. For the most part, the towns and villages in this district are situated upon or near the tops of the hills, which perhaps accounts for its comparative healthiness for the residence of Europeans. The Basle missionaries, who have many important stations in this district, reside here for a period varying from four to seven years, without a visit to Europe, making it their home with their wives and children, though the latter are sent to Europe when they have reached the age of four or five years. The lower districts are not so well populated as the highlands, some of them, with the exception of a few hunters' huts, being totally uninhabited. In the old maps of the African continent its situation is marked Akim, famous for gold, a character it well deserves. The people, who fully know the value of their country, though they cannot themselves develop it, are most desirous that Europeans should visit it for this purpose. Their chief occupation is gold digging, and as late as 1863 two new rich deposits were discovered. It is a beautiful country, and would well repay the European botanist and geologist.

The King of Kyebi possesses more nugget gold than any other monarch in the Gold Coast, and the currency of the country is gold dust. The whole surface is well watered, the principal streams being the Birrim, the Densu, the Bompong and the Pompong with their various tributaries. None of these rivers are ever dry, receiving their supplies from the various mountain ranges, and being frequently swollen and overflowed when the rains are on. The Birrim is the longest of the four rivers I have mentioned, but not the widest. This river rises near the little village of Appapam, a short distance south-west of Kyebi, the capital of the district, and receives its source from a mountain in the neighbourhood, nearly 2000 feet high. It flows north-east past the capital, and then turns north-west as far as Enyinam, where it turns its course south-west and joins the Prah a short distance north-east of Prahsu, on the borders of Akim and Ashanti. The whole of the valley of the upper part of this river is honeycombed with native pits, where gold digging has been carried on; and alluvial washings are common on the outskirts of every town that lies near. In the dry season I have crossed the bed of the Birrim at Enyinam when the water was only knee deep, a bright, clear stream, with a clean, sandy bed, while at the same place in the rainy season it is transformed into a rushing, muddy river, ten feet deep, nearly twenty yards wide, and with a current running at the rate of four miles an hour. The whole course of the river is between ninety and one hundred miles.

The river Densu rises from the same mountain near the village of Appapam, but flows in an entirely opposite direction. Leaving Appapam it flows first south-east and then almost due south to the sea, emptying its waters some ten miles to the west of Accra. This river is known by different names to the natives at various parts of its course. It rises as the Densu, is known lower down as the Humo, and flows into the sea as the Sekoom at the place mentioned. It has no very large or important town upon its banks, the only point of interest passed being the Akim peak, an isolated mountain of 1000 feet, at about its middle distance from the source to the sea. The Bompong and the Pompong also rise together, but flow in opposite directions. The source of these two rivers is found near the villages Oseem and Tafo, at a point on the main route between Kukurantumi and Osino. The former flows south and becomes a tributary of the Densu, whilst the latter flows north-east and empties its waters in the Afram, which is itself a tributary of the Volta. None of the rivers I have mentioned are navigable except for small canoes, owing to the numerous waterfalls and shoals to be found at all parts of their courses, and consequently they are of no use as waterways for commerce. A capital water supply for Accra and its neighbourhood could be obtained from the river Densu.

The chief mountains in the Akim country are the Atiwa Range, extending from Apedwa in the south to Kwaben in the north, running north-east and south-west for a distance of some thirty miles, and forming a natural boundary between the eastern and western provinces. The slopes of these mountains are covered with the densest forests, which have never been explored, though probably they form the matrix of the gold supply of the Akim country. This range of mountains continues more or less through the Kwahu country farther north and on to Begoro in the north-east. The entire country of Akim is said to be highly auriferous, but the gold has never been worked in a proper manner, the natives contenting themselves with digging circular holes from sixteen to twenty feet deep, whence they obtain it in the shape of small nuggets and dust, the latter being abundant in the rivers and water-courses, where I have constantly seen the people washing for it. Red sandstone and quartz are abundant in every direction. The forest woods are numerous and valuable, many of the trees growing to an immense height and girth, and being of two kinds, red and white. The former are close-grained and heavy, and are used for all purposes, while the latter are soft, and of but little value for working purposes. The timber from these trees would form a very valuable article of export if any means of transport existed to the coast, and the large areas thus cleared could be devoted to the growth of coffee, cocoa, rice and tropical spices, and to the cultivation of the rubber vine and the tobacco plant. The industry of the natives is limited to their wants, and as these are few and easily satisfied, the amount of energy they put into the cultivation of their soil, and in fact into any kind of work, is in proportion to their daily requirements. The palm flourishes everywhere, and in places the tobacco plant has been found growing in wild luxuriance, in addition to fruits of many kinds, including the guava, mango, banana, plantain and pine-apple. Whenever cultivated, the orange grows in profusion and in excellence, particularly at the mission station of Begoro. In this neighbourhood, too, one of the most northerly parts of Akim, and some 1400 feet above the sea, are a great variety of rubber, gum and dye trees, all of which might with industry and care form the source of great wealth to the inhabitants. Kibbi or Kyebi is the chief town and capital of Eastern Akim, and the residence of the king. It is well elevated, being about 900 feet above the sea, at the southern extremity of the Atiwa Range, and is the centre of a large gold-bearing area.

Another very important town in the Akim country is Begoro, situated on its northern borders, at the same elevation, and almost surrounded by mountains of a higher altitude. It is a very picturesque and healthy station of the Basle Mission, an illustration of which will be found on page 214. Coffee is being cultivated with great success, and grows luxuriantly throughout the whole province. I have travelled the forest belt, that extends from Aburi, twenty-seven miles from the coast, to Abetifi, some 175 miles from the sea, four times up and down, and have been much surprised at the almost total absence of animal life. A few deer, leopards and monkeys are the only occupants of the thick bush that everywhere prevails, and these are seldom seen, and inaccessible to the hunter owing to the security of their haunts. Through this forest from south to north is a seven days' journey, and travelling through it is most monotonous and somewhat depressing. There is no road, but ever the same narrow, winding, tortuous path, bordered on either side by the dense tangled undergrowth of the bush, through which is seen the tall straight trunks of giant trees, whose lofty tops are lost in the mass of foliage overhead; the spaces between being filled in with depending and climbing plants of every description. But few flowers enliven the way; bright patches of glaring sunlight and dense banks of deep shade seem to struggle for the mastery, and owing to the dense shade, there is but little danger from the sun. Over stagnant pools of water, and occasionally across the path, a few gaudy butterflies flit to and fro in the gleams of sunlight, forming about the only relief for the eye, from the sombre dark green in which everything is endowed by nature. And all is still; save for the occasional call of a bird to its mate, or the wild harsh cry of the sloth, no sound is heard. Insect life is very plentiful, and the silence of the day somewhat compensated for, by the innumerable insect noises of the evening and night. On the higher lands of the forest the travelling is dry and comparatively easy, but sometimes the bush and undergrowth are so thick that what track there is is lost; and in the low-lying districts swamps are frequent, where the traveller can only progress by walking for hours through mud and water, poisoned by the noxious gases rising from the rapid decay of such an abundance of vegetable matter.

Immediately to the north of the Akim country lies the mountainous district of Kwahu or Okwahu, which in the native language means the top of a rock or top of the palm trees. This state has the Ashanti country as a western boundary, the river Volta on the east, while it joins Akim to the south and stretches in rolling

BASLE MISSION STATION, BEGORO.

grass lands far away to the north. The mountains of Akim are continued into Quahu, and reach their highest points at Abetifi and Obo. The former is 2000 feet above the sea level and the latter even higher, forming the source of the river Prah. From Begoro, the most northern town of Akim, to Abetifi is a three days' journey through the forest, and this latter place is one of the most inland stations of the Basle Mission Society. The country in the neighbourhood of Obo is auriferous, and many native workings may be seen at the foot of the hills and by the river beds. Nugget gold is reported to be plentiful, the chief of Bomen finding a nugget worth £23 as late as 1896. The chief alluvial gold districts in the Quahu country are Obeng, the residence of the king, Bomen, Obo, Ativi, Kwasiho and Akropong, much quartz being in evidence throughout the whole district, and I feel certain that when this part of the colony comes to be opened up, and suitable transport established, many rich mines will be found in the neighbourhood.

Abetifi lies a good four days' journey to the east of Kumasi in the same latitude, and has been the scene of many Ashanti invasions. The Akims gained their independence no less than eight times from their merciless conquerors, the Ashantis. The plains to the north of Abetifi are well watered by the Afram River and its tributaries, which flows eastward through the country and joins the Volta near Anum in the Peki country. The climate in these regions is humid throughout the year, and in the wet season much rain falls, making travelling next to impossible. The rain comes up soon after noonday, and descends in torrents, being generally ushered in by violent thunder and lightning of the most vivid description. Malaria is more prevalent during the rainy season, and mild attacks of fever are frequent. Epidemics of small-pox carry off the natives, sometimes clearing out whole villages, but from this dread disease the European seems to be quite safe. Guinea worm is also very common among the natives.

Western Akim is a densely-wooded country bordering Ashanti and Assin, and was until lately under the former power. One of the chief roads from Ashanti to Accra passes through Western Akim. It is poorly populated and its productions are very few. A Government school has lately been opened at its capital, Insuaim.

In appearance, the inhabitants of Akim are much the same as the other tribes upon the coast, differing but little in their habits, manners, language and religion from their surrounding neighbours. The men are of medium height, though of slighter build than the coast tribes, but they are capable of sustaining great exertion when they feel inclined, which is not very often. The women are shorter than the men and well formed, and perform most of the work that is done. They obtain the food supply, fetch the wood and water, and do most of the washing for gold, the proceeds from the sale of which are spent by the men in rum and tobacco. Their chief food is "fou-fou," a tenacious mass of boiled plantains or yams, beaten to the consistency of a thick batter by the aid of a little water, and immersed in a dish of pepper soup flavoured with a little dried fish, monkey's flesh, or a few snails. They are very fond of palm-oil food, but are seldom able to get it, as they are too lazy to cultivate the particular palm which provides this dainty dish. Roast plantains are also a favourite fare, and when cooked over a wood fire form an agreeable dish to a hungry traveller. I have tried both the "palm-oil chop," as it is called, and the roast plantains, which make a good substitute for bread, though a trifle sweet. Eggs, fowls, sheep and goats are plentiful throughout the country, except when native troops are passing through, when they will suddenly disappear, and all kinds of food are then difficult to obtain. The travelling native is, however, as bad as the native soldier in this respect. If he is hungry and sees food, he takes it, and if remonstrated with, his answer generally is: "No belong to any one; plenty food live; God send it". What answer can you make? I remember on one occasion when leaving a town in the Akim district, being presented by the chief with a parting present of a sheep, which was handed to one of my bearers to lead by a string to our next halting-place, when the day's march should be finished. When resting in the evening before taking my dinner, I heard a commotion in that part of the compound inhabited by my carriers and servants, and upon proceeding to inquire the cause, I found that my sheep of the morning had become two. On inquiry as to whom the other sheep belonged, I was informed that it was the property of my bearers, who could not tell me how they obtained it, but volunteered the statement that they "supposed it had followed my sheep because it wanted company". Some roadside village that we had passed in the day had one sheep the less to fold that night!

To show how completely the Akims were at one time under the power of the Ashantis and feared their displeasure, I will give but one instance. About 1742, when Osai Aquissa ruled over Ashanti and its tributary powers, the King of Akim desired to make war upon one of his near neighbours. Before he could do this, the consent of the Ashanti monarch was necessary, which was obtained by the promise of halving the spoil. The Akims went to war, but gained little or no spoil, and Osai Aquissa hearing of this demanded the head of the King of Akim for his want of success in the campaign.

When the Akim ruler heard of the demand, he summoned his chiefs and explained his fate to them, and desired to sacrifice his life in order to ensure peace for his kingdom. Report has it, that he and his chiefs had a barrel of powder brought for each to sit upon, and having drunk a large quantity of rum, they blew themselves up with the fire from their pipes, rather than suffer the resentment of the Ashanti ruler. This is recorded by Bowdich and also mentioned by Dr. Issert, who reports it as tradition from Akim.

The language of the Akims is a branch of the Akán tongue, the mother language of both the Ashanti and Fanti peoples. It is commonly called Tshi (pronounced Chwee), and is spoken by the Ashanti, Gaman, Tufel, Akim, Assin, Aquapim, Akwamu, Fanti, Wassaw and Ahanta peoples. For convenience the " Tshi " may be divided into two dialects—that spoken by the tribes in the north, and that spoken by the tribes in the south of the colony. This northern dialect is often called Akán, of which the Akim tongue is an example, while that of the south is called Fanti, which is spoken from Elmina to Winnebah. The people of Winnebah, though Fantis, speak in addition to their own tongue a dialect called Effutu, and from Half Assini to the Volta, no less than six different languages are spoken in a distance of 300 miles. The Akán excels the Fanti in purity, and that spoken by the people of Eastern Akim is considered to be the purest and best of the Akán tongue. There are variations in both languages common to particular tribes, but the principal difference between the Akán and the Fanti, is that the latter is the more sibilant language. In addition to the common language, the manners, customs, religious beliefs and traditions are similar throughout the tribes mentioned. Marriage customs are both curious and interesting. The Akims are, of course, like all other tribes on the coast, polygamists, and the richer the man, the more wives he has. When a man takes a wife she does not receive a dowry from her parents, but the applicant pays a sum for her to her parents, varying from £5 to £15 in gold dust, in addition to presents of cloth and libations of rum. The one exception to this general rule is, that the chief of a district can demand the daughter of any man in his district as a wife without the usual payments, and often when a king ascends the stool or native throne, he takes over with it the principal wives of his predecessor. Another peculiar exception is, that the daughter of the so-called royal family in any of the Tshi tribes can bestow herself upon any man, and he must accept the gift on pain of death. Should a daughter of the king choose a man from the common people for her husband, she at once raises him by her action to her own status, and he is made a chief. This does not prevent him from having other wives, but should his princess wife object to any he may already have or selects afterwards, she can compel him to send the objectionable ones away, on penalty of death. Princesses have also the privilege of divorcing their husbands without any investigation; they simply have to present them with a piece of white chalk or clay, which is a token of dismissal. The common people must, however, have their cases tried before the chiefs, and if a divorce be granted to the woman, the amount the man paid for her is retained by her family, and she is presented with a piece of white clay, with which she proceeds to mark the trees in the principal street of her town, to show that she is no longer a wife. Should, however, the divorce be granted to the man, the amount paid to the wife's relatives for her must be returned in full to the man.

The greatest custom, however, of the Tshi-speaking people, is the yam custom. This is annual, and is held just before that vegetable arrives at maturity. The yams are planted in December, and are not eaten till the conclusion of the custom at the end of the following September. All chiefs and headmen of the towns and villages are expected to appear with their noisy retinues at the capital of the king, and none are excused. If a chief or headman has offended, or if his fidelity is suspected, he is seldom accused or punished until the yam custom, which they attend frequently quite unconscious, and always uncertain of what may be laid to their charge. This yam custom is a regular saturnalia, neither theft, intrigue nor assault is punishable during its continuance: the grossest liberty is allowed to prevail, and each sex abandons itself to its passions. The festivals are two in number, one held in December at the planting, and the second held in September at the gathering. This second lasts a fortnight, and is commenced by a loud beating of drums. On the fifth day the king eats new yams, but the people are not allowed to do so until the end of the festivals. They are really religious thanksgivings to the gods for the crop of yams, but were made into political customs by the Ashantis. The first and fifth days were days of fasting, but any amount of drink could be consumed during the whole time. This was served out by the chiefs. On the fifth day a human sacrifice was made to the souls of departed kings, whilst the eighth day was further marked by another public distribution of liquor. On the days between those mentioned, and until the close of the custom, other ceremonies, such as sprinkling with water, processions to their gods, bathing in the nearest stream, making sacrifices at the yam plantation, in order that some of the fresh blood might run into the ground, were religiously observed.

Other national customs are the Adaï, by which time is counted, the New Year of the Tshi people beginning on the 1st of October. The Adaï customs are two in number, known respectively as the great and the little Adaï. The former always occurs on a Sunday and the latter on a Wednesday, and six weeks are allowed to elapse between each great Adaï and the same between each little Adaï, with a period of twenty-one days between the two customs. All the festivals of these people are occasions for immoderate drinking, general license, uproarious noise, beating of drums and firing of muskets, commencing at sunrise and continuing the whole day and far into the night.

The customs of these people at a birth, marriage or death are worthy of notice. When a Tshi woman finds herself to be with child, she commemorates the event by an offering to the particular deity that presides over her house, the priestess of whom binds her neck, wrists and ankles with fetish charms made of black and white beads, in order to bring good fortune with the event. As the time for the birth of the child draws near, the woman usually leaves her husband's house and proceeds to that of her mother or some near female relation, in order that she may receive whatever advice and assistance may be necessary on the birth of the child. This operation is generally accomplished while the woman is seated on the ordinary stool, where she is surrounded by her female friends, relations and visitors, who would look with scorn upon her did she dare to utter any cry of pain during her period of labour. This being over, the child is at once named from the day of the week upon which it is born, washed and bound round the neck, ankles and wrists with strings of beads, like the mother, to bring it good fortune. After this ceremony is over, the mother is not allowed to do any work of a domestic nature for seven days, when she again takes her place and proceeds with her daily work. At the expiration of three months more offerings are made to the family god, and the mother, with her child, pays a round of visits to her friends and neighbours, accompanied with a band of females, singing and dancing by the way in honour of her safe delivery. Generally on the eighth day after the birth of the child, the father proceeds with a number of his friends to the house where the mother and child are staying to see his newly-born offspring. Arrived there, they seat themselves in front of the entrance : the child is brought to the father and handed round. Thanks are given to the fetish, and often a second name is bestowed upon it by the father, after some particular friend or deceased relative, and a little spirit is squirted from the father's mouth into the face of the child. The second name thus given to the child is always used after the first, and the pouring of some spirit upon the ground completes the ceremony. As the Tshi names are different from the Akra, I give a full list of them, male and female.

Day of Week.	Male Name.	Female Name.
Sunday	Kwasi	Akosúa
Monday	Cudjo	Adwoa
Tuesday	Kwábina	Abiena
Wednesday	Kwako	Akudea
Thursday	Kwáo	Yá
Friday	Kofi	Afuá
Saturday	Kwámina	Amma

Strangers on the coast are named from the day upon which they arrive. The people, too, are fond of giving nicknames to the Europeans with whom they come in contact, from some peculiarity that they notice concerning them, generally from some fact about their personal appearance, as a bald head, for instance.

Bosman states that as soon as a child is born, and the priest has consecrated it, if above the common rank it has three names bestowed upon it, though it is always called by one. The first name given to it is that of the day of the week on which it was born; the second, if a son, is his grandfather's name, and if a girl, her grandmother's name, though this is not strictly observed by the natives, some of them giving their own name or that of some friend or relation. After this their names increase with their years, for should any one behave valiantly in a fight or by killing a wild beast, he is generally given a new name for the deed.

In past times if the mother succumbed in giving birth to her child, and the child survived, it was customary to bury the child with the mother, and in the Ahanta country it was a law for the tenth child of the same mother to be buried alive, and the mother separated from her husband for the space of a whole year, living quite by herself in a separate hut, and being supplied with the daily necessaries of life. In many parts of the country the women, when their custom is upon them, are compelled to retire from the towns to some shelter in the plantations or in the bush, and in Ahanta, on the same occasions, the women are prohibited from entering any inhabited place under penalty of heavy fines and other punishment. The better classes generally have a hut or house in the bush to which their females retire, but the poorer classes are forced to suffer the inclemencies of the weather without any shelter. Fortunately, with the advance of civilisation all such customs are dying out, particularly in the parts nearer the coast, and many of those connected with the sacrifice of, or affecting, human life no longer exist. Marriage among these people is a question of physical fitness rather than of age, and when a girl has arrived at her eleventh or twelfth year she is considered capable of entering the married state. At this age maturity is reached, and the girl is taken by her friends to the nearest water-side and washed, and an offering to the gods is made upon the banks of the stream, consisting of mashed yam and palm oil, to thank them that the girl has arrived at a marriageable age. After the washing in the stream is complete, a bracelet of black and white beads and gold is placed round the girl's wrist, and where this is not procurable the body is simply marked with white lines. Physical development alone is often deemed by the natives to be sufficient evidence of a girl's fitness for the married state, and this being satisfactory, and the previous ceremony complete, she is most carefully dressed and paraded through the town in order to notify that she has reached the age when she can be married. All the finery in the way of gaudy cloths and gold ornaments that the family possesses is used for the occasion, and when there is none, it is frequently borrowed for the occasion. A silk cloth takes the place of the ordinary cotton one, tied with a silk handkerchief round the waist, leaving the upper parts of the body quite bare. Her hair is made up into some fantastic design according to the fashion of her country, and head, neck, arms and ankles are plentifully adorned with gold ornaments. Her skin shines like ebony, and she is perfumed with scents that only native nostrils can appreciate. Thus attired she is paraded through the streets of her town or village attended by a number of young girls, who chant a song in her praise. This is a public notice that she is of a marriageable age, and if not already betrothed, such a display seldom fails to bring forward a number of suitors for her hand. The favoured one makes his offer to the girl's parents, which, if accepted, is at once paid over, and the bridegroom prepares his wedding feast. Presents for the bride and for her family and relations are bestowed by the future husband, and a plentiful supply of liquor and tobacco provided for the ceremony, according to the financial position of the bridegroom. All preparations being made, on a given day the bride is led to the house of the bridegroom, and the two families join in a feast which lasts long after the couple have become man and wife. Next day the husband shows his satisfaction concerning his wife by anointing her head, shoulders and the upper parts of her body with a powder of fine white clay, and sends her again through the streets accompanied by her friends, who sing in her honour. Should, however, the husband have fault to find, he can obtain a release from his wife according to his country's law. On the coast the character of the bride is made most public, for part of the husband's present to her family being a flask of rum, and that being not sent until the next day, the condition of this, whether quite full or somewhat wanting, is held to denote the condition of purity in which he received his newly made wife from her family. Some of their funeral customs are as strange as those relating to birth and marriage. Loud shouts and cries announce the death of a person, and the females of the house parade the streets with disordered clothing and unkempt hair, uttering the most mournful cries, and making known the fact to all the people living in the neighbourhood of the deceased person. Almost immediately after death the corpse is washed and then dressed in its richest cloths, and ornamented with more or less profusion of gold and beads, according to the rank of the deceased. When this is done, it is either allowed to repose upon a couch, as if asleep, or is supported in a sitting position upon the native stool, to receive the last visits from friends, relations and neighbours. During this time the whole place is crowded with people, mostly women, who in turn approach the corpse and alternately sing its praises, or reproach it for having left them and the good things of the world behind. The noise is astounding, and the greater the person the louder and more continued the noise. A dish of the food most favoured during its lifetime is placed before the corpse, and the body is surrounded by the most valuable articles that were possessed by the deceased. The men seldom or never enter the room where the body lies, but sit outside smoking and drinking and receiving the donations of gin, rum, tobacco and gunpowder, that come pouring in from all persons who were known to the departed, and who have come to do honour to his remains. Each party that arrives notifies its approach by the firing of guns, shouts and cries and the beating of drums. It is difficult to say whence the practice arose of firing guns at a burial, but it is common all over the colony, and is also practised upon all the holidays and festivals. It is part of West African nature; nothing can be done without noise. The period between death and burial is a time of fasting for all relatives so far as food is concerned, but the same abstinence is not observed with regard to drink, the result being, at the actual interment of the body, by far the majority of the mourners are in a state of semi or complete intoxication. In many towns upon the death of a chief or person of importance, a fast is proclaimed through the district, which is kept for two or three days, only roast plantains and fruits being allowed to be eaten. The time permitted to elapse between death and burial is seldom allowed to exceed three days, more commonly it lasts but one, but the length of the custom depends upon the rank of the deceased. In all towns along the coast and in the southern part of the colony it has long been the practice to bury the body in a grave dug under the floor of one of the rooms of the house, possibly on account of the wealth that was often buried with it. This custom is now forbidden by law for sanitary reasons, and churchyards have been formed outside most of the large towns. The time for interment having arrived, the body is placed in a rough coffin, made large enough to contain the articles that are buried with the corpse.

Should it be a person of some rank and wealth, silk handkerchiefs and cloths, sandals and pipes are interred with the body, which is adorned with bracelets and anklets of gold and aggrey beads, and sometimes even powdered over with gold dust. These buried treasures form a source of wealth to the family in later days, and are drawn upon when necessity arises, often by the sons of the deceased. A quantity of spirits, generally rum, food and tobacco are also included for the use of the departed and his shade on their long journey to the unknown land. After the grave has been filled in, a sacrifice of fowls, sheep or goats is made, the last salutes are fired and the day ends in a general drunken orgie, which is continued for some time in accordance with the wealth of the family. The head is often completely shaved by the nearer relations of the departed, and the widows seldom leave the house for some weeks after the funeral, particularly if the burial has been performed inside the walls. They sit and watch the grave, taking little or no food, and being generally in a most disorderly and untidy condition. Thanks are sent round to all those people who assisted in any way at the funeral rites, and great debts are often incurred by the poorer people in order to ensure an imposing ceremony for their lost relative. The Ashantis and other people in the north bury their dead outside their houses, but the rites described are common to most of the Tshi-speaking tribes.

The same native traditions are common among these people, some of which are worthy of record. The first, relating to their own origin, is interesting. All the Tshi-speaking people are supposed to have come from a far country behind Salaga. This was an open, flat, grass country, plentifully supplied with oxen, sheep and goats, and to this country came another race, a red people, supposed to be the Fulas. These new-comers, being stronger than the original inhabitants, took from them their cattle and their women, and generally made slaves of the people, until the natives, to avoid such depredations, began to go away into the bush lands farther to the south and west. Here, in the forests, they were secure from their strange oppressors, and villages, far away from their own land, were secretly formed, secure from the attacks of their invaders, who many times attempted to force them back as slaves in their own country. The numbers of the runaways gradually increased, and, as they grew and multiplied, they extended their habitations farther and farther through the forests to the south, until the sea was reached. The sight of this thundering along the shore much startled them, and they called it in their native tongue, " boiling water that was not hot ". This appears to be a likely explanation of the emigration of the Tshi-speaking people into the Gold Coast, though many years must have elapsed for them to have become so numerous and to have been broken up into the many different tribes in which they are now found. In the map forming the preface to *A New Account of Guinea*, published in London in 1734, and written by Captain William Snelgrave, the country to the north of the Gold Coast is marked, " Foule Guiallon, or the original country of the Foules," which would go to prove that the Fulas inhabited the country that the Tshis describe, and that the latter were driven south by the former. The Tshis state that when they reached the sea-board, the country was uninhabited, but this could hardly be, as traces of an older language than the Tshi are found to this day at several points along the coast, notably at Winnebah, where a dialect is spoken known as Effutu, previously described in an earlier chapter.

A second tradition that exists concerns the origin of the names Ashanti and Fanti, and is explained in the following way : In the times long ago, when the Fantis and the Ashantis were one people, possibly before the migration of the Tshis to the coast, before mentioned, and whilst engaged in war with some more inland northern race, their provisions failed them, and they were reduced to the verge of starvation. In this difficulty they agreed to save themselves by separating, and to wander in different directions in search of food. The one party discovered and subsisted themselves upon a plant they found growing to the south of their own country termed "Fan," which word, together with the verb "didi," to eat, formed the origin of the present word "Fanti," the eaters of the plant fan, a kind of cabbage. The other section of the tribe discovered a plant they called "Shan" or "San," and coupling it with the same verb "didi," formed the present word Shanti or Santi, now called Ashanti. Hence the origin of the two names.

Palm wine is the national drink of the country, and its discovery is related in the following manner : The Fantis were once marching through the forest, headed by a very famous hunter called Ansah, who was accompanied by his dog. One day when out hunting, the dog led him to a fallen palm tree, which had been uprooted by an elephant, and a great hole bored in it by his trunk in order to enable him to drink the juice. The hunter noticed that the sap was still flowing from the hole in the fallen tree, but being afraid of tasting it himself, gave some to his dog, and next day, finding that the animal had suffered no ill-effects from the experiment, he returned to the forest and drank a great quantity of the juice himself. Its pleasantness induced him to take more than he should have done; he became intoxicated, and lay in the forest in a drunken sleep until the next day, much to the alarm of his followers, who thought he was lost or had been captured by an enemy. On coming to his senses again he resolved to take some of the sap to the king, and filling an earthen pot he conveyed it to the king's house and explained its origin and its effects. The king, anxious to test the truth of his story, drank too freely of the juice and was soon reduced to a similar state of inebriety as the hunter had been the day before, and slept soundly. The people, thinking Ansah had poisoned his king, killed him in their rage before he had time to explain. In time the king recovered his senses, and hearing what had been done to Ansah, ordered his executioners to be put to death, and in honour of the hunter named the new drink "ansah," now "ensa," and in order to distinguish it from the rum imported, which was also called "ensa," the word "fufu," meaning white, was added to it, so that "fufu ensa" now means palm wine, and the story related is supposed to account for its discovery. The natives in all parts of the colony consume great quantities of it at all times of the day.

Local tradition also asserts that the villages of Mouri and Asabu were founded by two giants, Amamfi, who had his sister with him, and Kwagia, who, with a large number of their followers and attendants, came out of the sea to live upon the dry land, and after journeying for some days, alighted upon a part of the beach between Anamaboe and Cape Coast. The two leaders, Amamfi and Kwagia, had reached dry land attended by a host of followers, when they were seen by a hunter, who, clapping his hands, exclaimed, "What a number!" and immediately all those who had not completely emerged from the water were turned into stone, and their bodies, in the shape of a reef of rocks, may be still seen stretching far out into the sea. Amamfi and his sister and Kwagia travelled on until they reached the Iron Hill, and descending to the road at the base, they parted, Amamfi and his sister turning to the interior and founding the village of Asabu or Assibo, while Kwagia took the beach road, until he arrived upon a headland which he considered a good place for fishing, where he founded the present Mouri, having cleared away all the bush in six days with the help of his followers. From this, Kwagia is said to be the father of fishermen, and Amamfi is called the father of agriculture, the latter using a billhook so large, that it took six bars of iron to make it, and the point of it, which by some means became broken off and was found in the bush, contained enough iron to make six ordinary articles of the same kind. It is further reported that Amamfi came to visit Kwagia at Mouri every Friday, and on this account no plantation work is done on that day. The Fantis who already inhabited the country around Asabu, looked upon Amamfi as an intruder, with the result that many encounters took place between Amamfi and his followers and the Fantis, which always ended in a victory for the former, on account of the great strength of their leader. The latter, however, determined to make one more effort to regain their country, and after consultation with their fetish, introduced a certain creeping plant into Amamfi's country, with the result that Amamfi and his chiefs were attacked with guinea-worm, and unable to fight in the battle that ensued, they retired again to the sea. From this arose the following saying in the country: "Amamfi fears nothing so much as guinea-worm".

Another tradition accounts for the rocks situated in the sea by Ussher Town, Accra. A prince coming from the sea was to be selected from Accra to rule over Akim, and two men were sent forward to spy out the land. They had to run a race, and the first who saw the land was to claim it for his master. The race began, and the Accra messenger, being outstripped, called to the other to help him to remove a thorn that had entered his foot. The Tshi man stopped, and said, "How came a thorn upon this rock?" but willing to help his companion, he stooped down to get his knife to lend to the Akra, whereupon the latter jumped over his shoulders and exclaimed, "It is I who first saw the land". Immediately the two messengers were turned to stone and became the twin rocks on the beach, behind the Basle Mission Factory at James Town, Accra. Still a further tradition is told to account for the Tshi village at the foot of the Akim Peak (1000 feet). A noble woman in the interior was loved by two princes, who agreed to cast lots as to which should ask for her hand. This was done, but the unsuccessful one called upon her one night and carried her away. The name of this prince was Akwamu, which afterwards became the name of that tribe and kingdom. After travelling for six weeks they took refuge with the King of Accra, for whom the husband worked as a servant. They had two children, a son and a daughter, and in course of time obtained the grant of a piece of land from the king and built on it their own village, some four or five miles away, leaving their son at the court of the king to be trained. This prince was called Akwamu. Akwamu, being a Tshi, soon managed to collect a number of fugitives around him, and in the space of fifty years formed the present small state, Nyanawan, at the foot of the Akim Peak, though still remaining under the King of Accra.

CHAPTER IX.

The Aquapim, Adangme, Awoonah, Krobo and Akwamu Countries—Their Peoples—Pram Pram—Ada and Kwitta—Krepi—Peki—The Volta River—Anglo-French Convention, 1898.

IMMEDIATELY to the north and north-west of Accra lies the small mountainous country of Aquapim or Akwapim, the hills of which can be distinctly seen from the coast, and which forms one of the healthiest of the inland territories.

This country is supposed to have received its name from the King of Akwamu or Aquamboe, who once ruled over this part of the colony and named it from the number of its inhabitants. The name means literally, "the thousand subjects". This country has Accra on the south, Akim on the north and west, and Krobo and Adangme on the east. The origin of the people inhabiting this region is involved in much doubt. Some of their towns are certainly now peopled by the descendants of refugees from Akim, but the majority of their settlements contain a mixture of the original inhabitants mixed with other invading tribes. When the southern kingdom of Accra was destroyed by the Aquamboes in the middle of the seventeenth century, the whole of the present Aquapim country came under the power of that nation, and remained tributary to them for many years. Before this time the country contained nearly a hundred well-populated and flourishing towns, but after their defeat the people seem to have been scattered in all directions, to be united again under the Akim prince Safori, the reported founder of the capital, Akropong. This would be early in the eighteenth century. In these days the Aquapim people were not united under one common king, but each town recognised a separate ruler, among whom quarrelling was very frequent. From their uniting, under Safori, again into a common race, nine rulers can be traced, according to native traditions, in the short space of about forty-five years, from 1734 to 1778. The people at this time seem to have been very poor, possessing neither gold, money, nor cloth to wear, which last deficiency they remedied by beating out the bark of a certain tree to make the necessary cloth for their loins.

The country now contains some twenty important towns, the chief of which are Berekuso, Aburi, Mampong, Akropong and Latè, in addition to many villages of varying size and population. The inhabitants make good farmers, and are active and industrious, speaking the Tshi language in addition to the Gá. Palm oil, a little gold dust and coffee, which latter grows here to perfection, are among their chief productions, while the surface of the whole country is diversified and well wooded and watered. The town of Akropong, some thirty-nine miles north-east of Accra, is the capital of the kingdom and the residence of the king. It stands on a ridge of the Aquapim Mountains some 1440 feet above the sea level. The present king, Quamina Fori, speaks English well, and tries to improve his country to the best of his ability, but I am afraid some of his tribes are very troublesome, owing to the power of the fetish that still remains among the people. This capital is one of the most important stations of the Basle Mission, where they have an excellent church and three schools, in which both English and the vernacular are taught, in addition to plantation work and general industrial subjects. The coffee plantations round Akropong are among the best in the colony, though the native is often too apt to think, that after having once planted his coffee it needs no further attention. A regular postal service exists between this town and Accra, which is continued to the Volta River.

The people of the capital seem to do little or no work, the latter for preference, but there is much drinking of palm wine, beating of drums, playing the native game of Warri and gambling for shells, by spinning beans upon a mat spread on the ground. This latter game seems to have earned the English name of "marbles," but I could not discover its native title. Any number of players can join in this game, sitting in a circle with the mat spread in the centre. A stake is fixed upon by the players, and the beans are set spinning, and the person whose bean knocks out most of the others, when all are set spinning, is declared the winner.

A moonlight night in a large inland town such as this is a time to be avoided, particularly if after a long march, the traveller desires to sleep. From moonrise to midnight, and sometimes long after, the whole place is made hideous with the noise of tom-toms, drums, mouth organs, bells, sticks beaten on each other, and in fact the knocking together of any two substances that will make a noise (the louder the better), which is vigorously accompanied by song and dance. The King of Akropong boasts a town band, with big drum, side drums, fifes and a bugle, upon which English tunes are done to death in many and various keys. Each member of this band vies with his neighbour to play the loudest, and as the big drum, when vigorously handled, can speak for itself in this respect, it is generally an easy victor in the production of sound, and covers (like charity) a multitude of sins in the way of false notes committed by the other players. The players themselves are dressed as gorgeously as possible, in the colour or colours (and garments) that each fancies, while the conductor smokes a pipe when beating time, which is generally in a different measure to that in which the band is playing. When at Akropong in 1897, the band turned out two nights in my honour, but on the third I sent them to my nearest European neighbours, the Basle Mission. The members of the band are insensible alike to praise or ridicule, and whatever one says, is taken as a compliment, and forms the signal for louder and more continuous playing. Every event is seized upon by these people for "making play" as they term it, a birth, a marriage or a death, it is all the same for them.

The road from Accra to this capital is an excellent one, passing near Abokobi, through Aburi to Akropong. It is wide and well kept, fit for wheeled traffic for the greater part of its distance, and was, I believe, first constructed by the missionaries, at a cost of something under £1000. From Accra to Abokobi is about sixteen miles, over a flat and slightly undulating country. The soil is sandy and produces little more than tall rank grass, with here and there small clumps of stunted bushes, affording no shade to the traveller. No place of importance is passed on the way, except the little village of Akokomi, near which runs the small Dakobi River. This stream is fed by the water from the Aquapim Hills, and partly from the overflow of the Ashongmang spring, which rises in the neighbourhood. According to local tradition this spring has a very interesting origin, and from the analysis of its water by Dr. Fisch, of the Basle Mission at Aburi, contains about 1 per cent. of Epsom salt in solution, thus furnishing a free and moderately aperient drink for the natives. Those who drink of its waters are said to live long. Jacob Owoo, a native member of the Basle Mission, is credited with having dug this well many years ago. Previous to this another spring existed some ten minutes' walk from the present well, but the heathens of the neighbourhood forbade the Christian members of the congregation to drink of its waters, and so Jacob Owoo and the elders of the mission dug their own. This seems to have diverted the water from the original spring, for it rapidly dried up and left the heathens without water. To this day neither Christian nor heathen is allowed to draw water from the Ashongmang well on Mondays. The town of Abokobi lies about a mile to the west off the main road to Aburi. It is very hot and dry, being shut in on the north and west by the surrounding hills, which are of quartz formation and are said to contain gold. Leggong Hill is one of these, and also the hills between Abokobi and Berekuso. An assay of some of the weathered stones taken indiscriminately from the slopes of the former hill gave 16 grains of gold to the ton, while those taken from the latter place gave 1 dwt. 6 grains to the ton. This surely points to the presence of gold reefs in the neighbourhood.

The word Abokobi is apparently a mixture of the Tshi and Gá languages. "Abo" means in Tshi a rock, while "Ko" in Gá means bush, and "Bi" means child. Thus the word means "rock bush child". To explain this, tradition says, a rock of ironstone exists a short distance from the hills round, in which is a large hole which fills with water after rain, and into this hole a child fell and was lost, hence, child in the rock of the bush, from which the town was named. The people of Abokobi are generally very superstitious, and believe in many fabled monsters that inhabit the country round, some of which are so tall, that only the branches of the trees will serve them for a seat.

Excellent dwellings, school and church have been established here by the Basle Mission, and in the mission gardens the date-palm, the vanilla and castor-oil trees flourish, while the mahogany, coffee and orange promise well in the surrounding neighbourhood.

From Abokobi a by-path leads into the main road again to Teimang, after from thirty to forty minutes' easy walk, where as a rule a cool, comfortable rest can be obtained at the so-called Hotel Provençal, a house belonging to the chief native of the place. Teimang means Tei's Town, and is seventeen miles from Accra by the main road. From here to Aburi is a three hours' journey, along a good road until the foot of the mountain is reached, which is continued after a thirty minutes' climb right into the town, some twenty-seven miles from the coast and 1400 feet above the sea. Its elevated position ensures it a certain immunity from the malarial vapours of the low-lying coast, and the town is considered to be, in consequence, better suited to the health of Europeans. The Government has established an excellent sanatorium at this place, attached to which are the botanical gardens, where experiments in the cultivation of tropical agriculture are carried on under the superintendence of a Curator from Kew Gardens, for the benefit of the natives of the colony. Coffee, both Arabian and Liberian, grows here in profusion, and cocoa also flourishes well. Both the Basle Mission and Wesleyan Societies have stations at Aburi, and much good has been done by them in the

BASE OF A BIG TREE, BOTANICAL GARDENS, ABURI.

neighbourhood. Some flint axe heads have recently been found here. From the verandah of the sanatorium, the white roofs of Accra, the sea and the passing steamers are clearly visible during the fine weather. All the roads from Aburi to the surrounding places of importance are more or less mountainous and very rocky, quartz being abundant everywhere. The one exception to this, is the road to Akropong, which continues upon the ridge of the mountains until the latter place is reached, and which may be described, for its whole distance of about eleven miles, as a fairly good road.

Less than two hours' journey south-east of Akropong stands the important town of Latè, sometimes written Lateh or Daté, upon another distinct range of hills. Though under the rule of the Aquapim king, the Latè people are distinct in speech and in many of their customs from the other inhabitants of the Aquapim country. The Aquapims generally speak Tshi; the Latès and their branches have a distinct language called Cheripong. The road to Latè leads down the mountain behind the present Basle Mission premises, across the valley at the base and up to the top of another range, quite distinct from that upon which Akropong stands. The ascent to the town is very steep and rocky, and much quartz is to be found in every direction. When near the top, the road divides left and right, the one leading to the Basle Mission Station and the other to the Wesleyan headquarters, both of which have important schools in the town. An assay of the stones picked up in the former road showed 12 grains of gold to the ton, while those from the latter gave 16 grains. Some pieces, however, broken from the immense boulders which are everywhere to be found in the streets, showed visible gold upon their broken surfaces, and upon assay, gave 16 dwt. to the ton. These rocks are in the streets of the town upon the top of a mountain some 1400 feet high, and only a seven hours' journey from the coast at Pram Pram. The native houses are nearly all built of stone, but the people reject the quartz as being too hard to work. It is, I believe, the first time that gold has been discovered in this neighbourhood, and the people little know that from the dirty, discoloured stones that they reject, the engineer and the chemist can extract the pure yellow gold that all civilised nations strive to obtain. I will give two further instances from the stones collected on this journey. Some taken from the river bed at Akropong gave upon assay 20 grains to the ton, and others from the stream at Abonsi, some two and a half hours away from Latè, yielded at the rate of 2 dwt. of gold per ton of quartz. Surely there must exist in this neighbourhood some important gold-bearing reefs of quartz, for it must be remembered that the evidences quoted were all taken from the surface of the ground, composed of stones that have been exposed to the weather for very many years.

The origin of the Adangme people has already been described, and the country now occupied by their descendants extends from the Ponni Village, the eastern extremity of the Gold Goast in early times, to the Volta River; the most important towns are Pram Pram and Ada. The former is situated some twenty-one miles from Accra, and three miles east of the Ponni River and Village. This little river is of small importance. It rises in the Aquapim Mountains, with several feeders between Aburi and Akropong, nearly disappears in the dry season and is of no use for transport purposes. The town of Pram Pram stands upon elevated ground close to the sea, and contains the remains of old Fort Vernon, built by the English about 1700, and now the residence of the District Commissioner, in addition to supplying accommodation for the various Government offices. It has a comparatively healthy situation, contains about

2500 inhabitants and is divided into an upper and a lower town. Large quantities of palm oil and kernels are exported from this place, which does a very considerable trade with the interior towns. Dodowah is the most important of these, where an immense market is held twice a week, attended by native traders from all parts of this division of the colony. It is situated in the centre of a rich oil-yielding district, and contains considerably over 1000 inhabitants. The most important places on the coast are Temma and Ningo, situated respectively west and east about the same distance from Pram Pram. The inhabitants are mostly engaged in fishing, and in the collection of salt, which is transported and sold in the interior. At Ningo was the Danish fort of Fredensborg, built by the Danes somewhere between 1735 and 1741, but which is now a mass of tangled bush and ruins. The whole country from here to Ada at the mouth of the Volta, is a low-lying marshy district, with a sea-board of about forty miles, upon which breaks the most terrible surf to be found at any point along the coast. The shore is fringed for its entire length by enormous groves of the cocoa-nut palm, separated at intervals by clumps of low bushes and scrub. The Volta River forms the eastern and northern boundary of this district, which during the rainy season has more than half its area under water, forming a vast shallow lagoon, separated from the sea by a narrow elevated belt of sand, varying from two hundred yards to two miles in width. In the dry season the waters of this lagoon are evaporated, leaving behind a thin deposit of salt, which is collected by the inhabitants and sold in the interior. On account of its situation, the whole district is very thinly populated, the natives either congregating in the villages upon the sea-shore or in the towns upon the right bank of the Volta. The town of Ada is situated at the mouth of the Volta River upon its right bank, and contains the remains of Fort Kongenstein, belonging to the Danes in 1784, but which was ceded, with the other Danish possessions on the coast, to the English in 1850. Ada is the residence of a District Commissioner, and contains about 1000 people, engaged in a considerable export trade at the hands of the English, American, French and German factories. The Basle Mission has established a small school and church at this port. The town is not considered healthy for the residence of Europeans.

Four miles up the river, on its right bank, stands Big Ada, a town of much more importance than the one at its mouth. It has a population of about 8000 people, the majority of whom are engaged in the collection of palm oil and kernels from the surrounding districts of Krobo, Krepi and Akwamu, and transporting them down the river to the port at its mouth. The quantity thus obtained and exported from Ada, amounts to no less than nearly one third of the total produce of these commodities from the whole colony. Steam launches are employed in bringing down the puncheons of palm oil to the mouth of the river, and a "tow" often consists of more than one hundred such puncheons, the kernels being brought down in canoes and bar-boats. The Basle and Wesleyan Missions have centres at Big Ada, and many of the inhabitants are engaged in the cultivation of the pine-apple and the rearing of ducks. By boat from the riverside Ada to Big Ada is a pleasant passage of about one hour, and should the river be at all low, good sport can be had on the way with the alligators lying asleep in the sun upon the muddy banks, and up the numerous creeks which are to be found at all points. At certain seasons of the year the mosquitoes are very troublesome in this district, particularly at Ada. Only once, I think, have the Ashantis troubled this waterside port, and that was in 1807, when they carried away the big bell from the fort as a trophy to Kumasi. It has, I believe, since been recovered, and, as far as my memory serves me, is now in the possession of the Basle Mission.

The province of Awoonah is the most eastern coast territory in the Gold Coast of the present day, extending from the Volta River to the German boundary of Togoland, at Afflao, a distance of some fifty miles along the shore, and inland, at its greatest width for about forty miles. The general aspect of this large stretch of country is very similar to that of Adangme, the greater part of the low-lying territory near the sea-shore being covered by the Kwitta or Awoonah Lagoon, and its various branches. Throughout its whole length, this lagoon is separated from the sea by a very narrow strip of sandy soil, which at times, after very heavy rains in the interior, is broken through by the great weight of water behind, which thus finds its way to the sea. During the dry season the water from a very large portion of its surface is completely evaporated, leaving behind a bed of black mud covered with tiny shells, from which the most noxious odours are emitted. This exposure of the black fetid mud to the fierce rays of a tropical sun causes the most unwholesome vapours to rise, that render the district a very unhealthy one for Europeans, and consequently the death-rate in this district is high. At one time the lagoon was directly fed by the waters of the Volta River, by means of a canal cut from its left bank opposite the town of Agravi, which kept it always full. This canal, however, has since been closed by the natives, owing to some dispute, with the result that the town of Kwitta is made practically uninhabitable for more than half the year, from the poisonous smells that are emitted owing to the shallowness of the water, which seriously reduces the value of the lagoon for transport purposes.

The present fort of Kwitta was originally a Danish settlement, known as Fort Prindenstein, and built by the Danes in 1784. It was ceded to England in 1850 with the rest of the Danish forts for the sum of £10,000, and is now the residence of the District Commissioner and the officer commanding a detachment of Hausà Forces. The town of Kwitta is long and straggling, but there are a few good native houses in the place in addition to those belonging to the mercantile firms. At the western extremity of the town are the quarters, church and schools of the Roman Catholic Mission, which exerts a great influence over the people in the district for some considerable distance, each village near Kwitta being provided with its chapel and school. The inhabitants are mostly engaged in the catching and the curing of fish, and in the preparation of salt from the shallow lagoons which everywhere abound. Some of the best native cloth to be obtained in the colony is woven in the Awoonah district, and excellent bricks are made by the boys of the Roman Catholic School. The Bremen Mission has also schools in Kwitta and its immediate neighbourhood. The population of the place is about 2000, but larger towns are to be found a short distance in the interior. The most important of these are Awoonah (2500), Agbosome (3000) and Jella Kofi (2000). A large and gradually increasing trade is being done at Kwitta, vast quantities of palm oil, kernels, rubber and copra being exported to the chief European and American ports. A market is held in the town twice every week, which attracts the natives from all the adjacent towns and villages. Sugar-cane and ground-nuts grow plentifully in this part of the colony.

To the north of Adangme and Aquapim and south of Akwamu lies the small country of Krobo, close to the right bank of the Volta, a country notorious until most recent times for the human sacrifices carried on within its borders. It is a well-populated district, and the bulk of the people are now industriously employed in plantation work, particularly in the growing of coffee, which finds a good market at Hamburg. This district contains some large and very important towns, the chief of which are Odumase, Sra, Kpong and Akuse, the last being the residence of the District Commissioner, and situated upon the right bank of the Volta, a short distance south of Kpong. A range of mountains from the Aquapim country traverses the Krobo district from south-west to north-east, and isolated peaks are dotted about the country. The chief of these are the Krobo Mountain, 1000 feet; Mount Yogaga, 1200 feet; Mount Noyo, 1400 feet, and Mount Lovolo. The town of Odumase, the residence of the king and an important station of the Basle Mission, is almost surrounded by mountains, which causes it to be very hot until evening, when the land breeze sets in with great regularity about five o'clock. The population of this town is nearly 2000, and the town itself is very clean and somewhat picturesque, with good roads running in all directions. Quite close are the towns of Sra and Somanya, both large and populous, and famous for their weekly markets.

The Krobo Mountain lies about mid-way between Odumase and Akuse, rising abruptly from the plain to a height of about 1000 feet, and quite inaccessible except from one side. On this mountain were the villages of the Krobos, once the home of the worst fetish in the colony. For many years the inhabitants were under the power of the people of Aquapim, who ill-treated them upon every available occasion, it being a law that every Krobo who was found alone in the bush should be the property of the finder and sold as a slave. The Krobos themselves were very fond of capturing individuals in the forest, and killing them in order to obtain their skulls for the annual festivals of their traditional fetishes Kotokro and Nadu, whose homes were in the mountain.

By degrees these people extended themselves from the mountain, and began to form settlements in the bush near their plantations, where they constructed rough sheds for their habitations, with two openings, one in front and one behind. This was done for the following reason: Often but one Krobo would be left in the hamlet or village, the others being at work on the plantations, and when he took his meal, he would drop pieces of food round the dish to make it appear that more than one person had been eating. Should a stranger pass and speak to him, the Krobo would not understand, but pointing to the crumbs on the ground, he would intimate by signs that his friends were near and he would call them if desired. To do this he would step inside his hut by the one door and out again by the other, and soon be lost to sight in the bush, so afraid would he be of being captured by any one who spoke with him. The power of the Krobo fetish was completely broken in 1893, when the ringleaders were hanged for making human sacrifice.

The Krobo district is generally considered to be the richest part of the colony for the production of palm oil, consisting as it does of an immense plain covered with palm trees, which often shade the roads on both sides. The people are industrous in the manufacture of the palm oil, and the Basle Mission has made great progress among them in the way of education and agricultural pursuits. The whole currency of the country is cowry shells, though English silver is now accepted all through the district. Gold is fetish to these people, and on no account will they touch it with the hands unless through their cloth; should they do so the hands are immediately washed to cleanse them. A rich man will possess a house full of cowry shells, which are also often buried in the earth. It is supposed that there are large deposits of gold in the Krobo country, which for generations have been held as sacred by the inhabitants, and which, when found, are again returned to the earth. The sand in the bed of the Okoi river yields gold when panned, and the country round is held to be of an auriferous nature.

The Krobos are not a warlike people, and when attacked or in danger, they ascend the Krobo Mountain, a natural fortress which would defy the ascent of an army. They are a wild and superstitious, but not a dangerous people. The men dress in much the same fashion as the other natives of the coast, but the women and girls are, for the most part, often naked and are very well formed. The port of the Krobo country is Kpong or Pong, an important town on the right bank of the Volta, engaged principally in the export of the palm oil to the river's mouth. The Basle Mission and the Wesleyans have schools in this district, and the people speak both the Gá and the Adangme tongues.

The present country of Akwamu, or the Aquamboe of early times, is situated to the north of Krobo, on both banks of the Volta. It is not of very large extent, nor is it now of very great importance. It is mountainous and but thinly populated, though at one time powerful enough to subdue the Aquapim, Krobo and Accra countries. The people are brave, and a short time ago were not included in the British Protectorate, on account of their constant intrigues with the coast tribes. Both the Gá and Adangme languages are spoken throughout the district, and the elements of English and the vernacular are now being taught in the schools. Government ferries exist at Senki and Akwamu on the river Volta, the latter being the chief town of the district. In the early eighteenth century the Aquamboe natives are described as being very haughty, arrogant and warlike, their power being very terrible to all the neighbouring countries, except Akim, with the people of which they were constantly at war. It would appear that the Akims assumed a sort of feudal right over the Aquamboes, to which the latter would not submit, though frequently paying an annual tribute to ensure peace for a time. Aquamboe at this time included the whole of the Accra country, where English, Dutch and Danes held forts, each of which had its adjacent village lying under the walls. The general name given to these settlements was Accra, which, says Bosman, " was formerly a kingdom whose inhabitants were conquered by the Aquamboeans, and driven to a place called Little Popo, which at present contains the remainder of the great kingdom of Accra ". The people were then so rich in slaves and gold, that this country possessed greater wealth than most of the other divisions of the colony put together.

An excellent trade road now exists from Accra through Aburi, Akropong, Odumase, Pong, Akwamu, to Anum in the Peki country, the most north-eastern limit of the colony. Krepi or Creppee is now included in the German territory of Togoland, and is a well-cultivated and fairly extensive country on the left bank of the Volta, and including the old Argotime country. Though in German territory the Basle Mission has some stations in the country, the chief of which is Bismarcksburg, some miles south-east of Salaga. Previous to the delimitation of the Anglo-German boundary to the east of the colony in 1890, Krepi was included in the Protectorate of the Gold Coast.

The inhabitants are said to be very industrious, smelting their own iron and collecting large quantities of cotton, which are shipped from the coast towns. The old country of Argotime, which formed a part of the Krepi country, was inhabited by a very brave and energetic people, very much resembling the Krobo people upon the western side of the Volta. They build their towns and villages among the groves of cocoa-nut trees, which everywhere abound, and which partly conceal them from the traveller. The people are supposed to consist of emigrants from the coast neighbourhood of Ningo, Shai and Ada, who left their own country more than one hundred years ago to settle in these regions, but who have no connection with the people of Little Popo, who also migrated from the Shai plains and the Gá country. The language of the country is the same as the coast territory of Adangme, but by so much and such constant intercourse with the neighbouring tribes in customs and intermarriage, they are rapidly acquiring the language of the surrounding people. The inhabitants are very industrious, and in every town and village are to be found cotton spinners, weavers and dyers. A peculiar feature of their towns and villages is said to be the central shaded streets, forming a spacious shed as it were, which is used as the market-place. The branches of the trees along the sides of the main street are drawn together at the top, and propped up by sticks to form a shady arch over the whole.

Immediately to the west of Krepi and bordering the left bank of the Volta, is the small country of Peki, a narrow strip running almost due north and south for some forty miles, by eight to twenty wide. Very few Europeans have visited this part of the colony, and consequently but little is known about it. It is a well-watered and mountainous country, and in the neighbourhood of Anum very picturesque. The chief towns are Boso and Anum, the latter standing 800 feet above the sea, and commanding a fine view of the upper and lower reaches of the Volta, and its tributary the Afram, which joins the former nearly opposite the town. Anum stands on a mountain in the midst of mountains on all sides but the north-west, where the land falls away in rolling grass lands as far as the eye can reach, across the Afram plain to Kwahu, a distance of nearly 100 miles. The town is an important station of the Basle Mission, containing commodious quarters, and an excellent chapel and schools. The town was visited by the Ashantis about 1870; the mission station was captured, and the residents, the Rev. Mr. and Mrs. Ramseyer and Mr. Kühne, taken away to Kumasi, where they were detained for nearly four years. The district round Anum might well be called the Switzerland of Africa, for at no other spot in the colony are such beautiful views to be obtained. It is a comparatively healthy district and should be the residence of a District Commissioner, who should control this part of the colony. Before this can be done a suitable residence should be provided. An experiment in this direction was tried in 1897, but failed for some reason, and I believe the idea of a resident has been dropped. The district is also known by the name of British Krepi.

The Volta, or as the natives call it, the Atirri River, is by far the largest stream in the Gold Coast, though very little is known definitely about it. This important river is generally supposed to take its rise in the highlands near the Kong country, far away to the north of the Gold Coast, near the twelfth parallel of northern latitude, and to be composed of three separate branches rising at a considerable distance from each other, and known as the Black, White and Red Volta. The Black Volta is the most western stream, rising in the Grunshi country; the White Volta forms the central waters, flowing south from the Moshi country, where it joins the first some thirty miles west of Salaga, while the third arm comes from the Gurma territory and joins the waters of the other two at a point some thirty miles south of Salaga, from which the main stream flows almost due south into the Gulf of Guinea. From Salaga to the sea its course must be about 140 miles, while its total length cannot fall below 400 miles, even if it is not considerably more. For the lower part of its course it flows almost due south, and forms part of the eastern boundary of the Gold Coast. Its most important tributary in the Gold Coast is the Afram, which rises to the north of the Ashanti country, and flowing south-east falls into the Volta almost opposite Anum. The whole of the upper course of this large river is reported to be much impeded for navigation by the presence of cataracts, rocks and rapids, though in many parts it is extremely wide, while for the last sixty or seventy miles it is navigable for steam launches and bar-boats down to the river's mouth at Ada. The bar at the mouth is very dangerous, and though there are channels by which boats may enter with safety, they are always changing their situation, and causing navigation at its mouth to be very uncertain. The depth of water in the river varies according to the season; it is highest in September and lowest in May.

Colonel Starrenburg of Elmina travelled for some sixty miles up the Volta, accompanied by a Danish officer, and still found the channel three to four fathoms deep, and reported the channel between the breakers at its mouth to be about a mile wide. Dalzel mentions that an American brig made good her passage over the bar, and a Danish schooner has also done the same, but of late years the passage has been very seldom attempted on account of the shifting nature of the bar.

From Ada to Salaga is considered to be a fifteen days' journey, eleven by water and then four by land. Another account says: From May to December the water is good to drink, being then higher than the sea; in the other months it is not so, but then it produces more fish. The river overflows in July and August, and the neighbourhood of its banks is excellent for the cultivation of rice. Three miles from the sea is an island called Bird Island, full of pelicans of peculiar kinds, and a fish is caught in the river, which when smoked is very similar to European salmon. There are also hippopotami and crocodiles, while quantities of oysters adhere to the mangroves which everywhere fringe the banks. Monkeys and singing birds are reported plentiful, and a species of nightingale, which sings only in May and December. A kind of cedar is found along its banks, which shoots up many branches from the ground, about as thick as a pipe, and quite destitute of leaves; this tree is so very salt in its nature, that in the morning a great quantity of liquid salt is found upon its leaves, which crystallises in the course of the day. A plant of this class and order is also found in the province of St. Jago in Chili. Some forty-eight miles from its mouth is the island of Amalfee, the inhabitants of which, with those of Agravi and many other riverside towns, call themselves river inhabitants, who acted in the past as the chief brokers of slaves for the people of the Krepi and the Argotime countries. In Bosman's map the river is marked as the Rio Volta, emptying into the sea at Ponni Village, the then eastern boundary of the Gold Coast, while in Captain William Snelgrave's *New Account of Some Parts of Guinea*, 1734, it receives its correct situation. By travellers along the coast, the Volta mouth is crossed from a point called Riverside on the right bank, to the Custom station of Attititi on the left, a distance of five or six miles, and a pull of from forty to fifty minutes, which at times is attended with some danger when near

THE VOLTA RIVER.   257

the bar and the surf is bad, and a native canoe the only transport available. The mouth of this important river has recently been thoroughly surveyed by the Colonial Office authorities, with a view of opening the estuary to ordinary navigation, to which, I am afraid, almost insurmountable obstacles bar the way. A better solution of the difficulty would be found in the construction of a railway from Kpong on the right bank of the Volta to Accra, and a landing stage at the latter place.

This brings us to the close of the description of the various coast and inland territories that comprise the Gold Coast Colony and Protectorate, with the exception of the Ashanti country and the recently added interior provinces. The former has played so important a part in the history of the Gold Coast from the year 1700 down to the present time, that its rise and fall must be given in their entirety, in the two following chapters while the present may be closed with an epitome of the general products of the eastern part of the colony.

The resources of the whole of this district between the Prah and the Volta are vast and extensive, and require only to be developed. The country provides a number of exportable plants not to be found in any abundance in other parts of the coast; the soil is rich and fertile, and would facilitate the growth of many articles rapidly and luxuriantly. The Volta River might be used to bring down the riches of the interior, and an impetus be given to the export of gold dust, palm oil, monkey skins, gum, copal and cotton. As previously stated, the amount of gold dust now exported from Accra is small, but this could be considerably increased by the opening up and the working of the mines in Eastern and Western Akim. Before this can be accomplished several difficulties must be overcome, particularly with regard to the foolish superstitions of the natives. The people in the gold districts are very much prejudiced against having any one who wears European clothes, or who can read or write in English, in the gold-bearing districts. They are afraid of the gold being worked by civilised people, and make their religion the excuse for doing so. They insist that their fetish forbids any white man, or for the matter of that, any black man in white man's clothes, to go near or find out the real source of their native mines. Nor will they dig too deep for fear of the gold running away, and the result is that many extensive gold fields of the country remain undeveloped. This is not only true in Akim, but in all the gold-bearing parts of the colony. Civilised organisation and proper machinery must be introduced to successfully work the mines, and suitable means of transport from the coast must be provided by the construction of roads, available at all seasons for wheeled traffic.

A good road is the first development that must be undertaken; money, engineering science and English energy will do the rest. One illustration of the native opposition will serve to show how true their superstition is, with regard to the working of gold by educated persons. It is reported that a Mr. Thomas Hughes, an intelligent native of Cape Coast, commenced mining operations in the sixties in the rich gold fields of Western Wassaw. Being promised support by the local government, he imported expensive machinery for the purpose, and after much difficulty had it transported by the natives to the locality selected, and commenced mining. Within a short distance from the surface, his miners came upon a thin stratum containing gold, which presently increased to a fine rich vein. When this was discovered, although residing only a few yards from his diggings, he was forbidden by the king to again go near them, as it was against the commands of the fetish. Mr. Hughes was compelled to obey, on the alternative of instant expulsion from that part of the country. This, however, came in due course, for no sooner was it known of his discovery of a good vein of gold-bearing rock, and that he was likely to succeed, than he and his people were told to leave the country, and his machinery was destroyed. Ebony is supposed to exist in the forests of the interior, and timber trees are very plentiful. The Rev. J. A. B. Horton says: "From considering and examining the geological structure of the eastern district, I am under the impression that there are extensive coal fields in the interior of the country and in Dahomey, and this view is confirmed by circumstantial evidence. When the rainy season is very severe, and the streams of the Volta swell up and become very rapid, large masses of coal have been known to be brought down from the interior and left upon its banks. The last seen was at a place called Kpong, in the Krobo country."

"Seven years ago, while examining the shells of this part of the coast, I was forcibly struck with their resemblance and identity with those on the coast of Brazil. The geological structure of the two countries is almost identical. These facts lead me to believe that when the resources of the country are much more developed, diamonds will be found, not only in the eastern district but also in the rivers and lagoons of Awoonah and Dahomey. I made fruitless searches myself while stationed at Kwitta and Ada, but it is my firm belief in years to come, all things being equal, and development progressive, the diamond will ultimately be one of the exportable articles."

Others in addition to Mr. Horton hold this belief, and Burton and Cameron report that in a small mining concession near Ahema or Huma, in the west, a crystal was found, which was strongly suspected of being a diamond. They say : " It was taken to Axim, where its glass-cutting properties were proved. Unfortunately during one of these trials the setting gave way, and the stone fell into a heap of rubbish, where it could not be found. Many have suspected that these regions will prove diamantiferous."

The Hinterland of the Gold Coast Colony has now been satisfactorily settled with France, and according to the Anglo-French Convention of the present year the following basis of agreement has been determined upon. The boundary line which has been accepted as a prolongation of the frontier between the Gold Coast (British) and the Ivory Coast (French) takes the upper courses of the river Volta as the most convenient dividing line and cedes a slice of the theoretic Hinterland of the Gold Coast Colony to France. The friendly departure which has been made from our academic claim gives the towns of Bona and Dawkita, lately the scene of the heroic exploits of Lieutenant Henderson, and now in the occupation of British troops, to France. These are the only points upon the map which Great Britain will be called upon to evacuate. The French will evacuate Wa and all other points to the east of the river Volta and south of the eleventh parallel, but

France obtains, north of the eleventh parallel, the concession of the extensive, healthy, and valuable territory of Mossi, for which Great Britain receives no equivalent. The new boundary, after following the eleventh parallel in an eastward direction along the northern frontier of Mamprusi, is deflected northwards to include Bawku, and has the appearance of ending without cause east of the Greenwich meridian. As a matter of fact, it comes in contact at that point with the boundary lately defined by the Franco-German agreement to mark the limits of French and German territory in that district. The boundary as now defined between ourselves and France carries the northern frontier of the Gold Coast to German territory. It will be a matter for future negotiation between ourselves and Germany to determine the line which shall be definitely drawn between German and British territory from the point at which the Anglo-German frontier of the Gold Coast and Togoland ceases on the eighth parallel to a point at which it shall meet the Anglo-French boundary defined under the present convention.[1]

[1] From the weekly edition of the *Times*, 4th June, 1898.

CHAPTER X.

The Kingdom of Ashanti—Its People—Origin—History—Dwaben —The Capital, Kumasi—Wars down to 1817—The Town— Constitution and Laws—Roads from Kumasi.

AUTHENTIC records concerning the early history of the Ashanti people are very difficult to obtain even from tradition, for among the Ashantis it was made a capital punishment to speak either of the life or the death of their King, so that very little information is to be gained even from the natives themselves. With some it is a common and generally accepted tradition that the Ashantis were once a more waterside people than at present, and that they migrated towards the interior, conquering the Inta people and some lesser tribes on their way, finally settling in the country we know as Ashanti somewhere about 1700, and founding the two important towns of Kumasi and Dwaben. This West African power has thus lasted for a little less than two centuries, bowing, in its turn, to the civilisation of Western Europe. By some it is stated, that the Ashantis went from the country behind the present Winnebah, from the banks of the river Ainsu, and that the town of Croomadie to be found there was their original settlement. But this is not a likely solution of the difficulty. Among the Ashanti, Fanti, Wassaw, Akim, Assin and Aquapim people it is a general belief, that they were forced from the interior by a stronger people towards the water side, and therefore we may suppose this movement to have been anterior to the migration to the interior previously mentioned. The present arts, manners, customs and languages of the tribes just enumerated, all go to prove that the people composing them were at one time from a common stock; this common stock being a family of some twelve tribes, already described in an earlier part of this book. For the purpose, however, of tracing the history of these people for the past two centuries, it will be sufficient to state, that about the beginning of the eighteenth century, there was a large movement of the Ashanti people towards their present capital, Kumasi, which it is reported they commenced to build in 1700. What history they previously possessed is entirely lost, for the first mention of these people to Europeans was made by Barbot and Bosman about the year 1700 in their descriptions of the Coast of Guinea.

This early migration from their previous locality, and settling down with Kumasi as the chief town, is assumed to have been conducted by their leader, Osai Tootoo, who, assisted by the superstitious encouragements of his priests, conducted the people to their present country, conquered many tribes on the way, commenced the building of Kumasi, was made king as a reward, and received the stool from the people. From this time begins what might be called an authentic record, and the establishment of the so-called Ashanti aristocracy. On the accession of Osai Tootoo to the stool, one of his first acts was to consolidate his own position, by at once passing a law making the king and his descendants exempt from capital punishment, and creating an aristocracy composed of his peers and associates.

In all the Ashanti history from this date, a sister tribe, known as the Dwabens, has always played a very important part, and it is recorded that this sister kingdom, which existed until very recently, was founded by a relative of Osai Tootoo, named Boitinne, about the same time; the latter choosing for his centre the already existing town of Dwaben or Jabin, some twenty miles east and a little north of the proposed site for Kumasi. These two chiefs were sons of sisters, and it is supposed that when this change of locality took place, the tribe over which Boitinne had charge was the stronger of the two, and was thus able to secure for its centre an already existing town, leaving Osai Tootoo to build his own at Kumasi. However this may have been, we find that the inhabitants of the two towns became firm allies in war, and equal sharers in spoil and conquest from 1700 until very recent times. This common interest remained undisturbed for more than a century, the two tribes subordinating all other interests, to that of one great policy of increase of territory and power, at the expense of all surrounding tribes.

From the establishment of Osai Tootoo and his followers at Kumasi, the latter became the head of the military power of his adherents. He caused his most important chiefs to build large towns near the capital, bestowing upon them titular dignity, and conciliating the conquered people by making them tributary to his own, and checking any attempt to revolt, by exacting their frequent attendance at the capital on the occasion of all political festivities and native customs. The despotic

THE ROAD TO KUMASI.

power and the military prerogative were invested in the king, but his chiefs and aristocracy controlled all legislative and judicial power, in addition to the management of the common business of the state. It was only upon very extraordinary occasions that a full assembly of the king and chiefs was required.

During his reign Osai Tootoo commenced the building of Kumasi, defeated the Akims and Assins, conquered the Tufel country, and subdued all the small states in the immediate vicinity of the capital. Denkira was next attacked, the king of which was assisted by the then Dutch Governor-General, with a few Europeans and some guns. They could not, however, stand against the Ashantis; the guns were captured and were to be seen as late as 1817, as trophies in the streets of Kumasi. The following account of this destruction of Denkira is given by Bosman :—

"Dinkira, elevated by its great riches and power, became so arrogant that it looked on all other natives with a contemptible eye, esteeming them no more than its slaves, which rendered it the object of their common hatred, each impatiently wishing its downfall, though no nation was so hardy as to attack it, till the King of Ashanti, injured and affronted by its governor, adventured to avenge himself on this nation in a signal manner. The occasion of this was that the King of Dinkira, a young prince whose valour had become the admiration of all the natives of the coast, sent some of his wives to compliment Zay (Osai), the King of Ashanti, who not only received and entertained them very civilly, but sent them back with several very considerable presents to express his obliging appreciation of the grateful embassy.

And being resolved to return his obligation, he some time after sent some of his wives to compliment the King of Dinkira, and assure him of the great esteem he had for his person. These ambassadresses were not less splendidly treated at Dinkira, being also loaded with presents; but the king cast a wanton eye upon one of them, and gratified his brutal desire; after which he suffered her to return with the rest to their country and their injured husband, who was informed of this affront. But he took care to make the King of Dinkira sensible that he would not rest till he had washed away the scandal in his injurious blood. After he was made sensible of the King of Ashanti's resolution, knowing very well with whom he had to deal, the King of Dinkira offered several hundred marks of gold to compensate for the injury. The enraged king, deaf to all such offers, prepared himself for a vigorous war, by raising a strong army to make a descent on Dinkira, and not being sufficiently stored with gunpowder, he bought up great quantities on the coast. The Dinkiras were foolish enough to assist him themselves, suffering his subjects to pass with it uninterruptedly through their country, notwithstanding they knew very well it was only designed for their own destruction. While he was making these preparations, the King of Dinkira died, which might encourage a belief that the impending cloud of war would blow over. Whether the governors of Dinkira were too haughty to implore a peace of the injured Osai, or being instigated by the enemies of that country, is uncertain, for he still persisted in his purpose of utterly extirpating the Dinkiras. And about the beginning of the present year (1750), being completely ready, he came with a terrible army into the field; and engaging the Dinkiras he defeated them, and fighting them a second time he again defeated them. The natives report that in these two battles, more than 100,000 men were killed, and that the natives of Akim, who came to assist the Dinkiras, lost some 30,000 men, in addition to one of their great captains and his whole following. The plunder after this victory took the Ashantis fifteen days to collect, the king's booty alone amounting to several thousand marks in gold, which is affirmed by one of our European officers, who was in the Ashanti camp and saw the treasure. Thus you see the towering pride of Dinkira in ashes, they being now forced to fly before those whom they not long before thought no better than their slaves, and themselves being now sold as slaves."

Osai Tootoo did not live long enough to complete the building of Kumasi. He met his death about 1720 in the following tragic manner. He had declared war against Atoä, a small district between Assin and Akim, and invaded the country. The King of Atoä, well knowing he could not stand against so formidable a force as the Ashantis could put in the field, spread his small army through the bush until he reached the rear of the Ashanti force. Here they found the king leisurely following the main body of his army with a few followers only, all of whom were destroyed by the Atoäs, who shot the king in his hammock. This event happened near a place called Cormantee, and on a Saturday, from which arose the most solemn oath of the Ashanti people, *Meminda Cormantee* or by *Saturday and Cormantee*. Since that day it is reported that Saturday is regarded by the Ashantis as fatal, and no enterprise has since been undertaken on that day of the week.

Osai Opookoo, brother of the former king, succeeded to the stool about 1720, and had there been no brother to succeed, the sister's son would have been the heir to the right of succession; this extraordinary rule of succession, which excludes all children but those of a sister, is founded upon the argument, that if the wives of the sons are faithless, the blood of the family is entirely lost in the offspring, but should the daughters of the royal family deceive their husbands, it is still in part preserved on one side. A nice distinction truly, and one showing the morality of Western Africa. Throughout the Ashanti race property descends to the sister's son, and with the exception of the king, titles only descend to the son of the deceased.

Osai or Sai was the family name of the Ashanti royalty, being shared by some of the family as well, in the same way that Innane was the family name of the kings of Dagwumba. Osai Opookoo continued and finished building the town of Kumasi, and made approaches to the King of Dahomey for union with that monarch, who refused alliance, possibly because he was more despotic and refused to allow his subjects the same freedom, that was then enjoyed by the Ashantis.

The next effort of this potentate was the invasion and subjugation of the powerful Gaman country, of which Bontuko was the capital. Abo, the King of Gaman, hearing of the approach of the Ashantis, retreated north towards the Kong plains, followed by the Ashanti army. The King of Kong interfered, and refusing to allow a struggle in his territory, compelled Abo to return and fight his adversary upon his own ground. The King of Gaman was defeated, and purchased peace from the Ashantis by the immediate present of a large sum of gold and the promise of an annual tribute. This latter consisted of a payment of 100 periguins, equal to a sum of £900 sterling, in addition to all large pieces of rock gold (nuggets) found in the Gaman country. From this period Gaman became tributary to the Ashanti power. The province of Takima, whence the Fantis are supposed to have migrated, was next invaded, and this invasion is said to have been the cause of the establishment of the Fantis near the coast at Gomoah, behind Winnebah. These people, rather than submit to the cruelties perpetrated by their conquerors, left their own territory and sought a more peaceful home farther south. Their annual tribute was fixed at 500 slaves, 200 cows, 400 sheep, 400 cotton cloths, 200 silk and cotton cloths, being exempt from a gold payment on account of that commodity not being found in their country.

The powerful Akim tribe was the next to suffer defeat and become tributary to Osai Opookoo. Not only were they taxed in gold according to the number of crooms in their country, but being from this time a conquered people, they were compelled to deliver to the Ashantis the monthly notes which they held from the English, Danish and Dutch for their forts in Accra. These notes, or books as they were often called, have played a very important part on many occasions in early West African history, and it is a pity that they are all now lost or destroyed, because from them an interesting history could be gained. A note or book was a certificate of a monthly pension from the African

Committee of a set sum in gold dust, paid to the Fanti chiefs and kings who resided in the neighbourhood of the British Settlements on the coast, to secure their attachment, influence and services for the safe-conduct of merchandise through their territories. When the coast tribes, who held most of these notes, were conquered by the rapacious Ashantis, they had to deliver them as part of the spoil of the victors, and the monthly amount was duly claimed and received by the Ashantis by right of conquest. In this way many of the English, Dutch and Danish notes found their way into Ashanti hands, and were ultimately destroyed by them, thus unwittingly in their ignorance disposing of valuable European records. The Akras state that they lost their notes to the Akims by fraud, and the latter lost them to the Ashantis, their conquerors, under Osai Opookoo. Thus, by right of conquest the Ashantis became the recipients of the monthly payments, and many troubles arose in consequence, a detailed account of which will be given later on in the next chapter.

Dagwumba, a large country north-east of Ashanti, was next attacked and added to the Ashanti rule. Osai Opookoo had sent messengers to the king, probably requiring a pretext for war, demanding tribute from this country, which being refused, war was declared, the people defeated, and their king glad to make terms with the Ashantis, in order to prevent further loss of dignity with his own people, and to save the further insults to which he would be subjected as a conquered chief from his adversaries. The alliance thus formed was beneficial to both countries; the King of Dagwumba's loss of dignity being compensated by a gain of commercial power, for, on becoming tributary to Osai Opookoo, mercantile intercourse was established between the Ashantis and the great markets of the far interior, through the medium of his own people, to which they already had access, because their country was farther inland than Ashanti. Thus by levying a toll upon all commodities passing through his country, he increased his revenues and at the same time obtained respect from his conquerors as a superior tributary power. The Inta country, which lay between Ashanti and Dagwumba to the north-east, also became tributary during this reign, so that between 1720 and 1741 four great tribes, the Gamans, Akims, Dagwumbas and Intas, were each in turn made subservient to the power of Ashanti. When a fresh state was thus conquered, it was placed under the particular care of some important Ashanti chief, who generally resided at Kumasi, and who only visited his tributary state in order to receive the annual payment due to his king from its native ruler, for whose proper conduct and obedience he was held, in a measure, to be responsible.

The ruler of Dwaben died during the reign of Osai Opookoo, whose decease is also reported about the year 1741. A brother again succeeded to the stool, by name Osai Aquissa, who ruled in Kumasi for twelve years, until 1753. Nothing very remarkable appears to have taken place during his short reign. He preserved tributary all the states previously conquered, but there are no traditions of his adding any fresh territory to the empire. The one event of importance that is mentioned and the history of it preserved, refers to the King of Akim. This monarch, having received from Osai Aquissa permission to wage war with his neighbours, on condition of sharing the spoil with that king, is reported to have sacrificed himself for the good of his people. For, failing to obtain the necessary spoil, he sent none to Kumasi, whereupon his head was demanded by Osai Aquissa, and the Akim king, after consultation with his chiefs, decided to end his life with them. Tradition has it that each sat upon a keg of gunpowder, smoking his pipe, and that after a long and final draught of rum, each applied the ashes of his pipe to his own funeral pyre and thus saved destruction at the hands of the Ashantis.

Osai Cudjo succeeded in 1753, and devoted his energies to retrenching the power of, and afterwards conciliating, the so-called aristocracy, which in power was growing to such an extent as to menace the existence of the state. Wherever possible, he raised his favourite captains to the vacant stools whenever an opportunity offered, often uniting three or four districts under the newly made kings, and taking an oath with them that their lives should be held as sacred as his own, in order to anticipate any doubts as to their fidelity to the constitution. The act of raising a man to the stool did not of necessity give the recipient a seat at the general council, but merely notified a succession to certain property, which was handed down to successive generations.

The tributary Wassaws and Assins attempted in this reign to regain their freedom, but were again attacked and defeated, and compelled to acknowledge Ashanti as a superior power. Osai Cudjo then turned his attention to Aquapim and Kwahu, subjected their people and placed them under tribute to his people. These successes kept in awe other tribes, which were waiting an opportunity of throwing off the Ashanti yoke. Though many attempted to regain their freedom, none succeeded, and this king is generally spoken of as a very great and powerful monarch, whose memory is respected for the many exploits and conquests that he so successfully undertook. He is reported to have reigned for thirty-two years, from 1753 to 1785, altogether a remarkable reign, during which Quama, the second king of the sister town Dwaben, is also reported to have died, but of whom there are no particulars of any note.

Osai Quamina, grandson of the previous king, succeeded to the stool in 1785. He was very young, and had a somewhat romantic career. His reign is chiefly conspicuous for the revolt of the Akim people, almost immediately upon his accession to the stool. The Akims were led by their chief Afoosoo, a most active and powerful leader, who, to strengthen his forces and to ensure victory, induced several smaller states to throw in their lot with him, and to make a bold bid to regain their independence. They were so far successful that they inflicted several defeats upon the Ashantis, but fell at last, victims to the treachery of their own people. Afoosoo was betrayed to the Ashanti general, Quatchie Kofie, who had charge of the war against him, and who carried his head, as was the custom, to Kumasi, and again brought the Akims into subjection. The valour and determined resistance of the Akim chief Afoosoo, made the Ashanti conqueror so vain of having at last obtained his adversary's head, that upon his return to Kumasi, he caused a small figure of Afoosoo to be made, with which he adorned the top of his state umbrella, and before which he danced in a most insulting manner upon every occasion of a state ceremony, particularly when the Akim representatives were present to witness his vanity. Such sights were no doubt duly reported to the conquered Akims, and only tended to make them the more rebellious and to fight with more bravery when in the field: and to constantly see the effigy of their favourite leader so grossly insulted, added to their hate for the Ashantis, and so incensed them against their cruel masters, that it is reported that they fought for their independence no less than eight times. The states of Banda and Soota were also made tributary in this reign, the subjugation of the latter occupying the Ashanti army, under Odumata, for ten years, during which time this general was forbidden to come to Kumasi until the subjugation was complete. The same general attacked and subdued the Nkoranzas, but to accomplish his end, he was compelled to raise a large auxiliary army from the Gaman country, already tributary to Ashanti.

Osai Quamina incurred the displeasure of his people, by raising a servant named Apookoo to the vacant stool of Assimadoo to the exclusion of the rightful family, and this event was the commencement of disagreement with his people, which may perhaps have had something to do with his own end. The last military act of his reign was the despatch of an expedition in answer to a request for help from the Danish Governor-General of Christiansborg, to send him an army with which to punish the Popos. Osai Quamina agreed, and despatched 5000 Ashanti troops to the castle at Christiansborg, but on their way down the Governor-General died, and his successor, rather prudently, paid to the Ashanti king the sum of 250 ounces of gold dust to take his men back again, rather than be a party to what would have been a very troublesome alliance.

In 1798 Osai Quamina left Kumasi and paid a visit to the sister town of Dwaben, remaining away for the space of twelve months, a most unusual thing for an Ashanti king to do, and in spite of the urgent requests of his people to return. It is supposed that he was induced to stay by the allurements of Gyawa, the king's daughter, of whom he seemed to have become infatuated. It was, however, at last announced to him by his nobles, that if he did not return to his country by the approaching Yam custom, he would be deprived of his stool by his people. He, however, did not return, owing either to the arts of his mistress, or to her refusal to accompany him to Kumasi, on account of the possible resentment of his mother to her when she arrived. Some suppose that the King of Dwaben was privy to and urged on her refusal, in order that by the dethronement of Osai Quamina, he might reap the benefit of joining the two kingdoms under his own sway. That the king was dethroned is certain, and the manner of this deprivation of the stool is worthy of record and most interesting.

The chief captains of Kumasi, headed by one Appia Danqua, waited upon the queen mother, and recounted to her the shortcomings of her son, commanding her, as daughter of their old king and as his parent, to remonstrate with him upon his conduct. His mother, however, told them she had already done so, but without avail, and also stated that in return her son had attempted to take her life, and that as remonstrances were of no avail, she would beg them to unseat Osai Quamina, and to place her second son Osai Opookoo on the stool in his place.

Thus Osai Quamina was dethroned and his brother raised in his place. This decision of the queen mother and the captains was then communicated to the dethroned king: a few women and slaves were sent to him, with the request that he would retire to the bush and build himself a "croom" and there die. Before his death, however, he sought and obtained a private interview with the new king, asking that those who had been the means of his downfall should be distrusted and punished, and then he implored death, which was effected by fixing his feet on the ground, bending his body backward with a prop in the small of the back, and suspending from a noose round his neck several large tusks of ivory, the weight of which pressing upon his neck strangled him. (This mode was chosen because his blood could not be shed, nor could he be drowned in the sacred river.)

1799.—Osai Opookoo lived only a few weeks after his elevation to the stool, and was succeeded in turn by his brother Osai Tootoo Quamina, a youth about seventeen years of age. On the occasion of his accession, the captains of the country, from fear of the increasing power of the aristocracy, insisted that the remaining members of the king's family should publicly proclaim their liability to capital punishment, and thus remove the idea of the sacredness of the royal family from suffering in this way. It was in this reign that the Fanti kingdom was invaded in 1807, and for the first time the Ashantis came into direct conflict with the English during the campaign. While this Fanti invasion was being considered, Baba, afterwards the chief of the Moors, appeared in Kumasi, and requested protection from its king against his chief, who had driven him from the

Gamba country by his rapacity, promising to make Osai Tootoo Quamina heir to a great property, now withheld from him by his kinsman the king, upon his recovery of it. The Ashanti king promised Baba to make the King of Gamba do justice to him after the Fanti invasion was over, on condition that Baba and his companions were successful in the fetishes made by them for the Ashanti success. After the Fanti invasion, the King of Ashanti carried out his promise to Baba, and the King of Gamba did not think it prudent to resist the demand, but satisfied his kinsman.

In 1807 while Osai Tootoo Quamina was absent upon the Fanti invasion, Ashanti was ruled by the queen mother (always an important person in Ashanti politics) as regent. She appears to have been, from all accounts, a very designing and licentious woman, openly intriguing with the captains of the court, and ruining many of those who refused, either from fear or disgust, to intrigue with her.

Between 1807 and 1811, during this regency, the King of Dwaben, Yabaguona, died, and was succeeded by his grandson, Boitinne Quama, then about twenty years of age. The Akims, too, under Attah, who had been to the first Fanti war in 1807 and acquitted himself well, rebelled, and refused to join his Ashanti master in an invasion directed against the Fantis in Winnebah and Bereku, whither Opookoo, an Ashanti captain, was journeying, and from whence he sent orders for Attah to join him. When Attah received this order he at once sent word back to Opookoo, before he had crossed the Prah River, that he would not come to his aid, and also advising Opookoo not to pass through his territory. Whereupon Opookoo reported Attah's conduct to the king at Kumasi, who as usual despatched messengers to Attah to inquire if such was the case. Without hesitation, Attah confessed to the king's messengers that he had refused to join Opookoo, and added, moreover, that he was tired of being a slave and incessantly summoned to war, and that also he could not forget that Osai Cudjo, Quamina's ancestor, had cut off his (Attah's) grandfather's head, and that he would fight with Opookoo whenever he came. About this time Quamina Guma (the father of Beegua, captain of Danish Accra), one of the king's sons, was returning to Kumasi with a large quantity of gold, in order to make custom for the king's mother, passing through Attah's territory. Here he was intercepted, robbed of his gold, and murdered with his party, with the exception of one, who was sent as a messenger to the king at Kumasi, to tell him that Attah was in earnest and determined to war with him. Attah, to strengthen his forces, had induced another chief who was also weary of Ashanti rule, Quaw Saffatchee, to join him. Opookoo was therefore ordered by the Ashanti king to at once march against Attah, who, when he entered his country, was for attacking him at once at sunrise, but to this Quaw objected, saying it would be best to wait until 3 P.M., when the Ashantis had eaten and would be resting, and also if they were defeated, it would be a better time for retreat (evening coming on), as the Ashantis never pursue in the dark. The attack took place as arranged, and the fight remained undecided till night fell, when Opookoo, on counting his men, found he had lost so many, that he decided to send messengers to call the Akras to his help, they being then vassals of Ashanti. The Akras came to the help of Opookoo, whereupon Attah and Quaw divided and retreated, the former to windward and the latter to Ada. Opookoo followed the latter, and thinking the then Dutch governor, Mr. Flindt, had assisted Quaw to escape, after being tediously and closely watched by Opookoo's men, took the governor prisoner and marched away with him to Aquapim, where the army encamped for five months, during which time Mr. Flindt was treated with all respect, and at last released on a ransom of £400. Opookoo was then ordered back to Kumasi, and it is said took with him the bell from the fort at Ada as a trophy.

At the time of this insurrection Appia Danqua had been sent with 6000 men against the Fantis, who were disposed somewhat to aid the rebels. Appia met them at Appam, a town on the coast between Winnebah and Saltpond, and after the fight, Baffoo, the Anamaboe Caboceer, was taken prisoner. While, however, Appia's army was in the neighbourhood of Tantum, some few miles away, they heard of the approach of Attah, who, it will be remembered, was retreating to windward before the troops of Opookoo, and whose very name was sufficient to infuse genuine fear into the victorious army of Appia, who, with a show of discretion, then hurried away into the interior.

In this manner the passage of the Ashantis through the Akim country to the coast became closed, and remained so for about a period of two years, partly owing to the activity and energy of Cudjoe Cooma, the new king of that country, who had been raised to the stool some six months after the death of Attah. During this six months' interval, between the death of Attah and the placing of Cudjoe Cooma upon the stool, the

Akims were governed by one Qwaku Ashanti, but who ruled them so very harshly, that at the end of a few months he was commanded by his people to take his own life, and was allowed by them one week in which to accomplish this end. It is reported that he spent the week thus allowed in making custom and then committed suicide.

At the time of Attah's rebellion, Quaw Saffatchee, another Ashanti tributary ruler, had joined forces with him, and about this time this chief, together with the Fantis, attacked Accra, but were repulsed. The King of Ashanti now determined to make one bold effort to reopen the road through the Akim country, and to receive the arrears of pay from the forts on the coast that were due to him. He accordingly collected an army of some 20,000 men, and placing them under the charge of Amanqua Abiniowa, instructed him to proceed through the Akim and Aquapim countries to receive the submission of the people, to do no violence, and to commit no act of war except in self-defence. At the same time Appia Danqua was sent with a smaller body of men, to encamp a short distance from the coast behind Winnebah and Tantum, in case the revolters again retreated and fled to windward. Abiniowa and his army reached to within a day's march of the Aquapim country, and then at a small place called Aquiasso, one of his advance parties was attacked by Cudjoe Cooma and his men, and beaten back with a slight loss. The main body of the Ashantis now prepared for attack, which took place next morning. The engagement lasted about six hours, and ended in a victory for the Ashantis. After the fight Amanqua sent a jaw-bone of a man and a slave to each of the Accra towns, following with his army shortly afterwards to receive the king's pay, and remaining in the neighbourhood for about twelve months. On his return to Aquapim he received a message from the Ashanti king, and a large present of gold for his victory. The message was to the effect that he had better not see Kumasi, unless he brought with him the heads of Cudjoe Cooma and Quaw Saffatchee. This instruction from Kumasi was not immediately communicated by Amanqua to his captains, but, ordering them to deposit all their property in Accra, he made custom for three days to gain favour for his undertaking, and then took fetish with all his captains, binding them never to return to Kumasi without the heads of Cudjoe and Quaw.

In 1816 Appia Danqua had died in the Assin country, and was succeeded by his brother Appia Nanu, under whom Bakkee was second in command. The King of Ashanti, hearing nothing of his progress, but rather of his idleness, sent Amanqua to join him, which was effected at Essecumah, and to upbraid him for his supposed cowardice. Soon after this union a skirmish took place near the Saltpond at Cape Coast, and then the combined army went to attack Commendah. Soon after this the palaver was settled at Cape Coast, and the army again divided; Cudjoe Cooma was killed by a party of Appia Nanu's men near Essecumah, upon which Appia Danqua returned to Kumasi instead of going to join Amanqua.

Quaw Saffatchee was at this time in Accra, and Adoo Danqua, his brother, paid a visit to the Akras, and opened negotiations for the delivery of him to his enemies, the Ashantis, promising that if the Akras delivered him into their hands they would prevail upon their king to give the stool to his brother, who was now trying to betray him. Quaw thereupon left Accra to meet his brother, accompanied only by a few Akras and Ashantis, and after one day's journey came where his brother was waiting him. A palaver took place, Adoo urged his brother to kill himself, but from this Quaw dissented, saying he hoped eventually to wear out the patience of the Ashanti king in thus pursuing him. At this Adoo rose, a shot was fired at Quaw, which struck him down, but before he was killed he was shot and rose again no less than four times, dying with the reproach on his lips, that his brother was his murderer. The body was sent to Accra, and the head later to Kumasi. Amanqua's mission being now complete he returned to the Ashanti capital in 1817.

About this time the King of Ashanti received homage and tribute unasked from the Aowin tribe, and emboldened by his military successes, sent an embassy to Bontuko, the capital of the Gaman country, demanding the royal stool of the king. This stool was thickly plated and embossed with gold, and was in fear sent by Adinkara the king, in answer to the summons, in the absence of his sister, a woman of great spirit, and really the chief adviser of the king. On her return, learning what her brother had done, she severely reproached him, and ordered a new stool to be made of solid gold to replace the lost one, with a golden elephant for an ornament. The King of Ashanti hearing of this, sent another embassy demanding this new stool, but the sister informed them with more force than delicacy, that the king should deliver up neither the stool nor its ornament, adding she and her brother would change places, as he was unfit to be a king. Further, she would fight to the last, rather than submit to be so constantly despoiled. This message was duly delivered, and the king, admiring her spirit, sent word back to say she was a strong woman and fit to be a king's sister, and that he would give her twelve months to prepare for war. During the preparation many embassies passed between the two countries, one from the Gaman court, with gold to the amount of £3200, to preserve peace. The aristocracy objected to this, urging that their other tributary powers would mock them, did they not get the King of Gaman's head.

Up to this time it will be remembered, that the Ashanti people had really consisted of two divisions, those of Kumasi and those of Dwaben, each with their separate capital, but working together to carry out their schemes of military aggression. It became clear about 1817 that Osai Tootoo, the King of Ashanti, contemplated the reduction of his ally of Dwaben to be a tributary power, and to this effect sent a messenger to the King of Dwaben, a very weak young man, demanding gold. To this demand an answer was sent by one of the royal captains to the effect, that as no war was on hand no gold could be required in Kumasi, except for the benefit of the king himself, and also reminding him, that of old it had been the custom for the King of Dwaben to exact gold and not to pay it. Upon this being reported to the King of Ashanti, he sent his messengers with a gold-headed sword and other marks of favour to this captain, who, to his great surprise, refused them, saying that the honours he already possessed at home became him better.

This brings us down to the period when the Ashantis first began to be troublesome to the English upon the West Coast of Africa, and the various wars that arose from this will be detailed in the following chapter, while some account of the town of Kumasi, as it was in 1817, may be of interest to the general reader.

The first town of Kumasi was built upon the side of a large rocky hill of ironstone. It was insulated by a marsh close to the town on the north, and by a narrow stream half a mile distant from it on the north-west, and about sixty yards broad, while at the east, south-east and south it was respectively twenty, seventy and fifty yards broad at these points. In many parts, this marsh was five feet deep after the heavy rains, but more commonly only two. It contained many springs and supplied the town with water, but the vapours rising from it enveloped the city morning and evening with a thick fog, which was favourable to the production of dysentery in Europeans. A bird's-eye view of the place was uninteresting, nothing being seen but the thatch roofs of the houses, the whole encircled with bush and forest. The town itself was an oblong about four miles in circumference, excluding the suburbs of Assafoo and Bantamah, which were once connected with the main town by streets, at this time mostly in ruins. Four of the principal streets were about half a mile long and from fifty to a hundred yards wide. The streets were all named, and each placed under the charge of a separate captain, and at the top of one, upon a mound, were placed the cannon taken from the Denkiras by Osai Tootoo, the first authentic king. The royal residence was situated in a long and wide street running through the middle of the town, from

THE TOWN OF KUMASI (1817).

(BOWDICH.)

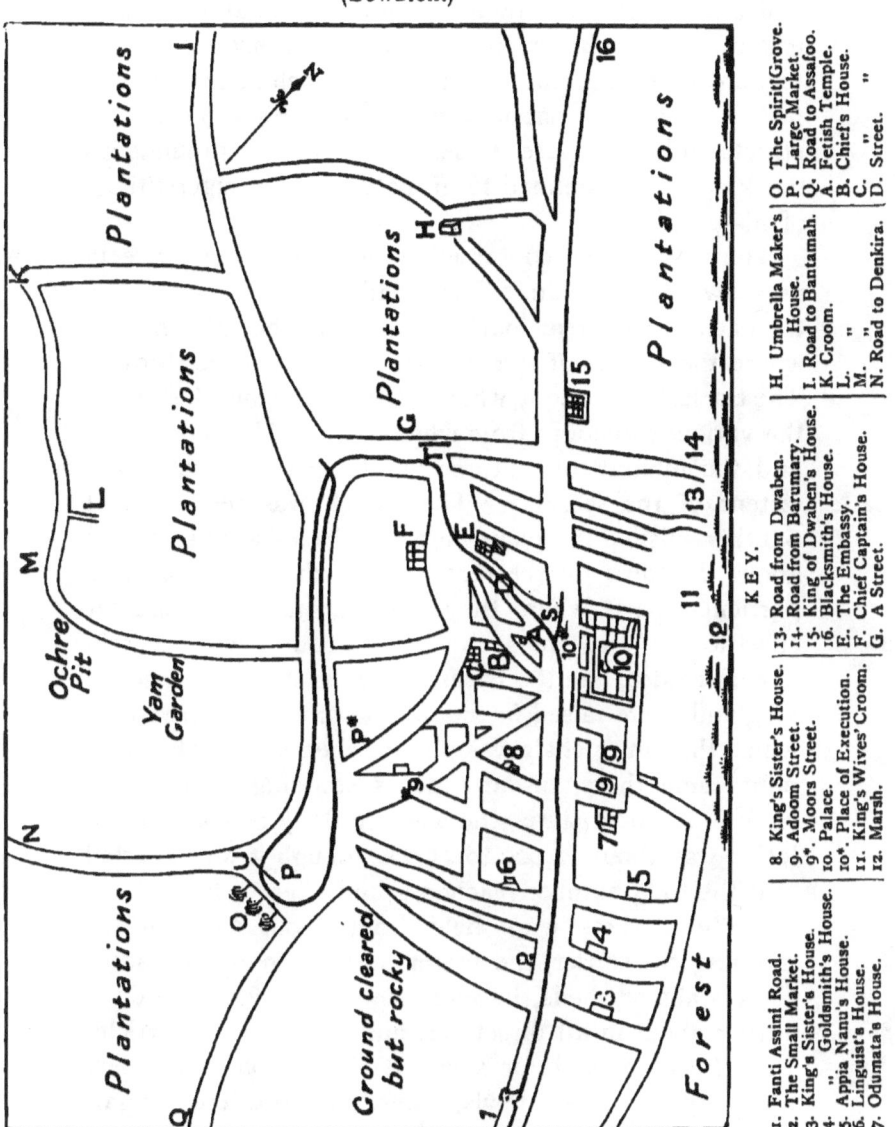

KEY.

1. Fanti Assini Road.
2. The Small Market.
3. King's Sister's House.
4. " Goldsmith's House.
5. " Appia Nanu's House.
6. Linguist's House.
7. Odumata's House.
8. King's Sister's House.
9. Adoom Street.
9*. Moors Street.
10. Palace.
10*. Place of Execution.
11. King's Wives' Croom.
12. Marsh.
13. Road from Dwaben.
14. Road from Barumary.
15. King of Dwaben's House.
16. Blacksmith's House.
E. The Embassy.
F. Chief Captain's House.
G. A Street.
H. Umbrella Maker's House.
I. Road to Bantamah.
K. Croom.
L. "
M. "
N. Road to Denkira.
O. The Spirit Grove.
P. Large Market.
Q. Road to Assafoo.
A. Fetish Temple.
B. Chief's House.
C. "
D. Street.

which it was shut out by a high wall, terminating at each end of the marsh, which was considered sufficient protection at these points. This street included the king's residence and also that of his brothers, with several smaller streets and open spaces to serve as recreation grounds for the king, when confined to his palace by the superstitions of his people.

The whole town contained some twenty-seven streets as shown in the plan. The small grove marked O, at the back of the great market-place, was the spirit house, where the trunks of the victims sacrificed were thrown. The tracks leading to it, which were daily renewed, showed the various directions from which they had been dragged, and the number of vultures on the trees indicated the extent of the sacrifice. The stench was terrible, and panthers visited the place nightly. Trees were scattered about the town for the recreation of the people of those particular parts where they existed, and small circular elevations of two steps, the lower about twenty feet in circumference, like the bases of the old market crosses in England, were raised in the middle of several streets, on which the king's chair was placed when he went to drink palm wine there, his attendants standing round in a circle. In these times the average daily resident population was about 12,000 to 15,000, though it was asserted that the total number reached a much larger figure.

Daily markets were held from about eight in the morning till sunset, the larger market containing some sixty stalls or sheds, besides crowds of inferior vendors, sitting about in all directions, and the following articles were freely offered for sale: Beef, mutton, pork, deer and monkey's flesh, fowls, yams, plantains, corn, sugar-cane, rice, peppers, oranges, pawpaws, pine-apple, bananas, salt and dried fish from the coast, large snails smoke-dried and stuck in rows on small sticks in the form of herring bone, eggs, palm wine, rum, pipes, beads, looking-glasses, sandals, silk, cotton, cloths, powder, pillows, thread and calabashes. Prices ruled much higher in Kumasi than in the surrounding towns, owing to the greater abundance of gold among the people. The following will show the prices in the capitals of Ashanti and Dagwumba respectively:—

Article.	Kumasi.	Yahudi.
A bullock	£6 0 0	£1 0 0
A sheep	0 15 0	0 4 0
A fowl	0 1 8	0 0 5
A horse	24 0 0	8 0 0
Yams	0 0 8 (for 2)	0 0 8 (for 10)

Plantations existed all round the town, the extent and order of which were surprising. No other implement was used but the hoe, and two crops of corn were produced every year. Yams were planted at Christmas and dug in the following September. The latter plantations were well looked after, and were well fenced in, planted in lines, with a broad walk round, while a hut was erected at each wicker gate, where a slave and his family resided to protect the plantation.

Down to the beginning of the nineteenth century the constitution of the Ashantis consisted of three estates, the King, the Aristocracy (reduced to four in number) and the great Assembly of the Captains or Caboceers. In the exercise of his judicial authority, the king always retired in private with his four counsellors to hear their opinions, which they were encouraged to state with the utmost candour, while the general assembly of the captains was summoned, simply to give publicity to the decisions arrived at by the king and his aristocracy, or simply to announce the will and pleasure of the former. The captains also made all necessary provision for the carrying out of such decisions. The most original feature of the law was that of succession, already described. The sisters of the king could marry or intrigue with whom they pleased, provided that the chosen one was an eminently strong or personable man. The king was heir to the gold of all his subjects, from the highest to the lowest; the fetish gold and the cloths being presented by him to his successor. The successor became liable for all the debts of the previous king, and in order to meet these, a large sum of gold dust was often presented to the one chosen to succeed to the stool. All the gold and ornaments buried with members of the king's family, and which were deposited with their bones in the fetish house at Bantamah, were sacred, and could only be used to save the capital from destruction at the hands of an enemy, or in a time of extreme national distress, and should the occasion arise for their use in this manner, the reigning king must on no account look upon them, unless he wished to incur the fatal vengeance of the fetish god. A slave seeking refuge from an allied or tributary power was always restored, but if he came from an unconnected power, he was received as a free man.

A tributary state which distinguished itself in the suppression of revolt in another was rewarded with certain privileges at the expense of the revolting power. If the subjects of any tributary power objected to the decision of their own ruler, according to the laws of their own country, they could carry their case for review to Kumasi, on payment of a certain sum in gold dust.

The direct descendants of the noble families who assisted Osai Tootoo in the foundation of the kingdom, were exempt from capital punishment, but could be despoiled of their goods and belongings.

Persons on the king's business were not allowed to seize provisions on the road, but, when requiring food, were first to offer a fair price for the same, which if refused, they were to claim one meal in the king's name and then proceed on their way.

The blood of the son of a king or any of the royal family could not be shed, but if found guilty of a crime of great magnitude, the offender was ordered to be drowned in the river Dah.

Conviction for cowardice brought death.

No one was allowed to pick up gold that had been dropped in the market-place, on pain of death. The collection of this was reserved for state occasions only.

A subject could clear any part of the bush for building a house or making a plantation, without paying rent to the king or chief, but if the path to his plantation ran through that of another, he must pay a small sum to the owner of that plantation.

The accuser in a suit was never confronted with the accused, nor the evidence revealed until the accused had replied, through the king's linguists, fully to the charge.

No man was punished for killing his own slave. Seven slaves were the price to be paid for an aggrey bead broken in a scuffle.

A man discovered in intrigue with a woman, either in a house or in the bush, both became the slaves of the person who thus discovered them, but were redeemable by their families.

To praise the beauty of another man's wife was forbidden, it being considered intrigue by implication.

If a woman became involved in a suit, she compromised her family, not her husband.

A woman could leave her husband for ill-treatment or dislike, by return of her marriage fee, but she could not marry again.

A husband unheard of for three years allowed the wife to marry again, and should the first husband return the claim of the second still stood, but all the children of the after marriage were considered the property of the first husband, and could be pawned by him.

To intrigue with the wife of a king was death, and only the captains could put their wives to death for infidelity, though they were expected to allow their redemption by their family on payment of a large sum of gold dust.

The property of a wife was quite distinct from that of the husband, but the king was heir to it.

If a person brought a frivolous charge against another and it was dismissed, the accuser was bound to provide an entertainment for the family and the friends of the accused.

A captain generally paid a periguin, £8 2s., for a wife, and a poor man two ackies, about 1s. 6d. Intrigue with the former incurred a fine of ten periguins, with the latter one and a half ackies and a pot of palm wine.

The Government had no power to direct trade into any particular market, but it could prevent the commerce of any objectionable power from passing through its territories.

THE PRINCIPAL ROADS FROM KUMASI.

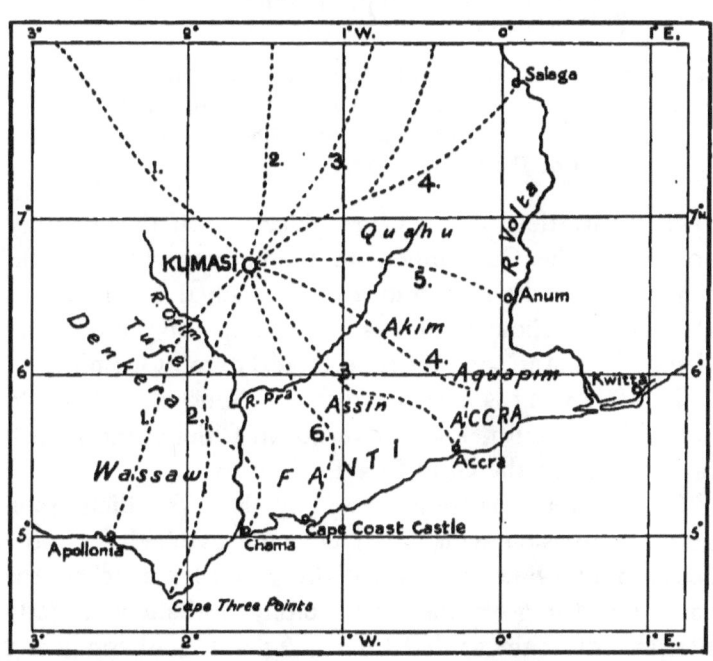

Coast Roads.
1. To Apollonia.
2. To Three Points and Chama.
3. To Accra.
4. To Accra.
5. To the Volta.

Inland Roads.
1. To Bontuko.
2. To Kintampo.
3. To Attabubu.
4. To Salaga.
5. Government Road.

CHAPTER XI.

Monthly Notes—Wars with England, 1807-1817—Mission to Ashanti—Second Ashanti War, 1824—Third Ashanti War, 1863—Fourth Ashanti War, 1873—The Last Ashanti War—Downfall of Prempeh, 1896.

ONE illustration of the value placed upon the monthly notes from the Government to the natives, will be sufficient to show the importance that attached to them, and also serve to show the ideas in the mind of the reigning King of Ashanti, at that time Osai Tootoo Quamina.

The following is a letter from the King of Ashanti to John Hope Smith, Esq., Governor-in-Chief of the British possessions on the Gold Coast of Africa.

This letter was sent down by Mr. Bowdich, soon after the mission which had been despatched from the coast to interview the Ashanti king in 1817 reached the capital, to the governor of the colony, and shows exactly the state of affairs at that time. Ashanti had conquered all the countries from the river Tando in the west, to the Volta in the east, leaving only the strip of shore, with its forts and factories, which were now seriously threatened. There is no doubt that the Ashantis contemplated the reduction of these, in order to satisfy their desire to become a maritime power.

The king sends his compliments to the governor. He thanks the King of England and him very much for the presents sent to him; he thinks them very handsome. The king's sisters and all his friends have seen them, and think them very handsome, and thank him. The king thanks his God and his fetish that he made the governor send the white men's faces for him to see, like he does now; he likes the English very much, and the governor all the same as his brother.

The King of England has made war against all the other white people a long time, and killed all the people all about, and taken all the towns, French, Dutch and Danish, all the towns all about. The King of Ashantee has made war against all the people of the water side, and all the black men all about, and taken all their towns.

When the King of England takes a French town, he says, "Come, all this is mine, bring all your books, and give me all your pay"; and if they don't do it, does the governor think the King of England likes it? So the king has beat the Fantees now two times, and taken all their towns, and they send and say to him, "You are a great king, we want to serve you"; but he says, "Hah! you want to serve me, then bring all your books, what you get from the forts"; and then they send him four ackies; this vexes him too much.

The first time he made war against the Fantees, two great men in Assini quarrelled; so half the people came to Ashantee, half went to Fantee. The king said, "What is the reason of this?" so he sent his gold swords and canes to know why they did so, and the Fantees killed his messengers and took all their gold.[1] After they fought with the Elminas and Accras, the Fantees sent word to the king they would serve him; the king sent word to the Assinis, "If it is true that the Fantees want to serve me, let me hear". After that they sent to say, "Yes; they tired of fighting, and wanted to serve him"; he said: "Well, give me some

[1] Here the king's linguist ceased, and by his desire requested us to repeat all the king had said; he was much pleased with our accuracy, and begged us to take some refreshment (spirits and palm wine were introduced in silver bowls), fearing he had kept us too long without eating, and would continue the letter to-morrow. He locked up what had been written, and heard it read again the next day, before his linguist continued.

gold, what you get from the books, and then you shall hear what palaver I have got in my head, and we can be friends"; then he sent some messengers, and after they waited more than two years, the Fantees sent word back, "No! we don't want to serve the king, but only to make the path open and get good trade"; this vexed the king too much.

Then the Fantees sent to a strong man, Cudjoe Coomah, and said, "Come, let us put our heads together against the king"; after that, when the king heard this, he sent one, not a great man, but his own slave, and said, "Well, you will do, go kill all the people, all the Aquapims, and Akims, and all"; and so he killed all, and after he killed all he came and told him.

When he sent against Akim, the people in Akim sent word that they told their head men not to vex the king, but they would not mind them, so he killed the head people, and the others begged his pardon.

When the king went to fight with the Fantees they sent this saucy word, "We will kill you and your people and stand on you"; then they did not kill one Ashantee captain, but the king killed all the Fantee captains and people. They do not stand on him.

That time, after the king fought, all the Fantees sent word, "Well we will serve you, but you must not send more harm to hurt us, we don't want to fight more, but to make good friends with you". Then the king said, "What caboceer lives at Cape Coast and Anamaboe, what books they get from the forts, let them send all, and then we can be friends". And the king sent word too, "If my messengers go to Cape Coast Fort, and if they bring pots of gold, and casks of goods, then I can't take that, *but I must have the books*".

After that the king sent word to the Governor of Cape Coast and the Governor of Anamaboe, "Well! you know I have killed all the Fantees, and I must have Adocoo's and Amooney's books, and I can make friends with you, good brother and good heart"; but now they send four ackies, that is what makes the king's heart break out when he looks on the book and thinks of four ackies, and his captains swear that the Fantees are rogues and want to cheat him. When the white men see the Fantees do this, and the English officers bring him these four ackies, it makes him get up very angry, but he has no palaver with white men.

All Fantee is his, all the black man's country is his; he hears that white men bring all the things that come here; he wonders they do not fight with the Fantees, for he knows they cheat them. Now he sees white men, and he thanks God and his fetish for it.

When the English made Apollonia Fort he fought with the Aowins, the masters of that country, and killed them; then he said to the caboceer, "I have killed all your people, your book is mine"; the caboceer said, "True! so long as you take my town, the book belongs to you".

He went to Dankara and fought, and killed the people; then he said, "Give me the book you get from Elmina," so they did, and now Elmina belongs to him.[1]

The English Fort at Accra gave a book to an Akim caboceer, called Aboigin Adjumawcon. The king killed him and took the book. The Dutch Fort gave a book to another Akim caboceer, Curry Curry Apam. The Danish Fort gave a book to another Akim caboceer, Arrawa Akim; the king killed all and took their books.

This king, Sai, is young on the stool, but he keeps always in his head what old men say, for it is good, and his great men and linguists tell it him every morning. The King of England makes three great men, and sends one to Cape Coast, one to Anamaboe and one to Accra; Cape Coast is the same as England. The king gets two ounces from Accra every moon, and the English wish to give him only four ackies for the big fort at Cape Coast, and the same for Anamaboe; do white men think this proper?

When the king killed the Dankara caboceer and got two ounces from Elmina, the Dutch governor said, "This is a proper king, we shall not play with him," and made the book four ounces. The king has killed all the people and all the forts are his; he sent his captains to see white men; now *he* sees them, and thanks God and his fetish. If the path was good when the captains went, the king would have gone under the forts and seen all the white men. The Ashantees take good gold to Cape Coast, but the Fantees mix it; he sent some of his captains like slaves to see,

[1] The king always spoke of the acts of all his ancestors as his own.

and they saw it ; ten handkerchiefs are cut to eight, water is put to rum, and charcoal to powder, even for the king; they cheat him, but he thinks the white men give all those things proper to the Fantees.

The king knows the King of England is his good friend, for he has sent him handsome dashes ; he knows his officers are his good friends, for they come to see him. The king wishes the governor to send to Elmina to see what is paid him there, and to write the King of England how much, as the English say their nation passes the Dutch; he will see by the books given him by both forts. If the King of England does not like that, he may send him himself what he pleases, and then Sai can take it.

He thanks the king and governor for sending four white men to see him. The old king wished to see some of them, but the Fantees stop it. He is but a young man and sees them, and so again he thanks God and his fetish.

>Dictated in the presence of
>>T. Edward Bowdich.
>>William Hutchison.
>>Henry Tedlie.

It was in 1807 that an Ashanti army reached the coast for the first time, though in the previous year, 1806, they had approached the neighbourhood of Cape Coast Castle, the governor of which, under some apprehension for the safety of the British Settlements along the coast, wished to send a flag of truce with a message to the King of Ashanti, who was then, in May, 1806, encamped only some fifteen miles from the town. The Fantis, with whom the Ashantis were at this time at war, were consulted upon this measure, and so much opposed it, particularly the natives of Anamaboe, that it was dispensed with, the Anamaboes thinking themselves quite a match for the Ashantis, and underrating their power. Shortly after this, a division of the Ashanti army made its appearance at the village of Cormantine, a little to the west of Saltpond, attacked the inhabitants, completely routing them and destroying their houses. The Dutch Fort at Cormantine was occupied by the captain commanding this division of the Ashanti force, who made it his headquarters and behaved in a most arrogant manner. As it was now time for the English governor to know something of the intentions of the Ashantis, the governor, Mr. White of Anamaboe, sent a messenger with a flag of truce to the Dutch Fort at Cormantine, where the Ashanti leader was encamped, requesting to be acquainted with the king's motive for coming to the coast with so large an army, and offering to act as a mediator between the Ashantis and the Fantis, in order to bring their war to a close. It is supposed that this message was duly given to the king, for on the succeeding day three messengers came from Cormantine with a white flag to see the Governor of Anamaboe. From this circumstance Mr. White fully expected that an agreeable answer had been sent to his message, but on this point he was doomed to disappointment, for the commander of the Ashanti army, being in possession of Fort Amsterdam at Cormantine, and having secured an opening to the sea, sent a most disagreeable reply to the following effect: "That when the governor would send him twenty barrels of gunpowder and one hundred muskets, he would be told what were the motives of the King of Ashanti".

To have satisfied this demand would have been equal to an admission of weakness on the part of the English, so the governor behaved politely to the messengers, gave them refreshment, and told them to tell their master that he much regretted that he did not appear willing to come to an understanding, and that if the Ashanti army attempted to approach the fort at Anamaboe in a hostile manner, the guns would be opened upon them. To impress upon the messengers the power of these guns, some few shots were fired from the fort, and as the bearers were about to depart, private intelligence was received by the governor that the men bearing the flag of truce, were to be murdered on their way to Cormantine. To present such a disaster, Mr. White and another gentleman accompanied them, and left them at a safe distance from their fort. A week elapsed and nothing occurred, and this circumstance was looked upon as a favourable omen. But the commander of the Ashanti division, who happened to be the King of Denkira, having ascertained the strength of Anamaboe, took possession of and occupied a small village about one mile to the east of the Anamaboe Fort, whence all the operations of his adversaries could be observed. This action was considered to be an annoyance, and a party consisting of nearly all the men in the town attacked the Ashantis, and succeeded in dislodging them from their newly-acquired post, after a somewhat stubborn resistance. While the Anamaboes were occupied with this attack, the Ashanti captain and the main body of his men were actively employed in securing all the passes that led again back to the town. Early on the next day the Ashanti army was seen to be in motion, the alarm was given, and every man able to carry a musket marched to meet the enemy. Confusion soon spread through the town; all the old people were collected in the fort and the gate closed. The sound of musketry approached nearer and nearer, and in a short time the

Ashantis entered the town on all sides, pursued the people to the beach and slaughtered all with whom they came in contact. Many took to their canoes and others saved themselves by swimming; the fort was several times assailed, though the guns were used against them with great effect. The governor was twice wounded, one man killed, and an officer and another man wounded in the assault. After repeated attacks by the Ashantis, the garrison was reduced to eight able men upon whom dependence could be placed, and who defended the western gate with much vigour. Chief among these defenders were Messieurs Governor White, Meredith, Swanzy, Smith and Baines.

Night came on and hostilities ceased, but the morning showed the results of the fight, dead and wounded on all sides, houses unroofed and others on fire. The fort gave refuge to about 2000 people of every description, and about 200 escaped to a rock surrounded by the sea and about a pistol shot from the shore, where they remained unmolested. Upon inquiry it was estimated that about 8000 Fantis had perished during the conflict. The attack on the fort was again renewed, but repulsed each time by the little garrison. The Ashantis now ceased active hostilities, remaining in and near the town for some days, and evidently anxious for peace, for, although they had defeated their enemies the Fantis, they too had suffered severely, losing in actual conflict and by sickness some 3000 men. On the 16th of June, reinforcements arrived from Cape Coast, and were landed safely and lodged in the fort under cover of the guns. A truce was soon afterwards agreed upon, by which the Ashantis undertook not to molest the British forts along the coast, provided that they observed a strict neutrality. The forces then withdrew, proceeding along the coast to leeward, inflicting desolation and ruin upon every town in the way. At last, the Ashanti captain returned towards his own country, only leaving a sufficient guard at Accra to look after the prisoners that had been captured, and to convey them to the Ashanti capital. The war, however, continued in different parts of the colony throughout the following years until 1811, when the Ashantis captured and conveyed into the interior Mr. Flindt, the Danish governor of the fort at Ada, who remained in their custody for a period of five months and three days. On this occasion the states of Akim and Aquapim rebelled unsuccessfully against Ashanti.

The next invasion of the Fanti country by the Ashantis took place in 1817, when they advanced as far as Cape Coast Castle and blockaded it, withdrawing only after the payment of a large tribute by the Fantis, to whom the money was advanced by the English. It was from this invasion that the necessity arose for the mission of Mr. Bowdich to Kumasi in 1817, in order to negotiate a peaceful solution of the ever-recurring Ashanti troubles. Reference to this mission has already been made, and the letter from the king to the governor commences the present chapter, in which a demand was made for the pay notes to be continued, and which was duly recognised by Mr. Bowdich. Relations of a friendly nature were established with the English, and a treaty concluded in September, 1817, one condition of which was the leaving of a British resident at Kumasi. The treaty thus made was soon broken by these troublesome people, for on the attempt of the King of Denkira to throw off the Ashanti yoke, the latter crossed the border, declared war and the British resident returned to Cape Coast. The king requested the governor to punish the people of Commendah for some trifling indignities offered to his people, and claimed 1600 ounces of gold from the people of Cape Coast for showing an unfriendly feeling towards him, and a similar amount from the governor of the colony. Tribute from the English governor was out of the question, but in 1819 Mr. Dupuis arrived from England as an envoy from the British Government, and announcing his mission to the Ashantis, he proceeded to their capital under the protection of the king. This officer succeeded in inducing the king to withdraw his claim to a fine, and to sign a treaty in which he promised fidelity to the British Crown, agreed to forget the past and arranged for a system of commerce with the coast towns. On the other hand Mr. Dupuis promised on behalf of the English that the sovereignty of the Ashanti king over the Fantis should be duly recognised, allowing the latter, however, to enjoy the freedom of British law. The Fantis being, as it were, thus disposed of, without their consent, the local government refused to sanction the treaty which acknowledged the transfer of the Fanti country to the Ashanti power.

This brings us down to the year 1821, when an English Bill was passed to abolish the African Company, and to transfer its possessions to the English Crown, with all its forts and possessions on the West Coast of Africa. About the same time Sir Charles Macarthy was made Governor of the Gold Coast, and began his rule by protecting the tribes that lived on the coast from the inroads of the Ashantis. This action soon roused the king again to commence active operations against his former adversaries. The first act of the Ashantis was to carry off from Anamaboe a sergeant of the British service and to execute him for speaking disrespectfully of the Ashanti king, and the second was to write to the governor to say that his head should be soon converted into an ornament for the royal drum. Opportunity for the execution of this threat came unfortunately but too soon. The Dutch governor at Elmina endeavoured to settle the negotiations peacefully, but failed ; and in 1823 the Ashantis again invaded the district of Wassaw, and encamped themselves on the right bank of the Prah. The English governor, Sir Charles Macarthy, determined to leave his camp at Duquah and cross the Prah at once, in order to give battle to his adversaries, and with but a force of some 500 men he carried out his design, crossed the river and took up a position at the village of Assamacow in January, 1824. In the meantime he had sent messengers to Major Chisholm, who, with some 2000 men, was on the left bank of the river, to come to his support. About the middle of the month he advanced still farther to the banks of the small river Adoomansoo, and on his way, with the greatest difficulty prevailed upon the timid and retreating Wassaws and Denkiras to remain in their country. Here a very decisive engagement took place, which unfortunately ended in the defeat and death of Sir Charles Macarthy. On the 21st of January, about midday, the Ashantis, reported to be some 10,000 strong, advanced to the attack, and the action was continued until dark. The Wassaws retreated early in the fight, ammunition soon ran short, and no more being available massacre completed the sad disaster. The Ashantis, sure of their victory, crossed the river, surrounded the governor's small and rapidly diminishing force, and cut them to pieces. The bush was too dense for open fighting and no orders could be given. Sir Charles Macarthy, Ensign Wetherall, Mr. Buckle and Mr. Williams, were surrounded, shot down, and all except the last named were beheaded, Sir Charles Macarthy's head being carried off by the victors to adorn the walls of the king's palace at Kumasi. Mr. Williams was taken prisoner and kept in the hands of the Ashantis for two months, tortured and released. Of the twelve officers who fought in this engagement, nine were killed and the remaining three badly wounded. Major Chisholm then succeeded to the command, and by careful measures saved the forts upon the coast from being attacked. The name of Sir Charles Macarthy lives to this day among the Fantis, and the great oath of the country is now the one that calls upon his name. Some time had to elapse before the Ashantis could be punished for this defeat of the English force, and the base of operations was moved from Cape Coast Castle to Accra. Here a force of some 10,000 men was collected, aided by a small contingent from the English regiments, and encamped at Dodowah, some twenty-five miles north-east of Accra, in the hopes of giving battle to the Ashantis in the plains instead of in their favourite bush. It was in the latter half of the year 1826 that the Ashanti army, some 10,000 strong, and elated by their previous victory, marched coastwards towards Accra, and met the encamped forces at the town mentioned and sustained a severe and crushing defeat. The allied tribes fought well, the King of Akim and his people carried all before them, the whole army of the Ashantis was completely routed, and their camp and gold captured, and by it the country was set at rest for many years. In September, 1827, the King of Kumasi sent his messengers to the coast to say that he wished to make peace with the white men and to be in future under their control. To ensure this British envoys were sent to Kumasi, and arrangements made by which a treaty was agreed upon in December, 1827, and though not finally adopted, preserved peace till 1831, when a final settlement of all difficulties was declared.

The disasters of the last few years, the decline of trade, and the death of Sir Charles Macarthy had at this time caused the Home Government to withdraw all the public establishments from the Gold Coast, and to invest them in the hands of the Company of African Merchants, of whom Captain Maclean was the first governor. The treaty of 1831, just referred to, was concluded by this gentleman, on behalf of the King of England, with the Kings of Ashanti, Cape Coast, Fanti, Anamaboe, Denkira, Tufel, Wassaw and Assin, of which the chief point was as follows: "The King of Ashanti having deposited in Cape Coast Castle, in the presence of the above-mentioned parties, the sum of 600 ounces of gold, and having delivered into the hands of the governor two young men of the royal family of Ashanti as security that he will keep peace with the said parties in all time coming, peace is hereby declared betwixt the said King of Ashanti and all and each of the parties aforesaid, to continue in all time coming". Peace was kept for some six or seven years

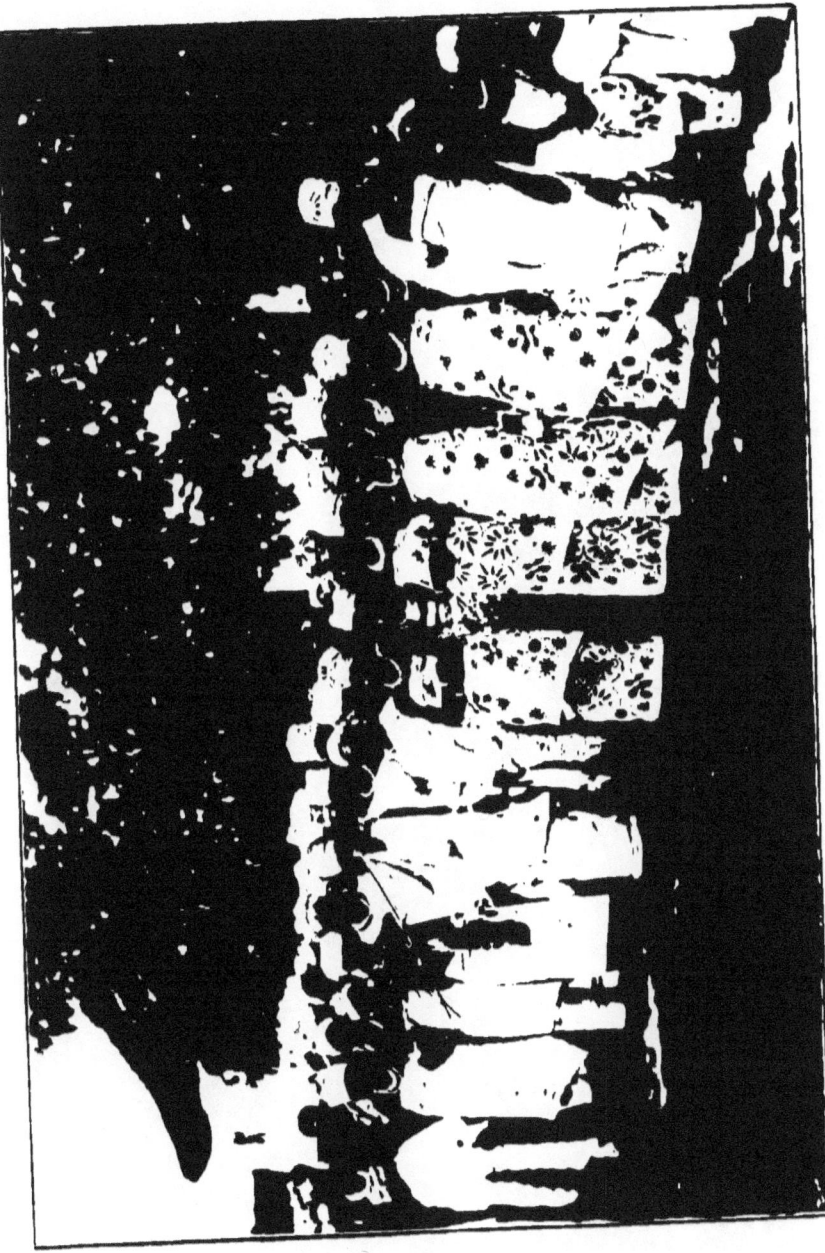

after this, when the 600 ounces of gold, that had been lodged in the castle as security, were sent back to the King of Ashanti. It is reported that the messengers who came for it were quite astonished that they received the full amount, and still more so that it was delivered to them in exactly the same condition as when it was given to the Government.

In 1840 a commission of inquiry was held, with the result that in 1843 the Home Government again resumed occupation of the forts upon the Gold Coast, and their proper maintenance, and Commander H. W. Hill, R.N., was appointed in the following year as Lieutenant-Governor of the colony. He was succeeded in 1846 by Commander William Winniett, R.N., whose mission to Kumasi will be remembered for its efforts to obtain the abolition of human sacrifice. From this time down to 1863 was a time of comparative peace in the colony, but the demand of the King of Ashanti from Governor Pine in December, 1862, brought about fresh difficulties. The King of Kumasi somewhat insolently demanded the return of a runaway slave boy, and also the delivery into his hands of an old man accused of thieving gold dust belonging to the king. This demand was naturally refused, and the Ashantis somewhat craftily prepared for war. They entered into an alliance with the Elminas, who supplied them with large quantities of arms and ammunition obtained on the coast, and generally couched their messages to the governor in very strained language. Roving bodies of Ashantis appeared in different parts of the Protectorate, and a new demand was sent to the governor that a certain chief Adjaman should be delivered up to them, or as an alternative they, the

Ashantis, would occupy the Protected Territory for years. When this last message was sent, these roving parties of Ashantis had already pillaged and burnt some thirty villages, in addition to killing several hundreds of their inhabitants. Governor Pine at once made known the state of affairs to the English Government, and requested that an expedition be sent to for ever quell the troublesome Ashantis, but to his great disappointment this wished-for help was for some reason refused. It was necessary to take action at once, and in December, 1863, having already a camp at Mansu, about half-way between Cape Coast and the Prah, he determined to push on and form a military camp at the Prah, with a depôt, now known as Prahsu, from which point he hoped that he would be able to induce the Ashanti king to come to terms once more. Accordingly a camp was constructed at Prahsu by some companies of the West India troops, which occupied them until March, 1864, when the rains commenced, somewhat earlier than usual, and the work had, for the time being, to be abandoned. With the rains came the fever owing to the inaction of the men, and in June of the same year they were withdrawn again, to be quartered at Cape Coast. Troubles between the Fantis and the Elminas occupied the next few years, and no lasting peace had as yet been concluded with the Ashantis. In 1869 a party of the Ashantis had crossed the northern portion of the Protectorate and reached the right bank of the river Volta, attacking and plundering the town of Anum, which lay some few miles to the east of the opposite bank. Here was a very important station belonging to the Basle Mission, occupied by the missionaries and their family. Although no actual war had been declared or was in progress, the Ashanti captain, Adoo Boofu, attacked the mission station and captured the missionaries, Messrs. Ramseyer and Kuhne, with the wife and child of the former, as well as a Frenchman named Bonnet and a Mr. Palmer of Accra. These were taken forcibly from their home, dragged by long and troublesome marches to Kumasi, and kept as prisoners there for a space of four years. Early in 1872 Mr. Pope Hennesey was sent from England in order to effect the completion of the transfer of the Dutch forts to the English, and the difficulty which had existed between the Ashantis over the Castle of Elmina was satisfactorily settled. A short account of this perhaps will not be out of place in this chapter. When the transfer of the Dutch forts to the English was in contemplation, a difficulty arose over the Castle of Elmina, which was claimed as tribute to Ashanti by the then king, who wrote to the English governor in 1870, stating that Elmina from time immemorial had paid an annual tribute to his ancestors. It was the old question of the monthly pay notes. The Denkiras had conquered the Elminas, who in their turn were tributary to Kumasi, and in this way the annual payment had been forfeited to the master power, and this caused the following letter to be sent to the English governor.

I beg to bring before your Excellency's kind consideration regarding the Elmina, if it is included in the change (*i.e.*, from Dutch to English). The fort of that place have from time immemorial paid annual tribute to my ancestors by right of arms, when we conquered the King of Denkira. This king having purchased £9000 worth of goods from the Dutch, and not paying for them, before we conquered him, the Dutch demanded of my father, Osai Tootoo, for the payment, who paid it full, the

£9000, and the Dutch delivered the Elmina to him as his own, and from that time tribute has been paid us to this present time. I hope, therefore, your Excellency will not include Elmina in the change, for it is mine by right.

This claim was of course denied by the Dutch governor, who, however, stated the sum of £80 had been annually paid to the Ashantis, not as tribute, but rather as a present, to preserve friendly relations in trade. There is no doubt that this claim was a piece of impudence on the part of the King of Ashanti, for on a Mr. Plange being sent by the English to Kumasi, the claim fell to the ground, and Elmina was duly included in the Dutch territory that was transferred. In the meantime several unsuccessful attempts had been made to effect the release of the captured Europeans at Kumasi, but the king sheltered himself with the excuse that as his general had captured them at great expense, he could not force him to release them until a ransom of 1800 ounces of gold had been paid. Many communications took place, many delays occurred, but the missionaries were still held at Kumasi. In April, 1872, both the English and Dutch governors sent letters and presents to the king asking him to give up the prisoners, but all representations were of no avail, until later in the year, when Mr. Pope Hennesey was informed by letter from the Ashanti capital, that the ransom of the Europeans was the only point to be settled in order to ensure a lasting peace. To this a reply was sent that the Basle Mission Society would be willing to pay any sum, not exceeding £1000, to cover the expenses of the Ashanti chief who had captured their representatives, but that it was not to be looked upon as an exchange of men for money, and that the amount stated should be at once paid if the captives were sent safely down to the Prah. To this the king replied: "His chiefs, in consultation with him, had decided that the £1000 should be accepted, and he asks for it to be sent to Kumasi and he will send the men down". Nothing, however, came of it, nor of a further request that the prisoners should be brought down to Cape Coast, and the money paid there. This was about the last negotiation made, which was in November, 1872, for events that were soon to happen were fortunately going to settle the difficulty that had so long existed.

Some trade disputes or misunderstandings arose at this time with the King of Elmina, on very slight grounds, and the Government, when, without the slightest warning, news was received on the coast that an Ashanti army, some 1200 strong, had crossed the Prah, occupying five days in the passage, and had invaded and attacked the Assin country, plundering and burning the towns and villages on their way. This occurred in January, 1873, and early in March it was known in England that another trouble with the Ashanti power had become a reality and not a farce, and that if the prestige of the English nation was to be upheld, immediate action was necessary. The towns near Cape Coast and Elmina were filled with men, women and children, who were forced from the interior districts by the ravages of the enemy to take refuge under the walls of the castles, and as all the food crops had been destroyed by the advancing Ashantis, famine became inevitable. Stores of rice were sent from England for the people, and arms and ammunition for the male part of the population. A body of

Hausà troops were brought from Lagos, and several of the native kings prepared their forces to repel the invader. Elmina, which had long shown signs of discontent to the English rule, now openly joined the Ashantis, who, advancing from the river Prah, destroyed nine towns on their way, and finally encamped within twelve miles of Elmina and Cape Coast Castle, having twice defeated the native forces opposed to them on their way. This latter defeat occurred on the 5th June, 1873, at Duquah, when the Fanti forces were totally routed, and retreated in great disorder into Cape Coast, swelling the already enormous crowd of refugees that occupied the place, and losing many of their number by small-pox and dysentery, which had broken out among their ranks. About the same time, to add to the difficulties, the Dutch natives of Chama and Elmina joined a division of the Ashanti army and attacked Commendah, where the people were practically at the mercy of their inveterate enemies. Colonel R. W. Harley was then administering the government of the colony, and the force at his disposal was very small, consisting as it did of some 100 soldiers of the Second West India Regiment, less than 250 Hausàs armed with breech-loaders, a local volunteer corps from Cape Coast armed with Enfields, and about fifty native Fanti policemen. On the coast, however, were H.M.S. *Druid* and *Argus*, and the gunboats *Merlin, Decoy* and *Seagull;* opposed to these was an advancing Ashanti army of 12,000 men, who, flushed with recent successes, had actually encamped within twelve miles of Cape Coast Castle. The gun-boat *Merlin*, under Lieutenant Day, was at once despatched to the relief of Commendah, which was in a most pitiable condition. The whole population had clustered on the shore, and implored protection, and all that could be done in the circumstances was to accommodate as many as possible on board ship. A merchant ship, the *Albertina*, which had two surf-boats, succeeded in embarking some 350 souls, though many were drowned in their efforts to reach the vessel, while the gun-boat remained to give such protection as the guns afforded to the people on shore.

Three days later, namely, on the 8th of June, H.M.S. *Barracouta* arrived from England in charge of Captain Fremantle, who brought with him a force of some 110 mariners and marine artillery and a large supply of arms and ammunition of war. These forces were under the command of Colonel Festing, R.M.A., who as senior officer also took command of the land forces. On the 12th June the officer administering the government placed Elmina under martial law, and its execution being placed in the hands of Captain Fremantle and Colonel Festing, they issued orders to the people to deliver up their arms, and after a sufficient delay had been allowed, finding that but little attention had been paid to the order, they proceeded to burn the town about noon on the 15th of June. The flames of the burning town were no sooner seen by the Ashantis, than an advance was made with 3000 of their men to attack the British forces. Captain Fremantle and Colonel Festing at once joined their forces, to the number of 500 men, and succeeded in inflicting a serious defeat upon the advancing enemy. A portion of the seamen and mariners were then embarked, and the remaining 200 under Colonel Festing again defeated and pursued the Ashantis for some three miles north of Elmina, when they returned to their camp with the loss of their general, a nephew of the king, and several of their more important chiefs. Commander Commerell then arrived on the west coast as Commander-in-Chief, but was dangerously wounded soon after his arrival while visiting the Prah to ascertain what facilities it afforded for navigation by boats, and Captain Luxmore of the *Argus* was also severely wounded.

A little later in the year Major-General Sir Garnet Wolseley was sent out as Governor-in-Chief to take command of the forces in the colony, and to undertake the punishment of the troublesome Ashantis. He arrived with thirty-six special service officers at Cape Coast Castle on the S.S. *Ambriz*, but without an army to assist the present small force in the colony. He soon showed, however, after his arrival the superiority of a small force of disciplined men over a multitude of barbarous natives, and towards the end of October, succeeded in inflicting three defeats upon the enemy. This, however, was only the commencement of the campaign; the country near the coast was cleared of the Ashantis, and all preparations were made for an advance into the interior and for the destruction of Kumasi so soon as the next dry season should come round. This expedition was organised with care and crowned with success. The main body of his forces, consisting of 1400 white troops, advanced direct on the capital by the main road from Cape Coast through Prahsu, whilst native levies were organised to attack and annoy the Ashantis in the eastern and western portions of their country. So soon as the Ashantis heard of these preparations for their destruction they began to rely upon their tactics of the past, sending in message after message of submission, and promising all sorts of good behaviour for the future. These attempts at obtaining peace had, however, no effect upon

THE BRITISH RESIDENT AT KUMASI (CAPTAIN DONALD STEWART, C.M.G.) AND OFFICIALS.

Sir Garnet Wolseley; he marched with his forces straight upon the capital, defeated the Ashantis in several well-contested irregular bush fights, and ultimately captured and burnt their capital. The king was captured, and a peace signed in which the Ashantis acknowledged the British authority, consented to pay an indemnity of 50,000 ounces of gold, to abolish human sacrifice and to keep the trade roads from their country to the coast, particularly the Prah road, clear of bush. In this expedition he was assisted by Captain Glover, R.N., the Governor of Lagos, who raised a native force at Accra and in the eastern division of the colony to march upon Kumasi from the east.

From this time down to 1896 peace was kept and but little trouble given to the British by the Ashantis, though the promise of the payment of the war indemnity and the abolition of human sacrifice was not honoured by these shifty people. In 1893-94, they attacked and pillaged their neighbours the Nkoranzas, and inflicted several severe defeats upon them, and as the latter came into British territory for protection, the Ashantis threatened to follow them and punish them there. In addition the roads had been allowed to become again overgrown, and the captured Nkoranzas were sacrificed to the number of some thousands in Kumasi. An expedition consisting of native troops, under Sir Francis Scott, K.C.M.G., was despatched to the Nkoranza country at the end of 1893, and order was again restored, but the events of this expedition finally led to the campaign of 1895-96 and the complete destruction of the Ashanti power, and the capture and deportation of the king, Prempeh, to Sierra Leone. To accomplish this end a well-selected and complete force was despatched from England, consisting of some 2000 regular troops, accompanied by a large staff of special officers of every description. General Sir Francis Scott, K.C.M.G., assisted by Colonel Kempster, was in command, and the most minute preparations were made for the success of the undertaking. Between Cape Coast Castle and Prahsu, some seventy-nine miles, no less than five depôt camps were formed; the various streams were satisfactorily bridged, telegraphic communication established along the whole route, and thousands of carriers enlisted for the transport of the baggage and supplies. As so many accounts have been specially written fully describing all the events of this last Ashanti campaign, it will only be necessary for me to mention the start and the satisfactory results that were achieved. About noon on the 16th of December, 1895, the native levies left Cape Coast Castle for the front to act as a covering force for the expedition that was ready to follow, and by the middle of the following month the Ashanti capital was reached, and the discovery made that King Prempeh was willing to submit to the English completely and unconditionally. The king, his chiefs and captains sat for a whole day watching the arrival of the British force, and by the end of January, 1896, the last and final Ashanti war was brought to a conclusion without bloodshed, and the power of this barbarous tribe crushed for ever. Negotiations followed; the king was deposed and with his mother and counsellors taken to the coast and imprisoned at Elmina, to be finally transported to Sierra Leone for the rest of his natural life.

The consummation, so often desired, of having a British resident at Kumasi, is now an accomplished fact, the first permanent resident appointed being Captain Donald Stewart, C.M.G.

CHAPTER XII.

Progress of the Colony—Education—The Basle Mission—The Wesleyan Mission—The Roman Catholic Mission—The Schools of the Colony—The Future of the Colony—Want of Railways and Central Harbour.

IT becomes an interesting study to even the most ordinary observer who visits or travels in the Gold Coast Colony, to ascertain the results of more than four centuries' intercourse that this part of the African continent has had with so-called civilised Europe, and to mark the advantages and disadvantages received therefrom. Associated, as it has been, with the leading countries of Europe at different epochs of its existence, one might have reasonably expected to find a constitution and laws built up upon a principle suitable to the needs of a West African race, and the people themselves taking an active interest in the future welfare of their own people. But this is not the case. The four centuries' connection with Europe has been a purely commercial one, which seems to have instilled in the minds of the natives of the present day one very doubtful business maxim, *viz.*, to pay as little as possible for any article you buy, or better still—do not pay for it at all if it can be possibly avoided. So anxious are we in Europe to extend our foreign trade, that it is far easier for a native of West Africa to become a so-called merchant without the need for absolutely any capital, than it is for a respectable European to establish himself in any branch of trade in his own country. For years past, so-called native princes and the sons of princes have been able to establish themselves as petty traders all along the coast, at the expense of European merchants, obtaining supplies of goods of all descriptions upon credit, in some cases without the slightest intention of making payment, and even selling them under the cost price in order to become possessed of ready money. A portion of the money thus obtained is remitted to Europe accompanied by a still larger order, and thus the debts to Europeans increase by leaps and bounds. Many causes have led to this result. It is easy for a commercial house to obtain orders from the Gold Coast, but obtaining payment for the same is a very different matter. Some lay the blame for this state of things upon the local government, others upon the merchants who periodically reside in the colony; some attribute it to the missionary societies at work on the coast, whilst others say it is the fault of education. Rather than side with any particular section, I am inclined to think that all four have assisted in producing the present unsatisfactory state of affairs in this respect. The Government has at times been too lenient, the merchants are too anxious to gain orders, often at the expense of each other, the missionary often places the native upon a pedestal among the races of the world that he is not yet fitted to occupy, and the education given has not been founded upon a proper basis. These remarks may give rise to a different opinion in the minds of my readers; should such be the case, my answer to them is, visit the country and see for yourselves.

A constant change of masters since the beginning of the fifteenth century; a vacillating policy of treatment of the natives by the various governments; want of continuity and purpose in the work in the officials, and the very uncertain nature of the West African climate have all tended to produce the unsatisfactory West Africa of the present day. The other great drawback to the general progress of the colony is the system of domestic slavery that exists in every part of the country, and causes most of the laziness and immorality that everywhere abound. The ordinary man possesses many domestic slaves, they alternately work and sleep; the master does little or nothing. These slaves are fed by their owners, morning and evening, and thus their only desire is satisfied. They possess no energy, no vigour, no intellect, and care nothing for the rights and responsibilities of ordinary everyday life. The bulk of the population of the colony being included under this head, it is little wonder that progress is slow and disappointing. The country is rich, mines are waiting to be worked, but the people, easily satisfied with a variety of food that costs them little or nothing, are content to live in the most miserable state of domestic slavery amid the most miserable surroundings in the shape of dwellings.

Education in the colony at the present day is in the hands of various mission societies, the Government leading the way, and entirely supporting from public funds large schools at Accra and Cape Coast Castle, in addition to a smaller one at the capital of Western Akim, some four days' journey from the coast to the interior.

The various mission agencies impart their own denominational teaching to their own particular group of schools. In the middle of the eighteenth century, an Anglican Church Mission was attempted, and the Rev. Thomas Thompson visited the Gold Coast and stayed four years, during which time he acted as chaplain at Cape Coast Castle. He was the pioneer for the introduction of the Christian religion in the colony, and when he returned to England in 1756, in consequence of ill health, he took with him some of the native youth of the colony, one of whom, Philip Quacoe, graduated at Oxford and was admitted to Holy Orders, in 1765, when he returned to Cape Coast to exercise his calling among his own people. He acted as chaplain at Cape Coast Castle for more than fifty years, dying in 1816. Since this time many others have succeeded him in the office as chaplain, both native and European. The mission agencies now at work are:—

1. The Basle Mission Society.
2. The Wesleyan Mission Society.
3. The North German Mission Society.
4. The Roman Catholic Mission Society.

These are mentioned in the order in which they became connected with the coast.

The advent of the Basle Mission dates from 1828, when the Basle Evangelical Mission Society obtained permission from the King of Denmark to establish Christian missions in the Danish Protectorate of the Gold Coast Colony; the present Christiansborg and the country to the east of that place, and then the capital of the Danish Protectorate. The first four missionaries for this work landed upon the 18th December in 1828, and within eight months from their arrival, three of their number had already succumbed to the treacherous climate, leaving but one to continue the work and the school of some ninety scholars that had been established. He also fell

A NATIVE BEAUTY.

a victim early in March, 1832, some short time before the arrival of three new-comers to take the place of those who had first died. The early history of all the missions on the Gold Coast is one of sickness and death, and of the three new-comers but one was left, after the short space of three months, to continue the work so nobly begun. The only survivor up to this time was Mr. Riis, who, finding the low-lying coast land so treacherous for the residence of the European, visited the hill region, called Aquapim, lying due north of Accra, and finding it by comparison healthier than the coast, decided to form a settlement in the mountains, and opened a Basle Mission Station at Akropong, the capital of Aquapim, some 1400 feet above the sea, and a journey of only one day and a half from the sea coast. The station at Christiansborg was then abandoned and Akropong became the headquarters of the mission. Mr. Riis was well received by the natives of Aquapim, and was joined in his work in 1836 by two new arrivals, both of whom, however, fell victims to the climate before a two years' residence had been completed. About this time, Mr. Riis visited Kumasi, and on his return to the coast left for Europe to recruit and to consult with the home committee about the future of the mission, which, on account of the very heavy loss of life, was about to be given up. The success of the work, too, in the Aquapim district was at this time seriously threatened by the political disturbances among the natives themselves, and also by some misunderstanding that had arisen between the natives and the Danish Government.

A new plan was now to be tried. Mr. Riis, in company with a Mr. Widmann, proposed to introduce from the West Indies some of the liberated Christian Africans to assist in the establishment of the work upon the Gold

Coast, as the climate had up to this time been found to be very disastrous to the continued residence of Europeans. They visited Jamaica in the West Indies, and selected, with the assistance of the Moravian Mission, some twenty-four likely colonists, with whom they landed at Christiansborg in April, 1843. No stay was made here, but the party proceeded at once to the hill station at Akropong, where for a time, things generally flourished under the new *régime*. The success, however, was only short-lived, for after a few years, the people, with the exception of a very few, turned out very unsatisfactory, and generally disappointed the expectations of the originators of the scheme. Some were the cause of much trouble to the mission in the colony, others returned to their old homes in the West Indies, while a few remained to carry on the work. Of those that remained, I know of one who is still living at Aburi in Aquapim, though I believe there are others at different stations in the colony in receipt of a small pension from the society. The year 1847 saw the arrival of Mr. Mohr (still actively at work in the colony) and several others to take up the work already begun. Christiansborg was again taken up, another station opened at Aburi and a preparatory school opened at Akropong, in which native assistants could be trained for the mission. Mr. Mohr devoted his energies to the erection of good houses as mission stations, and also utilised the West Indian colonists in the formation of coffee plantations, and other tropical produce which they had brought with them from the west. Thus gradually, though very slowly, coffee planting began to work its way among the members of the Basle Mission, and a part of the first plantation made at Akropong exists to the present day and is cultivated by the scholars of the existing school.

More missionaries arrived, and the difficulties of the native tongue were somewhat overcome by the successful attempt on the part of Rev. J. Zimmermann and the Rev. J. G. Christaller to reduce the Gá or Akra and the Tshi languages to writing. The Bible was first translated into the two tongues, and a series of grammars, hymn books, Bible histories, catechisms and various small school primers, printed at Basle for the use of the society on the coast, soon followed in its wake. From this date, 1847, the work of this excellent body began to prosper, and a few years saw the establishment and the opening of many new stations. In 1853, the members numbered nearly 200 souls, but the political disturbance of the following year somewhat retarded the progress of the mission for a time. The natives of the then Danish possessions on the Gold Coast had been transferred to the British Crown in 1850, but through some misunderstanding over the introduction of new taxes, a rebellion broke out, which was only suppressed after the bombardment of Christiansborg, and the destruction of many native houses and mission property. The people scattered in all directions, and their return being very uncertain, a large proportion of their number settled and formed a small plantation-village at Abokobi, some fifteen miles from the coast, which has since become a very flourishing mission station. In 1860, after a suitable building had been erected for the purpose, the Girls' Boarding School was transferred from Christiansborg to Abokobi. A most admirable introduction was now made by the Basle Mission. The necessity for providing good and substantial houses at the various stations established by the mission, led the committee in Europe to send out to the coast specially qualified men as artisans and mechanics to superintend their erection, and to establish industrial workshops at the same time, where, under proper supervision, the native youth of the colony might in time learn useful trades, and become workmen in their turn. After many difficulties and comparative failures, workshops at Christiansborg were established for carpenters, joiners, wheelwrights and blacksmiths, which have progressed so far at the present day as to become nearly self-supporting, and in addition have greatly benefited the country. The mission houses, all erected by native labour, are now to be reckoned among the best habitations in the colony, and stand as an example of what can be accomplished by native hands when superintended by European minds. One of the greatest difficulties in this country has been, and will be for years to come, to find the proper persons as managers of these establishments. Europeans cannot permanently reside in the country, and even to this day, little or no progress is made, where a native is at the head of an industrial department.

The next few years, 1853-57, saw an attempt on behalf of the Basle Mission to establish themselves at Gyadam, in Akim, but native wars between rival tribes destroyed their efforts. Gyadam was abandoned and Kukurantumi tried, to give way in its turn to Kyebi, the capital of Eastern Akim, and residence of the king, where, under much difficulty, a station was established in 1861. The King of Kyebi was no friend to the mission, and used his powers to prevent his people from receiving the benefits of civilisation. Open dissensions soon appeared, and persecution followed. The king accused a native member of the mission of having stolen a quantity of gold dust, and began to ill-treat the accused person and other members of the station. The Government was appealed to, and upon an investigation being made the king's charge could not be upheld, and the accused person was acquitted. The king, ordered to the coast by the Government to explain his conduct, died in the meantime, and the native members of the mission were accused of being party to his death. The mission station was attacked, much property destroyed, and many of the people ill-treated. Prompt action on the part of the Government, however, avoided further trouble, peace was restored, and the Kyebi people ordered to refund to the mission the value of the property destroyed. The cause of civilisation did not progress rapidly at Kyebi, partly on account of the disturbances mentioned, and partly on account of the climate being unhealthy for the continued residence of the European members. The station was surrounded by dense bush, and after the loss of several of the Europeans by fever, the headquarters were removed from Kyebi to Begoro in 1876, where a new station was formed some 1500 feet above the sea, and which has proved comparatively healthy. But though the Europeans withdrew to Begoro, the station at Kyebi was not abandoned, but the care of the congregation and the management of the schools were entrusted to a native minister and his assistants, accompanied with a series of regular visits from and the supervision by the Europeans, with the result that Kyebi still remains a prosperous centre of the Basle Mission.

In 1857 Messrs. Locher and Zimmermann made a

visit to the Krobo country, near the river Volta in the north-eastern portion of the Gold Coast, and were received by Chief Odonko of Odumase. He gave one of his sons to their care for education, and in many ways assisted the efforts of the missionaries, with the result that Odumase is now the centre of a large number of out-stations, where English is taught and plantation work encouraged. This centre contains an excellent church and two good schools, in addition to many smaller ones in the surrounding villages. Two years after their establishment at Odumase, *viz.*, in 1859, the Mission Trade Society, a joint stock company working for the benefit of the mission, and carrying on general trade to the exclusion of guns, powder and spirits, began its operations in the colony. This company renders very valuable assistance to the Basle Mission Society, even to the direct support of the mission work, as at Ada in 1865, and at Anum in 1867. The agents of the Mission Trade Society are all under the same rules and regulations as the other missionaries, and even occasionally take part in the ordinary mission work.

In these days the town of Ada, at the mouth of the Volta River, was considered as an out-station of Odumase, and was periodically visited by the missionaries from the latter town, by means of the water-way of the Volta. But in 1868 the Mission Trade Society commenced large and substantial premises at Adafo, a village close to the mouth of the Volta, since which time a representative of the mission has either resided there or at Big Ada, the principal town, some two hours' journey up the river. The number of members in this district rapidly increased, and many of them being well-to-do traders, they commenced to build a large and commodious chapel, which was finished in 1898. Troubles arose among the congregation, and the church elder and the native pastor refused to obey the committee, and claimed the chapel as their property. This has, however, been smoothed over, and at the present day Adafo and Big Ada are both flourishing stations with suitable churches and schools. In 1865 the Mission Trade Society commenced a station in the Anum district, at the town of that name, some two hours distant from the left bank of the Volta, at which a missionary and native catechist carried on the operations. By 1869 a flourishing mission station had been established, when the Ashantis invaded the country, attacked and captured the station and carried off Mr. and Mrs. Ramseyer and a Mr. Kühne as prisoners to Kumasi. The journey from Anum to Kumasi was a very trying one for the missionaries, and lasted several weeks; they had to walk the whole way on foot, were scarcely allowed any rest, being hurried on and abused by their inhuman captors; exposed to the burning sun by day, and to the dangerous chills at night, and insufficiently fed with unwholesome and sometimes decayed native food, it was a wonder that the whole party did not succumb. When Kumasi was reached they were treated much better than they had been during the journey, but were kept by the king as prisoners for four years, never knowing, during the whole of that time, whether their savage captors might at any time give orders for their destruction or not. At last, in January, 1874, when the English forces under Sir Garnet Wolseley advanced upon Kumasi, they were set free and returned to the coast, and about a fortnight later Kumasi was captured and destroyed by the English troops. After a beneficial stay in Europe Mr. and Mrs. Ramseyer returned to West Africa, with the avowed intention of opening up mission stations in the Ashanti country, but owing to the unsettled state of the place, they selected Abetifi, the capital of the Okwahu country, for the scene of their new operations. This country was formerly a tributary state to Ashanti, but since 1874 had thrown off the yoke and become independent under British protection. The station at Abetifi was commenced in 1876, and the selection of such a site has proved a very fortunate one, for there is no doubt that Abetifi, situated upon the tableland of Okwahu, some 2000 feet above the level of the sea, is one of the healthiest stations in the colony. Its only drawback is its distance from the coast, necessitating a somewhat fatiguing journey through swamps for several days.

In 1881, just twelve years after the destruction of the station at Anum, the town was again occupied by the mission, and is now a very flourishing centre, beautifully situated, and extending its civilising influence in the surrounding villages in all directions. Other stations were established in the Western Akim and the Agona Fanti countries, and after some fifty years of most arduous labour, the Basle Mission Society may claim to have been firmly settled in the country. The bill of mortality had, however, been very heavy, for from 1821 down to 1883 no less than seventeen Europeans had given their lives to the work, and to try and lessen this great mortality in the future Dr. R. Fisch was appointed in 1885 as the first medical missionary for the Gold Coast, a position which he still occupies.

THE WESLEYAN MISSION. 329

I have here attempted to give a slight outline of the work of the Basle Mission on the Gold Coast from its commencement, and would add in conclusion, from a five years' personal acquaintance with their work in all parts of the colony, that much good and lasting work has been accomplished by them, and that I hope to see in the near future a still further development in their industrial branches and the spread of English in their schools.

A WEDDING GROUP.

The work of the Wesleyan Mission Society on the West Coast of Africa dates back to about the year 1831, when a few young men, who had been educated in the Government School at Cape Coast Castle, formed a society at Cape Coast, called "A Meeting or Society for Promoting the Christian Knowledge," with the object of meeting at regular times to examine carefully the nature and claims of the Christian religion.

In 1833, while William de Graft, one of the members of this society, was at Dixcove, he received a request from his friends at Cape Coast to order out from England, through some suitable person who might be proceeding thither, a number of copies of the New Testament for their use. De Graft applied to Captain Potter, the master of a Bristol merchant vessel, which shortly afterwards arrived in port. Captain Potter was surprised to receive such an application from a native youth, and after some conversation with De Graft, inquired whether he and his friends would not like to receive instruction from a missionary. De Graft replied in the affirmative, and Captain Potter saw the other members of the society when his vessel proceeded to Cape Coast, and having consulted President Maclean, he sailed for England, resolving to bring out with him on his next voyage, not only the copies of the Scriptures, but a missionary.

On his arrival in Bristol, Potter communicated with the Wesleyan Missionary Society in London upon the subject, offering to take out with him on his next voyage a missionary to Cape Coast Castle, and to bring him back to England without any expense to the committee, should he, after trying the natives, conclude he could not commence a mission at that place.

This noble offer was readily accepted by the committee, who sent out Joseph Dunwell. Mr. Dunwell arrived on the coast on 31st December, 1834, and commenced work upon the following Sabbath, 4th January, 1835. His work lasted only for six months, for he died on the 25th of the next June, and was succeeded in September, 1836, by Mr. and Mrs. G. O. Wrigley. The new missionary and his wife were joined early in January, 1837, by Mr. and Mrs. Peter Harrop. Mrs. Harrop died on the 4th of the next month, and on the 8th, Mr. Harrop and Mrs. Wrigley were buried together. Mr. Wrigley did not long survive the complicated bereavement; he died in the following November. Mr. and Mrs. Thomas B. Freeman landed on 3rd January, 1838. Mr. Freeman consolidated the mission and studded the Gold Coast with churches and schools for the Wesleyan Society.

The present headquarters of the mission are at Cape Coast Castle, under the general superintendence of the Rev. Dennis Kemp, assisted by various European and native missionaries. Their principal stations are at the following places:—

Cape Coast,
Elmina,
Akim,
Beyin,
Kumasi,

Anamaboe,
Saltpond,
Winnebah,
Accra,
Aburi,

with many minor stations on the coast and in the interior.

GRAND TOTAL OF SCHOOLS AND SCHOLARS.
(1896.)

Schools.	On Register.		Total.	Number Present.		Total.	Average Attendance.		Total.
	Boys.	Girls.		Boys.	Girls.		Boys.	Girls.	
Basle Mission . . . 40	1774	1079	2853	1583	891	2474	1644	670	2314
Wesleyan Mission . 53	4386	599	4985	3986	492	4478	3330	360	3690
R. C. Mission . . . 16	1717	322	2039	1532	246	1778	1413	240	1653
Government 6	1145	183	1328	798	135	945	776	125	901
Totals 115	9022	2183	11205	7899	1764	9675	7163	1395	8558

In addition to the 115 inspected schools enumerated above there are also 83 schools belonging to the various missions that are not in receipt of a Government Grant.

Grants Earned.

The grants earned by the inspected schools have increased in about the same proportion to the increase of inspected schools. In 1894-95 the total amount expended by the Government was £3179 6s. upon the passes obtained. This year the amount has risen to £3400 11s., an increase of £221 5s. upon the previous year, and £100 11s. in excess of the vote sanctioned. This grant when divided by the total number of scholars for examination (exclusive of those in the Government Schools, for whom no grants are paid), viz., 8730, gives an average grant per scholar of 7s. 9½d., a slight decrease upon the amount *per capita* for 1894-95, but exactly the same as that for 1893-94. This sum of £3400 11s. is divided in the following amounts :—

	£	s.	d.
Basle Mission	1043	7	6
Wesleyan Mission	1613	17	6
R. C. Mission	743	6	0
Making a total of	3400	11	0

The following table shows the comparison of the grants earned by the various educational bodies for the years 1894 to 1896 :—

THE ROMAN CATHOLIC MISSION.

No. of Schools.	Denomination.	1894-95.		1895-96.	
		Total.	Per Scholar.	Total.	Per Scholar.
		£ s. d.	£ s. d.	£ s. d.	£ s. d.
40	Basle Mission . . .	1012 19 0	0 8 2½	1043 7 6	0 8 5
53	Wesleyan Mission .	1396 2 0	0 7 8	1613 17 6	0 7 2¼
16	R. C. Mission . . .	770 5 0	0 9 9½	743 6 0	0 8 4¼
109	Totals.	3179 6 0	0 8 5⅝	3400 11 0	0 7 9½

The decrease in the grant *per capita* to the Roman Catholic Schools, I attribute solely to the heavy mortality the mission has sustained during the past twelve months, by the sad loss of many European principals, who have fallen victims while bravely doing their duty, to the treacherous nature of the West African climate.

In the year 1881, the Roman Catholic Mission on the Gold Coast was confided by His Holiness Pope Leo XIII. to the fathers of the Society of the African Missions, whose mother house is in Lyons, 150 Cours Gambetta, France. This important society was founded in 1856 by Monsignor Marion de Brissillac, a missionary bishop who had already passed several years in the Chinese missions. Having barely started the work, Mgr. Marion entrusted its future to a young and able priest, the Rev. Father Planque, and taking with him his vicar-general, two priests and one lay brother, he left France for the Guinea Coast on board a sailing vessel, and after a month's voyage landed at Sierra Leone. Their stay there was of a very short duration, for at the end of six weeks all five were in the grave, having fallen victims to malarial fever. The newly founded Society of the African Missions, not having men enough to sacrifice them in such large numbers to the deadly influence of the climate of Sierra Leone, abandoned that station, and in 1863 the newly ordained priests proceeded to Lagos and Porto Novo, coast of Benin.

It was only in the year 1881, on the proposal of Chief Justice Marshall, that the Rev. Father Planque cast his eyes towards the Gold Coast. Two priests, the Rev. Fathers Moreau and Murat, who had been chaplains to Her Majesty's troops at Saint Helena, were appointed by him for the new mission. They landed at Elmina early in 1881, and at once opened a mission and a school. In a very short time after their arrival Father Murat fell a victim to the treacherous climate, and was the first of that long line of priests and nuns who have laid down their lives for that noble cause, the conversion and civilisation of the Gold Coast people, for although the mission only reckons seventeen years' existence, twenty-five missionaries have followed Father Murat to the grave. In spite of this high death rate, and a great many other difficulties, the missionary work has made marvellous progress on the whole Gold Coast, but more especially at Elmina. Here three distinct schools have been established by the fathers and the nuns.

1. The boys' school, which reckons over 120 pupils from the I. to the VII. standard.

2. The girls' school, much inferior in number, the natives deeming the education of their female children a matter of slight importance.

3. The infant school, whose pupils amount to 250 boys and girls combined.

The fathers' and sisters' dwelling houses are situated

on the top of a nice hill, and are of a structure peculiar to hot climates, a large verandah encircling them.

Between these two houses stands a large church which can easily accommodate 800 people. The number of converts, which increases daily, amounts to over 1000.

The work being fairly well established at Elmina, the fathers turned their attention to Cape Coast, and in June, 1889, the Rev. Fathers Grainer and Albert opened a mission in that former capital of the Gold Coast Colony. Here, too, the missionaries had to face many and serious difficulties. The year 1895 proved almost fatal to the mission; three priests and four nuns having died almost suddenly from bilious or malignant fever. Thanks to the arrival of a few new-comers (priests) and special pecuniary assistance from home, the work was carried on, and to-day it is in a very promising condition. Over 400 boys and girls attend our three schools daily, and the registers show more than 800 converts. A Catholic church has not yet been erected in Cape Coast, therefore the meetings of the members, on Sundays and festivals, take place in the schoolrooms. In December, 1890, the Rev. Father Ulrich, in company with the Rev. Father Groëbli, left Elmina to start a mission at Saltpond. Unfortunately the young priest died from fever shortly after his arrival there, and Father Ulrich, whose health had completely broken down, was forced to betake himself to a milder climate. The work was not altogether abandoned, but was entrusted to a native catechist. Last year the mission was reopened by the Rev. Father Wade, and since then a new dwelling-house and new schools have been erected. Number of scholars, 250; of converts, 450.

A large piece of land situated outside the town has been purchased by the fathers for agricultural purposes.

A mission was opened at Accra in 1893 by the Rev. Father Hilberer. The work was in a most promising condition when the missionaries were recalled to Cape Coast, in order to replace those who had fallen victims to the climate there.

The Rev. Father Wade founded the Catholic Mission of Kwitta in the year 1891. A large tract of land having been ceded to him by a rich native chief, he at once built a large and comfortable mission house. Some other nice buildings, such as a church, schoolrooms, etc., have been added since.

Besides these missions they have several out-stations, of which Anamaboe and Adjuah are the most important. In each of these stations is a native catechist, who at the same time fills the post of schoolmaster.

The fathers visit these out-stations periodically, in order to see how the work is progressing, and also to administer the Sacraments to the faithful. Anamaboe actually counts 150 schoolboys, and almost as many converts; Adjuah sixty-five school children and 180 converts.

They have in contemplation the extension of their work to the interior, and to Kumasi, as soon as the means at their disposal will allow of them doing so.

The mission counts moreover the charge of fifteen slaves, male and female, who have been entrusted to their care by the Government. These children having been bought and sold by the natives, in defiance of the law, the Government, after having them, hand them over in order that they may be educated.

A good start has been made in farming near Elmina.

Coffee, cacao, and a great number of rubber trees have been planted.

There is little doubt that with the addition of the Ashanti territory, and the recent acquisition of the country in the Hinterland up to the eleventh degree of north latitude, the commercial future of the Gold Coast promises to be one of great activity. The great difficulties to be first overcome are the want of suitable landing places and the absence of internal transport communication. Once these are established, commercial activity will soon follow; valuable products will be brought to the coast, mines will be opened up, and British energy and capital pave the way for a prosperous future for a somewhat long-neglected colony. Two landing places should be constructed, one near Takoradi Bay and one at Accra. The former place provides all requirements for harbour, safe anchorage, easy landing, and for a coaling station, while at the latter place the rocks upon which James Fort is built, would serve as a suitable foundation for a landing stage for the eastern part of the colony.

In a previous chapter I have already given an outline of the railways required in the colony. Here I will add but one more suggestion. The short strip of seaboard between Accra and Ada, including the estuary of the river Volta, is of but little commercial value or importance. Yet the town of Ada at the mouth of the Volta is the port from whence nearly one third of the palm oil and palm kernels produced in the colony are exported. Kpong on the right bank of the Volta is the collecting point for this large export trade, from whence with much trouble and expense, it is with considerable difficulty transported to the Volta mouth and across the bar for shipment from Ada. The trade of Accra, although the town is the capital and headquarters of the colony, does not improve, the exports being very small in comparison with other ports on the coast.

Now the present large export trade of Ada could be transferred with but little difficulty to Accra, by the construction of a railway between that port and the town of Kpong on the Volta river, and shipped with ease, provided that a landing stage was constructed at Accra in connection with the proposed railway. This increase of traffic would bring the capital into a state of commercial prosperity, at the expense of the present unhealthy town of Ada, a change that no one would seriously deplore; the trade itself would remain in the same hands, but the present commercial houses at Ada would have to close their premises and transfer their staff to Accra, the present headquarters of many of the Ada trading companies.

APPENDICES.

A.

List of Ashanti Kings from 1700 to the present time.

	Name of King.	Accession.	Ceased to Reign.	Remarks.
1	Osai Tootoo.	1700	1720	Killed
2	Osai Opookoo	1720	1741	Died
3	Osai Aquissa	1741	1753	,,
4	Osai Cudjo	1753	1785	,,
5	Osai Quamina	1785	1799	Deposed
6	Osai Opookoo II.	1799	1799	Died
7	Osai Tootoo Quamina	1799	1824	,,
8	Osai Okoto	1824	1838	,,
9	Osai Kwaku Dua I.	1838	1867	,,
10	Osai Kofi Karikari	1867	1874	Deposed
11	Osai Bousu	1874	1885	,,
12	Osai Kwaku Dua II.	1885	1888	Died
13	Osai Prempeh	1888	1896	Deposed

English Wars with Ashanti.

First war ⎫
Second war ⎬ often recorded as one war . . ⎧ 1807-1808
Third war ⎭   ⎨ 1811-1812
                                         ⎩ 1817-1820
Fourth war 1824-1826
Fifth war 1863-1864
Sixth war 1873-1874
Seventh war 1895-1896

Chief Battles fought in Ashanti Wars.

Place.	Date.
1. Battle of Egyaa	14th June, 1807
2. Battle of Anamaboe	15th June, 1807
3. Battle of Nsimanke	21st January, 1824
4. Battle of Dompim	25th April, 1824
5. Battle of Afutu	21st May, 1824
6. Battle of Cape Coast	11th July, 1824
7. Battle of Dodowah	26th August, 1826
8. Battle of Bobikuma	9th May, 1863
9. Battle of Yancoomasie	10th February, 1873
10. Battle of Tetsi	6th April, 1873
11. Battle of Dwukwa	30th May, 1873
12. Battle of Elmina	13th June, 1873
13. Battle of Abakrampa	9th November, 1873
14. Battle of Abogu	17th January, 1874
15. Battle of Boborasi	29th January, 1874
16. Battle of Owuratser	31st January, 1874
17. Battle of Amoafur	31st January, 1874
18. Battle of Bekwai	1st February, 1874
19. Battle of Fomanah	2nd February, 1874
20. Kumasi Burnt	3rd February, 1874
21. Kumasi again Burnt	1896

Chief Civil Wars on the Gold Coast.

1. War between Akwamus and Akras	1693
2. War between Fanti and Elmina	1809
3. War between Fanti and Accra	1812
4. Expedition to Apollonia	1835
5. Second Expedition to Apollonia	1849
6. War between Donasi and Abura	1851
7. War between Dunkwa and Abura	1859
8. Akim Civil War	1860
9. Second War between Fanti and Elmina	1868
10. War between Ashanti and Nkoranza	1894

APPENDICES. 341

B.

Distances in Miles and Time between Accra and the principal towns and villages on the coast. From "Actual Travelling".

I. To Windward.

Town.	Place.	Time.	Miles.
Accra	to River Sekoom	3 hours	10
River Sekoom	„ Bereku	4 hours	12
Bereku	„ Winnebah	3 hours	10
Winnebah	„ Mankwadi	2½ hours	7
Mankwadi	„ Appam	1 hour	4
Appam	„ Mumford	1 hour	3
Mumford	„ Tantum	2 hours	6
Tantum	„ Arkra	1½ hours	5
Arkra	„ Narkwa	1 hour	3
Narkwa	„ Saltpond	3 hours	9
Saltpond	„ Cormantine	⅓ hour	1
Saltpond	„ Anamaboe	2 hours	5
Anamaboe	„ Cape Coast	3½ hours	9
Cape Coast	„ Elmina	2½ hours	8
Elmina	„ Commendah	3¾ hours	10
Commendah	„ Chama	4 hours	12
Chama	„ Sekondi	3 hours	9
Sekondi	„ Adjuah	3 hours	9
Adjuah	„ Boutri	2½ hours	8
Boutri	„ Dixcove	1 hour	3
Dixcove	„ Acquidah	2 hours	6
Acquidah	„ Three Points Light	2 hours	5
Three Points Light	„ Princes	2 hours	5
Princes	„ Axim	3 hours	10
Axim	„ Esiamah	2½ hours	8
Esiamah	„ Attuabu	5 hours	18
Attuabu	„ Beyin	½ hour	2
Beyin	„ Half Assini	6 hours	20
Half Assini	„ Newtown	5 hours	18

II. To Leeward.

Town.	Place.	Time.	Miles.
Accra	to Christiansborg	1 hour	3
Christiansborg	„ Teshi	2 hours	5
Teshi	„ Pram Pram	5 hours	15
Pram Pram	„ Great Ningo	1½ hours	5
Great Ningo	„ Ada	9 hours	30
Ada	„ Attititi	1½ hours	5
Attititi	„ Huti	3 hours	9
Huti	„ Kwitta	5 hours	16
Kwitta	„ Danoe	5 hours	16
Danoe	„ Aflao	1½ hours	5

C.

Fares for Hammockmen and Carriers.

From.	To.	Amount.	
		s.	d.
Cape Coast	Anamaboe	3	6
„	Abakrampa	3	6
„	Adwa	12	6
„	Accra	20	0
„	Appam	13	6
„	Axim	20	0
„	Chama	6	9
„	Commendah	4	6
„	Dixcove	14	0
„	Elmina	2	6
„	Dukwah	4	6
„	Mumford	12	6
„	Mansu	14	6
„	Prahsu	20	0
„	Saltpond	4	6
„	Sekondi	9	0
„	Tarkwa	20	0
„	Winnebah	15	0

In addition to these stated fares, a sum of 3d. per diem is allowed for subsistence, and when travelling in the interior the rate of pay is 1s. per diem plus 3d. per diem subsistence for each day away from headquarters.

Fares for Canoemen.

WINDWARD.

From.	To.	Amount.
		s. d.
Cape Coast	Elmina	1 6
,,	Commendah	3 0
,,	Chama	5 0
,,	Sekondi	6 9
,,	Apoasi	7 0
,,	Adjuah	8 0
,,	Dixcove	9 6

LEEWARD.

From.	To.	Amount.
		s. d.
Cape Coast	Mouri	1 0
,,	Anamaboe	2 0
,,	Saltpond	3 0
,,	Narkwa	4 6
,,	Arkra	5 0
,,	Appam	6 9
,,	Mumford	7 0
,,	Winnebah	9 0

D.

Distances in Miles and Time between Accra and the principal towns and villages in the interior.

From.	To.	Time.	Miles.
Accra.	Abokobi.	4½ hours	16
Abokobi.	Aburi.	3½ hours	11
Aburi.	Asantema.	1 hour	3
Asantema.	Tutu.	½ hour	2
Tutu.	Apasare.	3¼ hours	10
Apasare.	Mampong.	3¼ hours	10
Mampong.	Amanokrum.	½ hour	2
Amanokrum.	Mamfe.	2 hours	6
Mamfe.	Akropong.	1 hour	3
Akropong.	Latè.	2 hours	5
Latè.	Abonse.	2½ hours	7
Abonse.	Assesseso.	2½ hours	7
Assesseso.	Adukrom.	1 hour	3
Adukrom.	Apirade.	½ hour	2
Apirade.	Afiduase.	6 hours	18
Afiduase.	Koforidua.	1 hour	3
Koforidua.	Kukurantumi.	3½ hours	10
Kukurantumi.	Asafo.	3 hours	9
Asafo.	Akoko.	3 hours	9
Akoko.	Kyebi.	2 hours	6
Kyebi.	Apedwa.	2½ hours	7
Apedwa.	Appapam.	4 hours	10
Appapam.	Kyebi.	2 hours	6
Kyebi.	Asiakwa.	3½ hours	10
Asiakwa.	Osino.	1½ hours	5
Osino.	Fankeniko.	2½ hours	7
Fankeniko.	Begoro.	3 hours	10
Begoro.	Enyinam.	6 hours	18
Enyinam.	Kan Kan.	3½ hours	10
Kan Kan.	Giagiaetti.	3 hours	8
Giagiaetti.	Mpraeso.	8 hours	20
Mpraeso.	Obomen.	¼ hour	1
Mpraeso.	Obo.	1 hour	3
Mpraeso.	Ativi.	¼ hour	1
Mpraeso.	Prahso.	7 hours	19

APPENDICES. 345

Distances in Miles and Time between Accra and the principal towns and villages in the interior—(continued).

From.	To.	Time.	Miles.
Prahso	Bompata	7 hours	17
Mpraeso	Abetifi	3 hours	9
Akropong	Assesseso	1½ hours	4
Assesseso	Odumase	4 hours	12
Odumase	Pong	2 hours	7
Pong	Akuse	1½ hours	5
Pong	Apeguso	7 hours	19
Apeguso	Anum	6 hours	17
Anum	Boso	2 hours	6
Winnebah	Swedur	5 hours	14
Swedur	Konyako	4 hours	11
Konyako	Nsaba	5 hours	13
Nsaba	Akorase	4 hours	10
Akorase	Asiesu	1 hour	3
Asiesu	Asantamang	3 hours	9
Asantamang	Mansu	2 hours	6
Mansu	Oda	4 hours	12
Oda	Akinassi	2½ hours	8
Akinassi	Yancoomasie	5 hours	16
Yancoomasie	Mansu	7 hours	20
Mansu	Dunkwa	5 hours	16
Dunkwa	Akroful	3 hours	9
Akroful	Cape Coast	3½ hours	10

E.

List of the Governors of the British Settlements on the Gold Coast from the date of the formation of the late African Company of Merchants (1750) to the present time (1898).

Names.	Rank.	Date of Appointment.	Remarks.
Thomas Melvil	Gov.-in-Chief	23rd June, 1751	Died
William Tymewell	,,	23rd Jan., 1756	,,
Charles Bell	ad interim	17th Feb., 1756	Superseded
Nassau Senior	Gov.-in-Chief	15th Oct., 1757	,,
Charles Bell	,,	10th May, 1761	Resigned
William Mutter	,,	15th Aug., 1763	Died
John Hippersley	,,	1st Mar., 1766	Resigned
Gilbert Petrie	,,	11th Aug., 1766	Died
John Grossle	,,	21st April, 1769	Superseded
David Mill	,,	11th Aug., 1770	,,
Richard Miles	ad interim	20th Jan., 1777	Died
John Roberts	Gov.-in-Chief	25th Mar., 1780	Superseded
J. B. Weuves	,,	26th May, 1781	Returned to Europe
Richard Miles	,,	29th April, 1782	Superseded
James Morgue	,,	29th Jan., 1784	Died
Thomas Price	,,	24th Jan., 1787	Resigned
Thomas Norris	,,	27th April, 1787	Superseded
William Fielde	,,	20th June, 1789	

APPENDICES. 347

John Gordon	ad interim	15th Nov., 1791	Superseded
A. Dalzell	Gov.-in-Chief	30th Mar., 1792	Returned to Europe on leave of absence
Jacob Mould	"	16th Dec., 1798	Superseded
John Gordon	ad interim	4th Jan., 1799	"
A. Dalzell	"	28th April, 1800	Resigned
Jacob Mould	Gov.-in-Chief	30th Sept., 1802	Superseded
Colonel G. Torrane	"	8th Feb., 1805	Died
E. W. White	"	4th Dec., 1807	Returned to Europe
Joseph Dawson	ad interim	21st April, 1816	Superseded
John Hope Smith	Gov.-in-Chief	12th Jan., 1817	Returned to Europe
Brig.-Gen. Sir Chs. Macarthy	"	27th Mar., 1822	Returned to Sierra Leone
Major Chisholm	Commandant	17th May, 1822	Superseded
Brig.-Gen. Sir Chs. Macarthy	Gov.-in-Chief	28th Nov., 1822	Killed in action
Major Chisholm	"	21st Jan., 1824	Died
Major Purdon	Commandant	1st July, 1824	Returned to Europe
Major-Gen. Chas. Turner	Gov.-in-Chief	22nd Mar., 1825	Returned to Sierra Leone
M.-Gen. Sir Neil Campbell	"	7th April, 1825	"
Captain Ricketts	Commandant	15th Nov., 1826	Superseded
Lieut.-Colonel Lumley	Lieut.-Gov.	15th Oct., 1827	Returned to Sierra Leone
Captain Hingston	Commandant	10th Mar., 1828	"
Major Ricketts	"	18th May, 1828	"
John Jackson	President	30th June, 1828	Superseded
Captain G. Maclean	"	19th Feb., 1830	Returned to Europe on leave of absence
William Topp	ad interim	26th June, 1836	Superseded

List of Governors of the British Settlements on the Gold Coast, etc.—(continued).

Names.	Rank.	Date of Service.	Remarks.
Captain Maclean	President	1838-44	
Commander H. W. Hill (R. N.)	Lieut.-Gov.	1844 and 1845	Superseded
James Lilly	,,	1845	
Comm. Will. Winniett (R. N.)	,,	1846-49	
J. C. Fitzpatrick		1849 and 1850	
Sir William Winniett	Gov.	1850	Died 4th Dec., 1850
James Bannerman	Lieut.-Gov.	1850 and 1851	
Major Stephen John Hill	Gov.	1851-53	
J. C. Fitzpatrick	Lieut.-Gov.	1853 and 1854	
Brodie G. Cruickshank	,,	1853	
Major Stephen John Hill	Gov.	1854	
Henry Connor	Acting-Gov.	1855	
Sir Benj. Chilly Campbell Pine	Gov.	1857 and 1858	
Major Henry Bird	Acting-Gov.	1858	
Edward Bullock Andrews	Gov.	1860-62	
William A. Ross	Acting-Gov.	1862	
Richard Pine	(Lieut.)-Gov.	1862-65	
William Hackett	Lieut.-Gov.	1864	
Major Rokeby S. W. Jones	,,	1865	Died
W. E. Mockler	,,	1865	
Lieut.-Col. Edward Conran	,,	1865-67	

APPENDICES. 349

Colonel S. W. Blackall	Gov.-in-Chief	1866	
Herbert Taylor Ussher	Administrator	1867 and 1868	
Sir A. E. Kennedy	Gov.-in-Chief	1868	
W. H. Simpson	Acting-Adm.	1868	
Herbert Taylor Ussher	Administrator	1869-71	
Charles Spencer Salmon	”	1871	
John Pope Hennesey	Gov.-in-Chief	1872	
Herbert Taylor Ussher	Administrator	1872	
Col. R. W. Harley	”	1872 and 1873	
W. R. Keate	Gov.-in-Chief	1873	
George Berkley	”	1873	
Col. Sir Garnet Wolseley	Administrator	1873 and 1874	
Lieut.-Col. Maxwell	”	1874	
Charles C. Lees	”	1874	
Col. Johnston	”	1874	
Capt. George C. Strahan	Gov.-in-Chief	1874	
Sir Sanford Freeling	”	1876	
Herbert Taylor Ussher	”	1879	Died 1st Dec, 1880
William B. Griffith	”	1880	
Sir Samuel Rowe	”	1881	
G. A. C. Young	”	1884	Died
William Brandford Griffith	”	1885	
Col. F. B. P. White	Gov.-in-Chief	1887	
Sir William B. Griffith	Acting-Gov.	1887, '90, '92, '94	
F. M. Hodgson	Gov.	1889, '91, '93	
Sir W. E. Maxwell, K.C.M.G.	”	1895	Died at sea, 1897
F. M. Hodgson, C.M.G.	”	1898	

APPENDIX F.

OUTFIT FOR THE WEST COAST.

1. CLOTHING.

The same clothing is worn on the West Coast as in temperate countries in the height of summer. For the dry season flannels, thin dark blue serge, or thin tweeds will be found most useful, while for the rainy season ordinary summer suits will not be found too heavy. In addition to several changes of the above, the dress suit, thin black morning coat and vest, and a thin overcoat should be taken.

Soft white or fancy shirts for general wear; thin woollen underclothing and socks, woollen pyjamas, cholera belts and flannel dressing-gowns will be found the best. Travellers should always wear flannel shirts. Ordinary white shirts are of course wanted.

Shoes or boots are a matter of taste—shoes are cooler for the towns, but travellers must have boots. Brown tan or white canvas will recommend themselves according to taste. Evening shoes and slippers are also wanted. Heavier boots and leggings, knickerbockers and putties are required by travelling officers. Much heavier clothing is required upon the homeward voyage.

The best travelling cases are the tin air-tight uniform

cases. A light pith helmet, tropical umbrella, and a sewn rain coat are absolutely necessary.

2. HOUSEHOLD ARTICLES.

Furnished quarters are supplied by the Government on the Gold Coast, but an officer requires many articles for household use. He cannot do better than take the following:—

(a) *For Bedroom use.*—Sheets, blankets, towels, mosquito curtain, pillow, pillow cases, and lamp or candlestick.

(b) *For Kitchen use.*—Large and small kettle, one set of iron enamelled saucepans, frying-pans large and small, tea-pot, coffee-pot, some enamelled pudding dishes.

Note.—These can be obtained at Accra, but not at many of the out-stations.

(c) *For Table use.*—Breakfast, dinner and tea china (I have found it best to select a Guinea Parcel as advertised, containing all these requisites). Knives, forks, spoons, table glass, cruet, table lamp, table cloth, napkins and an easy chair. Rough towelling for glass cloths and dusters can be obtained there.

Note.—All these articles can be obtained from F. Lack & Son, tropical outfitters, 90 Strand, London, W.C.

TRAVELLING REQUISITES.

Officers travelling require in addition: Small filter, camp bed, mosquito curtain and bars, two waterproof sheets, cooking stove, travelling lamps.

Stores.—Intending travellers to the West Coast of Africa. cannot do better than visit and consult Maconochie Brothers, 131 Leadenhall Street, London, E.C., with regard to a supply of tinned provisions. Only those of the first quality should be selected. Fairly good provisions can be had at Accra, but at the out-stations they are, as a rule, very poor.

The "Maconochie Rations" will be found particularly well adapted for officers away from headquarters.

I will not attempt to give any rules here for health, for so much depends upon the individual, that what is one man's food in this respect is another man's poison. There is but one golden rule for West Africa—*Moderation in All Things.*

www.ingramcontent.com/pod-product-compliance
Lightning Source LLC
Chambersburg PA
CBHW030406230426
43664CB00007BB/770